YEARBOOK
IN
EARLY CHILDHOOD EDUCATION

Bernard Spodek • Olivia N. Saracho
EDITORS

VOLUME 1
Early Childhood Teacher Preparation
Bernard Spodek and Olivia N. Saracho, Editors

VOLUME 2
Issues in Early Childhood Curriculum
Bernard Spodek and Olivia N. Saracho, Editors

VOLUME 3
Issues in Child Care
Bernard Spodek and Olivia N. Saracho, Editors

VOLUME 4
Language and Literacy in Early Childhood Education
Bernard Spodek and Olivia N. Saracho, Editors

VOLUME 5
Early Childhood Special Education
Philip L. Safford, Editor
with Bernard Spodek and Olivia N. Saracho

The *Yearbook in Early Childhood Education* is a series of annual publications. Each volume addresses a timely topic of major significance in the field of early childhood education, and contains chapters that present and interpret current knowledge of aspects of that topic, written by experts in the field. Key issues—including concerns about educational equity, multiculturalism, the needs of diverse populations of children and families, and the ethical dimensions of the field—are woven into the organization of each of the volumes.

Contents

YEARBOOK
IN
EARLY CHILDHOOD EDUCATION
VOLUME 5

EARLY CHILDHOOD SPECIAL EDUCATION

EDITED BY

Philip L. Safford

WITH

Bernard Spodek and Olivia N. Saracho

TEACHERS
COLLEGE
PRESS

Teachers College, Columbia University
New York • London

Published by Teachers College Press, 1234 Amsterdam Avenue,
New York, NY 10027

Library of Congress Cataloging-in-Publication Data

Early childhood special education / edited by Philip L. Safford with
    Bernard Spodek and Olivia N. Saracho.
            p.   cm. — (Yearbook in early childhood education ; v. 5)
        Includes bibliographical references and index.
        ISBN 0-8077-3370-9 (cloth : acid-free paper). — ISBN
    0-8077-3369-5 (paper : acid-free paper)
        1. Handicapped children — Education (Early childhood) — United
    States.   2. Special education — Law and legislation — United States.
    I. Safford, Philip L.   II. Spodek, Bernard.   III. Saracho, Olivia N.
    IV. Series.
    LC4019.3.E27   1994
    3 — dc20   94-17772

ISBN 0-8077-3369-5 (paper)
ISBN 0-8077-3370-9 (cloth)

Printed on acid-free paper

Manufactured in the United States of America

01 00 99 98 97 96 95 94   8 7 6 5 4 3 2 1

Introduction—Early Childhood Special Education

Philip L. Safford

This volume, *Early Childhood Special Education*, the fifth in the Yearbook in Early Childhood Education series, appears at an opportune time. As the "Century of the Child" nears its end and we anticipate the 21st century, young children and children at-risk have been identified as priority concerns in the United States. Yet, to be a child today is to be at-risk. Families of all young children, "typical" and "exceptional," share hopes that major reform efforts in the areas of education, health care, and child care will alleviate multiple stressors in their own lives and in the society and enhance all children's opportunity to realize the American dream.

Early childhood special education (ECSE), having emerged at an earlier period of national crisis, has in its brief, quarter-century history developed a substantial knowledge base and fostered an extensive and exponentially growing professional literature. Having developed, in some respects, independently of "general" early childhood education, and in fact separately from its other "parent," special education, ECSE presently seems to have reached a critical juncture, to be poised at a turning point in its history. So, too, is "general" early childhood education, as the very publication of this volume implies.

In fact, even as the manuscript went into press, new information continued to appear bearing on the themes addressed in this volume, especially that of the relationship of ECSE to early childhood education. Particularly important recent developments have included parallel and collaborative initiatives by the National Association for Education of Young Children (NAEYC) and the Division for Early Childhood (DEC, a division of the Council for Exceptional Children), reflected in the development of position statements concerning "preferred practices" and other developments cited in the fall 1993 issue of *Topics in Early Childhood Special Education*, entitled "Relationship Between General and Special Early Childhood Education." The contents of the present volume, both explicitly and implicitly, have important implications concerning that "relationship."

Early childhood educators introduced to ECSE are usually immediately struck by, and sometimes intimidated by, what seems a veritable thicket of social policy provisions, including legal mandates, that continue to give a "special" character to services for infants and young children determined to be *eligible* because of a disability or developmental delay. Nearly every chapter in the present volume makes reference to federal legislation, some of which may be more familiar to readers than others. While social policy is determined by several factors — including state law, rules and regulations, and litigation — a brief summary of the key federal legislation referenced by chapter authors is provided here.

An important event that stimulated the development and dissemination of "model" programs for infants and young children with disabilities was enactment, in 1968, of the Handicapped Children's Early Education Assistance Act. As a result of this legislation, which established the Handicapped Children's Early Education Program (HCEEP) within what is now called the Office of Special Education Programs (OSEP), a network of "First Chance" projects was established and funded. Moreover, a system for identifying *validated program models* was implemented, and federal support for *dissemination* of these models was provided.

Most readers are probably generally familiar with the Education of All Handicapped Children Act of 1975, which established the right to a Free Appropriate Public Education (FAPE) for all children with disabilities (specifically defined in the statute) that interfere with educational functioning. Among its most important provisions were those involving procedural due process, including informed parental consent for a multifactored evaluation (MFE) to be conducted to determine whether a student with a "suspected" disability is eligible. The legislation defined what an "appropriate" education for an individual student would be through the Individualized Education Program (IEP) requirement, identifying all the components of the IEP, including annual goals and short-term objectives, based on the description of the student's current levels of educational functioning, with specific provisions for evaluation. Due process is further addressed through the requirement that the IEP be signed by at least a parent, a teacher, and a school representative. While the word *mainstreaming* does not appear in the law, each IEP must include a statement of the extent to which the student will participate in regular education, based on the Least Restrictive Environment (LRE) requirement. This states that each student shall be educated to the maximum extent appropriate in regular education settings, with peers who do not have disabilities. Under this legislation, state education agencies (SEAs) and local education agencies (LEAs, i.e., public schools) were required to *identify* and *assess* all children with disabilities, from birth through age 21, and to serve children beginning at age 3, unless that was in conflict with a state's policy.

With enactment of the Education of the Handicapped Act Amendments of 1986, P.L. 99-457, these provisions, under Part B of the original legislation, were extended to all eligible children, beginning at age 3. Moreover, a new component, Part H, was introduced, which provided incentives for states to initiate a comprehensive system of early intervention for infants and toddlers, birth–age 2, with developmental delays or at-risk for disabilities, as determined by state policies. Unlike services under Part B, now addressing children age 3–21, which are based on an IEP, services under Part H are based on an Individual Family Services Plan (IFSP), developed in collaboration with families and reflecting an individual family's resources, priorities, and concerns. The IFSP must also include the Transition Plan to address what will occur as the child reaches age 3. This federal legislation is the social policy cornerstone of ECSE and early intervention services for infants, toddlers, and preschoolers with disabilities and their families.

Another legislative event of particular importance for persons with disabilities was the Technology-Related Assistance for Individuals with Disabilities Act of 1988. This legislation established assistive and adaptive technology among the related services a student may need in order to benefit from special education. Technological advances have had profound impact on virtually all facets of modern society; for persons with disabilities, such advances have opened doors and created avenues never before imagined.

The overall special education legislation was further changed through the Individuals with Disabilities Education Act of 1990, called IDEA. The change in name, substituting "individuals with disabilities" for "handicapped children," is important because it "puts the person first," acknowledges that law provides for persons into adulthood as well as for "children," and reflects awareness that the degree to which a disability is a "handicap" depends on factors like discrimination, cultural stereotypes, and architectural barriers, as well as the objective condition of the individual. This legislation made certain modifications in the basic legislative structure for special education and related services (e.g., establishing *autism* and *traumatic brain injury* as "categories" of disability, and requiring a *transition plan* addressing the transition from school to work and community living for all students at least by age 16). The IDEA Amendments of 1991 established the Final Rule for Early Intervention Program for Infants and Toddlers with Disabilities. Thus, IDEA is the law encompassing all education and early intervention services for infants, toddlers, children, and youth considered eligible based on criteria defined in the law.

Parallel to this succession of legislative amendments specifically concerning education and related services for children and youth with disabilities have been laws addressing the civil rights of persons of any age who presently have, or who have had, disabilities or who have been considered to have disabilities. Section 504 of the Vocational Rehabilitation Act of 1973, not codified until 1983, made it illegal for any agency receiving federal funds to discriminate against a person on the basis of a disability, defining "eligible" disabilities in language somewhat different from that in the education statutes. The impact of this policy on young children was seen in several areas, including federally funded child-care and early education programs. With regard to public education, if a state mandated provision of kindergarten at age 5, a school district in that state could not exclude a 5-year-old child with a disability. Also, students with disabilities who did not need special education (under P.L. 94-142, now IDEA) could not be discriminated against based on, for example, architectural barriers. Enactment of the Americans with Disabilities Act of 1990 extended these requirements of nondiscrimination to the private sector, with important implications for infants and young children with disabilities whose families seek to enroll them in privately sponsored child-care or education programs.

Each chapter in this volume reflects awareness of this policy context and its specific implications for practice that, in combination with other influences, have defined ECSE and continue to influence its development. In Chapter 1, Nicholas Anastasiow and Christine Nucci provide an overview of the social–historical influences and of the psychological theories reflected in ECSE. Next, Judy Stahlman in Chapter 2 discusses the new, collaborative partnership that must characterize relationships of professionals with families of young children with disabilities. In Chapter 3, Michael Guralnick addresses an area that has assumed great importance in early education of children with disabilities and of those at environmental risk: social competence. In Chapter 4 on the role of play in ECSE, Toni Linder provides a context for understanding and identifying special needs of young children, and for intervention, that acknowledges the central importance of play for young children, typical and exceptional. Philip Safford, Maria Sargent, and Christine Cook provide an overview in Chapter 5 of instructional models in ECSE, tracing their development, describing current issues, and suggesting trends that seem likely to emerge toward *inclusive* approaches. In Chapter 6, Gerald Mahoney and Amy Wheatley pursue such trends, specifically addressing the problematic mix of a "deficit-based" IEP with a *constructivist* pedagogy appropriate to all young children. Chapter 7 by Susan Fowler and Michaelene Ostrosky provides valuable guidance for all involved in conducting careful and thorough transition planning in early intervention and ECSE, preparatory to both entry and departure. Nancy Peterson, Patricia Barber, and Marilyn Ault provide a comprehensive overview of issues in Chapter 8, an equally valuable guide for professionals and caregivers, concerning young children with special health-care needs. In Chapter 9 on applications of assistive and adaptive technology with young children with and at-risk for disabilities, Philippa Campbell, Gail McGregor, and Ellen Nasik include specific information concerning resources available to families and professionals. Jeanette McCollum and Susan Maude, in Chapter 10, consider the implications of needs of children and families, and of better models of service delivery, for personnel preparation, focusing especially on the new and multidisciplinary area of services for infants and toddlers. Finally, in Chapter 11, Bernard Spodek and Olivia Saracho comment on the significance of developments discussed in the foregoing chapters for the general field of early childhood education.

The assistance of Bernard Spodek and Olivia Saracho, editors of the Early Childhood Yearbook Series, in preparation of this volume is gratefully acknowledged, as is that of Susan Liddicoat, Acquisitions Editor for Teachers College Press. Similarly, the very helpful critiques and suggestions provided by members of the Editorial Advisory Board for the yearbook, as well as other reviewers, were sincerely appreciated. Their expert reviews have contributed greatly to the quality of this yearbook. Finally, the authors themselves must be thanked for their enthusiastic and scholarly response to the invitation to contribute to this volume.

REFERENCES

Americans with Disabilities Act of 1990, 42 U.S.C. § 12101 (1990).
Education of All Handicapped Children Act of 1975, P. L. No. 94-142, 20 U.S.C. § 1401 et seq. (1975).
Education of the Handicapped Act Amendments of 1986, P. L. No. 99-457, *amended by* 20 U.S.C. §§ 1471–1485 (1990).

Handicapped Children's Early Education Assistance Act, P. L. No. 90-538 §§
    2–5, 20 U.S.C. § 621nt (1968), *repealed by*, P. L. No. 91-230, title VI, §
    662(5), 84 Stat. 188 (1970).
Individuals with Disabilities Act of 1990, P. L. No. 101-476, 20 U.S.C. §§
    1400–1485 (1990).
Individuals with Disabilities Act Amendments of 1991, P. L. No. 1102-119,
    Early Intervention Program for Infants and Toddlers with Disabilities,
    Final Rule, 34 C.F.R. § 303 (1993).
Technology-Related Assistance for Individuals with Disabilities Act of 1988, P.
    L. No. 100-407, 29 U.S.C. § 2201 (1988).
Vocational Rehabilitation Act of 1973 § 504, P. L. No. 93-112, 29 U.S.C. § 794
    (1983).

CHAPTER 1

Social, Historical, and Theoretical Foundations of Early Childhood Special Education and Early Intervention

Nicholas Anastasiow and Christine Nucci

It has been a long path for society to recognize that early educational experiences can markedly mitigate, ameliorate, or compensate for the impact of developmental delays and disabilities on the functioning and ultimate potential of young children. That recognition has been expressed in the United States in the form of a succession of social policy enactments, culminating in amendments in 1986 and reauthorization, as the Individuals with Disabilities Education Act (IDEA) of 1990, of federal legislation governing special education. These policy developments, like those in other nations, have reflected various influences, both social and scientific. This chapter first presents a social–historical overview of major milestones in the establishment of early childhood special education and early intervention with young children with disabilities. The second section discusses major theoretical influences on this field. However, as will be apparent, these have been closely related and, in some respects, are inseparable.

The sources of the social foundations of early childhood special education (ECSE) are not difficult to trace, as they are a fairly recent development, as Safford, Sargent, and Cook note in Chapter 5. The *Zeitgeist* changed to become more receptive to provisions for U.S. children early in the 20th century, when social concerns over child labor, infant mortality, and childhood diseases became focal issues for reformers, physicians, and the general public. As this movement of advocacy for children expanded, it addressed other concerns, such as the condition of children in orphanages and in residential facilities for persons with mental illness or mental retardation. The latter concern was important in weakening the belief that one's intelligence, psychometrically defined as IQ, was set at birth and little could be done to influence it. There was growing acceptance of the concept that intelligence is the product of environmental as well as genetic influences, with environmental experiences playing a major role in enabling the individual to acquire what is genetically possible (Hunt, 1961). We return to this central issue in the second section of the chapter, which describes and summarizes the major elements of current developmental theories.

To date, few if any coherent theories have been proposed dealing specifically with the psychological development of individuals with disabilities. Instead, the development of children with disabilities is most commonly assumed to proceed in the same fashion as does that of "ordinary people," in Werner and Smith's (1992) term, although they may need additional time or extra assistance in the form of therapies or prostheses to help them achieve developmental milestones. While reference is made to adult functioning, particularly as the foundations of mental health appear to be established through biological–environmental reciprocal interactions, or *transactions*, in the first years of life (Vaillant & Vaillant, 1981; Werner & Smith, 1992), the focus of this chapter is on the early years, defined here as birth through age 5. Theories are necessarily presented in the second part of the chapter in highly condensed fashion, due to space constraints, with the salient features of each theory discussed in terms of applications to ECSE and early intervention.

SOCIAL/HISTORICAL OVERVIEW

Philosophers have long been aware of the importance of the early years of life in influencing adult functioning, as illustrated by a sampling of quotations drawn from Cairns (1983) and Clarke and Clarke (1976):

> The time when they [infants and children] are taking shape is when any impression we choose to make leaves a permanent mark. (Plato, 428–483 B.C.E.)

> We are by nature the most tenacious of what we have imbibed in our infant years. (Quintilian, 35–100 C.E.)

> Great care is to be had on forming children's minds and giving them that seasoning early which shall influence their lives always after. (John Locke, 1631–1704)

> Just as the twig is bent, so is the tree inclined. (Alexander Pope, 1688–1744)

> It seems to be a law of human nature that the first sensation experienced creates the greatest effect. (John Stuart Mill, 1816–1873)

These philosophers based their views concerning the great importance of the early years of life on observations of adults, making inferences about what seemed to be the effects of early childrearing on adult behavior. In essence, these were retrospective observations that pointed to the early years as critical, but did not specify the factors that influenced development. The "theories" were global, and few axioms or principles could be derived from them.

Changing Beliefs About Childrearing

While various other contemporary pioneer psychologists such as Alfred Binet, James Mark Baldwin, and Janet Lapedeire have significantly influenced Western thought, the influence of Sigmund Freud, which continues to be reflected in innumerable facets of contemporary life, has surely been greatest (Cairns, 1983). All subsequent psychological theories have been influenced by Freud's theories and discoveries. Like those of earlier philosophers, Freud's statements about the early years of life suggested, to paraphrase the poet Wordsworth's poetic line, that the child is *psychologically* father to the man, since the events of the first years are of paramount importance to the child's subsequent life (Miller, 1983). Freud's basic and critical discoveries include the principle that human behavior systems are basically affective (i.e., emotional), and are oriented toward attainment of pleasure and avoidance of unpleasure. Moreover, an individual's response to needs results in internalized "ideas" about the self and others, a principle with implications for the understanding and treatment of psychological dysfunction: (1) Ideas can create and shape physical or behavioral symptoms; (2) ideas can modify and remove such symptoms; (3) these ideas are unconscious; (4) however, they can be made conscious by the therapeutic use of free association. Underlying these concepts is the belief that the mind is structured by the individual on the basis of experiences with significant others in the course of early development. Traumatic experiences, real or imagined, could develop into mental illness or be expressed in the form of physical symptoms. These and other psychoanalytic constructs have permeated Western thought and continue to influence childrearing, child care, and early education.

The Freudian influence, together with various of its offshoots in the work of Anna Freud, Harry Stack Sullivan, Heinz Hartmann, Erik Erikson, René Spitz, John Bowlby, Melanie Klein, and others, stimulated examinations of how children are reared (e.g., Skeels, 1966) and the effects on a child's development of prolonged separation from primary caregivers due to institutional placement or hospitalization, as well as the effects of abuse or neglect. The findings generated by such clinical and empirical investigations contributed to increased societal concern about the nurture of children and the importance of social programs for young children.

Cairns (1983) states that the predominant American orientation toward childrearing at the turn of the century was still influenced by the Calvinist tradition, in which children were perceived as little tyrants. Thus, the aim in their rearing was to break their willfulness and force them into a mold characterized by a deep sense of responsibility. This was believed accomplished largely through corporal punishment or the threat of punishment. Freud's theories challenged such punitive and repressive approaches, suggesting alternative interpretations of character development that began to be reflected in a myriad of advice manuals on the care of infants and young children. The new status of the child was expressed, at one level, by efforts on the part of physicians and public health workers to combat infant mortality, and at another by the formulations of such sociologists as G. H. Mead (1934) concerning the origins of the self.

Along with the emergence of pediatric clinics, moves to regulate child labor, and provision of health services in the public schools, the early part of the century saw the rise to prominence of educational progressivism, most closely identified with the child-centered and child-focused philosophy of John Dewey. Dewey asserted that childrearing should not be aimed at breaking down children's willfulness, but rather at freeing and stimulating their natural intelligence, moral goodness, social impulses, and creativity (Rockefeller, 1991). He perceived that the fundamental purpose of all social institutions was to serve as agencies not for the development of products, but for the creation of responsible, self-motivated, resourceful, and creative individuals.

At local levels in cities and towns, growing concerns over mortality in infancy and early childhood, together with increasing interest in childrearing issues, stimulated social and political action. As Sears (1975) reports, Cora Bussey Hills, of Iowa, a major leader in initiating research on children, had experienced the loss of her own children as a result of physicians' lack of knowledge about child development and hygiene. Politically astute, Mrs. Hills had, by 1917, convinced the Iowa state legislature to establish and fund a child-welfare station for research on children and their development. She argued that if research could improve the quality of corn and hogs, it could certainly benefit children as well. Over the next few years, the Rockefeller Foundation provided funds to establish 10 other child-welfare stations throughout the United States. This period also saw the beginning of Lewis Terman's longitudinal study of gifted individuals, from childhood to maturity, and the Berkeley Growth Studies of normal development in children, as well as establishment of the Fels Institute, the Minnesota Child Development Center, the Merrill Palmer Institute, and such professional and scholarly organizations as the American Psychological Association and the Society for Research in Child Development. Detailed accounts of this important phase in the emergence of developmental psychology are provided in several excellent sources. (With regard to children, suffice it here to note that the major focus of these agencies and organizations concerned normal development [excepting Terman's study of gifted children], with occasional attention to emotional problems. Serious research attention was not yet given to the potential benefits of early intervention to ameliorate mental retardation or other developmental disabilities [Cairns, 1983; Sears, 1975].)

Changing Attitudes Toward Disability

Societies have had very ambivalent feelings about individuals with disabilities, influenced by superstition, economics, and a host of other factors. For centuries, many infants with disabilities were abandoned or destroyed, later sold as prostitutes or carnival attractions, and from early in the Christian Era placed in foundling hospitals (where most died), then in almshouses or residential institutions, where they received little effective treatment or none at all (Ziron, 1990). Among the reformers who sought to correct this situation and to develop methods of intervention have been a number of physicians. In fact, especially in the United States, the "medical model" came to dominate the professional view of children with disabilities, with the implication that, if a defect could be cured, the child should be treated.

Cretinism, a condition associated with mental retardation and growth abnormalities, provides a useful example. Until it was discovered that cretinism results from an iodine deficiency in the expectant mother, a host of measures, some imposed by governments, had proved ineffective (Scheerenberger, 1983). Because of the iodine deficiency, the thyroid gland fails to develop in the fetus, with the consequences of mental retardation, shortness of stature, and facial dismorphology. Cretinism can be prevented by adding iodine to the expectant mother's diet, as is now universally done with salt, and should the condition yet occur, its development in the newborn can be prevented through medication. Another landmark discovery was later made concerning phenylketonuria (PKU), a condition in which an excess of enzymes in the brain can lead to mental retardation, controllable through a restricted, special diet for the child (Batshaw & Perret, 1986).

Physicians responded readily to those disorders that appeared to be potentially "curable"; if a cure was not probable, as was assumed in the case of mental retardation, even such enlightened reformers as Philippe Pinel and Benjamin Rush recommended institutionalization but not treatment—Edouard Seguin, S. G. Howe, Hervey Wilbur, and later Maria Montessori being notable exceptions (Scheerenberger, 1983). The residential schools for deaf children and for blind children that emerged in Europe and the United States over the first half of the 19th century were also exceptions, since they were in fact *schools*, and the famous Perkins Institute in Watertown, Massachusetts, pioneered in the education of deaf-blind pupils. But these too were "institutions," serving broad geographic areas, in the sense that pupils fortunate enough to be enrolled were separated from their families and segregated from typical agemates. Unlike other disabilities, such as mental retardation, epilepsy, and cerebral palsy, however, society's response to deafness and blindness had been positively influenced by these demonstrations of the benefits of education. However, as Safford et al. note in Chapter 5, such programs did not begin to serve young children until near the end of the century.

By the mid-20th century, events—most dramatically two world wars—had contributed to greater social awareness of, and more positive attitudes toward, disability. But public figures, such as Helen Keller, were also of great importance. President Franklin Delano Roosevelt, who could not use his legs as a result of poliomyelitis, became a powerful symbol of what a person with a disability could achieve. With his support, the March of Dimes raised funds to support the search for a cure for polio and for birth defects. The common misconception that any disability was associated with mental retardation was dispelled by Roosevelt's long leadership. A later president, John Fitzgerald Kennedy, had a sister with mental retardation, a fact he made public. The President's Commission on Mental Retardation established by Kennedy encouraged the establishment of major centers for research on mental retardation and related disabilities at several universities, as well as the formal establishment of the Bureau of Education for the Handicapped (now the Office of Special Education Programs), dramatically expanding the modest operation Elise Martens had run virtually singlehand-edly for some 20 years after it was authorized in 1931 (Aiello, 1976). Other prominent political figures have had personal reasons for concern for persons with disabilities, notably Hubert H. Humphrey, U.S. Sena-tor and vice president, who had a granddaughter with Down syn-drome, and Lowell Weikert, U.S. Senator and governor of Connecti-cut, who has a child with disabilities.

Senator Weikert's leadership was of critical importance in the de-velopment and passage of P.L. 94-142, the Education of All Hand-icapped Children Act (amended in 1990 as the Individuals with Dis-abilities Education Act). Earlier amendments, enacted in 1986 (P.L. 99-457), extended the provisions for Free Appropriate Public Education (FAPE) to children beginning at age 3, also providing, under a new Part H, for services for infants and toddlers with or at-risk for disabili-ties and their families. Enactment in 1990 of the Americans with Disa-bilities Act extended the prohibition of discrimination on the basis of disability, already in place under the Vocational Rehabilitation Act of 1973 for agencies receiving federal funds, to all facets of society, includ-ing programs affecting infants, toddlers, and young children, such as day care, as well as schools. These laws reflect revolutionary changes in social commitment to the education and civil rights of individuals with disabilities, which in turn reflects the dramatic changes in public atti-tudes that have occurred during the present century.

Research and scholarship also contributed to these changes in atti-tude, among professionals as well as the general public. With publica-tion of his study of long-term outcomes for infants in orphanages, Har-old Skeels (1966) provided convincing evidence confirming initial indications he and his colleagues at the Iowa Child Welfare Station had reported of the crucial importance of early environmental influence. Most who had been adopted achieved normal functioning, while those who remained institutionalized were highly vulnerable to mental retar-dation and mortality. In the masterful *Intelligence and Experience*, J. McVicker Hunt (1961) documented the influence of environmental experiences on the developing brain. Evidence of the impact these expe-riences have on children's and adults' intellectual functioning dispelled the notion that one's IQ was fixed and immutable, further underscored by Benjamin Bloom in *Stability and Change in Human Characteristics* (1964). These works were highly instrumental in the events that led to the initiation of Project Head Start, among other early interven-tion programs initiated as part of the War on Poverty under the administration of President Lyndon B. Johnson. Meanwhile, at the

University of Illinois Samuel Kirk (1972) was demonstrating that children with mental retardation could learn and improve their cognitive and social functioning, rather than experience a decline and widening discrepancy in comparison with peers, as was typical of children with Down syndrome, for example, as well as for children residing in poverty.

Since the 1920s, agencies providing services to children with disabilities had in fact existed in many American communities, and by the 1940s many of these were providing therapies and sometimes nursery classes for preschool-age children, the latter practice having in fact begun in several of the settlement houses established around the turn of the century. The later centers had come into existence, in most instances, largely because of the efforts of a parent of a child with a disability, whose advocacy had led to the formation of a community or even a national organization. When a program of federal grants to encourage development of model early intervention programs for young children with disabilities was authorized through legislation enacted in 1968, the Handicapped Children's Early Education Program (HCEEP), the extent of this network of community programs came as somewhat of a revelation to officials responsible for the administration of these grants. Neither they nor the general public were aware of the work of Louise Phillips in Magnolia, Arkansas, Ruth Jackson in Palo Alto, California, Barbara Smiley in Peoria, Illinois, Setsu Furuno in Honolulu, Hawaii, or of such pioneer professionals as Merle Karnes in Champaign, Illinois. Under the leadership of Bureau of Education for the Handicapped directors James J. Gallagher and Edwin Martin, and HCEEP director Jane DeWeerd, these and many other pioneers formed a national network of more than 200 "First Chance" model programs. Under the Joint Dissemination Review Panel, selected alternative models demonstrated to be effective with diverse groups of infants and young children with disabilities were validated and funded for replication.

While the importance of national research efforts and official leadership cannot be overestimated, it should be remembered that the major impetus for change throughout these mid-century decades came from parents pressing for services for their children with disabilities. These parents challenged officials and legislators, as well as many generally accepted notions, such as the view that autism was a severe form of emotional disturbance caused by psychologically cold parents. Parental advocacy was the prime factor in bringing about litigation in the courts, whose support of the right to treatment and to education in turn led to state and federal legislation (Kirk, Gallagher, & Anastasiow,

1993). From advocacy, to litigation, to legislation, the nation moved from ignoring and segregating persons with disabilities to acknowledging and guaranteeing their rights as citizens. A key provision in that movement has been recognition of the importance and effectiveness of early intervention, a concept supported by changing theoretical perspectives concerning human development.

THEORIES OF CHILD DEVELOPMENT

Teachers are able to teach without reference to a specific theory of human development. However, an adequate theory provides the teacher with a set of hypotheses for understanding children's behavior and for planning instruction. Today's special educators, while strongly influenced by behavioral perspectives concerning techniques, most often turn to general theories of child development for guidance concerning intervention with children with disabilities, as noted earlier. There are several reasons why this is quite appropriate:

1. Children with disabilities are usually cognitively normal.
2. Many infants at biological risk (significantly preterm and/or of low birthweight) attain normal development following appropriate early intervention.
3. Many disabilities, including many emotional problems, result from environmental influences early in life.
4. Children who are developmentally delayed follow the same course of development as do typical peers, although often not at the same rate or reaching the same level of functioning.
5. With the aid of prostheses, many children with disabilities attain milestones determined by the average attainment of children without disabilities of the same age and in the same culture.

Theories of child development proposed during the 20th century have been a mixed bag, some emphasizing the long-term influence of early events on personality and character development (Freud), others addressing diverse human capacities (e.g., Baldwin), and still others resting on the psychometric construct of IQ (e.g., Thorndike's later work). Beginning with Edward S. Thorndike and Ivan Pavlov, a host of learning theories (e.g., E. C. Tolman, Clark L. Hull, Edwin Guthrie, and later B. F. Skinner) have also been invoked concerning facets of children's development, though, with the exception of Skinner (e.g., 1938), rarely today. They have been supplanted by other theories. In this section, brief descriptions of several theoretical perspectives that appear particularly relevant to early intervention for children with disabilities are presented, necessarily in fairly broad terms, with minimal discussion of technical points. For more detailed examination, readers are referred to appropriate references. Our criteria for selecting a theory for discussion were that it should address (1) the source of behavior change in children; (2) the age or stage of development when change is most likely to occur; (3) the nature of the predicted change (i.e., *what*); and (4) the means of facilitating the child's development (i.e., *how*). As will be seen, the theories vary widely with respect to their ability to account explicitly for the mechanisms responsible for change.

Maturationist Perspectives

While the concept of age-expectancy norms is strongly based on the normative sequences of development documented by Arnold Gesell, the "ages-and-stages" framework has also been fostered by interactionist theories, such as those of Heinz Werner and Jean Piaget (Horowitz, 1987). Assessment scales used in early intervention (e.g., Furuno, 1990) identify what children are typically able to do at a particular age (e.g., drink from a cup, draw a circle, run, jump, etc.). These expectations of what a child should be able to do at a certain age are based on findings for large samples of children, who have performed those tasks at those ages. A particular child may be, in comparison with the norm for his or her age, at, above, or below age level, the last suggesting the possibility of developmental delay. Although such scales are helpful as a guide to instruction, they have two fundamental limitations: Neither they nor the theories on which they are based explain (1) *why* most children perform certain tasks at certain ages or (2) the wide variations observed among typically developing children in the performance of specific tasks, variations to some degree attributable to cultural differences in salience of a given skill and/or in opportunities to practice it.

The concept of developmentally appropriate practice (DAP) (Bredekamp, 1987) in early childhood education assumes that one can determine within age groups what children can do and what is an appropriate learning environment to stimulate their development. As useful as this concept is as a guide for the *what* and *when* of teaching of young children, however, it does not explain the sources of developmental change, such as progression from globally undifferentiated to ever finer discrimination in perception and concept formation. While DAP's strong emphasis, in its original form, on age-appropriateness may appear to imply an inordinately maturationist view of young children's development, its intended underlying constructivism is congruent with Piaget's *interactionist* theory, as Gullo (1992) has shown.

Interactionist and Transactionist Theories

Among the very important dimensions interactionists add to descriptions of changes occurring in children over time is the fundamental principle that child development occurs within a social context, initially through interaction with the primary caregiver (Osofsky, 1979). The basic techniques that the caregiver uses to facilitate development are responsiveness, vocalization and verbalization, nonpunitive and nonrepressive physical stimulation, psychological warmth, and encouragement (Werner & Smith, 1992). As the infant becomes mobile, the caregiver provides a safe environment within which the child can explore and manipulate and play with appropriate toys (Bradley & Caldwell, 1977).

Interaction, in the social sense, is the exchange of actions between two people. *Transactions* occur when, in these interactions, one person influences the other, who in turn influences the first person. Caregivers and infants engage in transactions. For example, an infant smiles or coos, and the caregiver's response by speaking in turn encourages the infant. A key point is that the infant (and later the child) is very much involved in his or her own development, initiating actions to which the caregiver responds as well as responding. This *transactional* perspective more accurately describes the process of encouraging development (Sameroff & Fiese, 1990) than have traditional formulations that stress either internal (i.e., biological) influences or, like the next group, external ones.

Learning Theories

Learning theories accounting for *instrumental* or *operant* learning have assumed that changes in behavior are initiated from outside the individual. Older views of learning as essentially based on stimulus–response connections are rarely invoked today to explain changes in the course of children's development. In more recent perspectives, based on the work of B. F. Skinner, these changes are achieved by carefully arranging the child's environment through systematic use of reinforcers and schedules of reinforcement, nonreinforcement, and punishment. These concepts provide an excellent technology, as Skinner (1938) proposed, useful in suggesting techniques for teachers in planning and delivering instruction. However, they do not account satisfactorily for lasting learning or qualitative changes in the course of development, nor do the concepts of stimulus or response generalization account adequately for children's ability to adapt prior learning to novel situations.

Social learning theory, originally derived from Freudian principles in combination with ideas of J. M. Baldwin and other theorists, later integrated with Skinnerian concepts, is similarly effective in describing particular facets of learning but not development. Such key concepts as imitation and modeling, based on social learning theory, are useful for teachers, however, as are those involving principles of reinforcement. Moreover, Bandura's (1977) concept of *self-efficacy* links social learning theory to more recent affect formulations, described in a subsequent section.

Cognitive Theories

Theories of cognitive development have focused on the course of progression from a globally undifferentiated state to the advanced skill mastery and abstract reasoning of adulthood. These theories tend to emphasize what is learned and how it is learned, rather than the total personality of the individual. Jean Piaget, the dominant cognitive developmental theorist from the 1960s through the 1980s, considered cognition in two ways. First, it was the combination of processes by which children learned: assimilation (taking knowledge in), accommodation (adjusting to new knowledge), and equilibration (a balance of assimilation and accommodation). Piaget proposed that all learning is based on primitive, congenitally organized, reflexive biological functions present at birth, which are transformed through successive interactions with the infant's environment. The second meaning of cognition refers to *what* is learned. While Piaget proposed that the child's task is to reinvent the world, his explanation of why this occurs as epistemic curiosity — the need to know — did not account explicitly for motivation, nor does his theory explicitly address the internal, neurologic mechanisms involved. Consequently, while the ideas of Piaget and other cognitive theorists also imply highly useful principles of teaching and learning, cognitive theory has, in our view, failed to yield a comprehensive theory of children's development.

Another cognitive theorist, L. S. Vygotsky (1978, 1987), gave particular emphasis to the social–cultural dimension of early development. Like Piaget, Vygotsky proposed that at birth the infant possesses sensory-motor patterns, but emphasized that, if allowed to develop unassisted by persons in a culture, the result would be a nonhuman animal.

He contended that the caregiver influences the coordination and generalization of sensory-motor patterns through language that the infant internalizes. In this way, language and thought become indistinguishable. The child gradually comes to control his or her own actions and initiate further learning with the help of an adult, or more advanced peer, who provides learning experiences just beyond what the child has mastered. This area, which Vygotsky called the *zone of proximal development*, is thus the appropriate area in which to instruct a child.

Brain Maturation Theories

Basic research (e.g., Greenough, Wallace, Alcanta, Hawrylak, Weiler, & Withers, 1992; Hebb, 1949, 1980) has continued to provide strong support for the position that intervention begun in the earliest years can affect neurological development of children with developmental disabilities. This line of scholarship has been strengthened by the work of brain maturation theorists (Kuo, 1967; Lecours, 1975), which has demonstrated that human brain development progresses in regular stages, being 30 percent mature at birth and essentially completed in the fourth year of life. The assumption is that the genes prepare neurological structures to receive information required for species-specific learning. For human beings, the most common example cited is language. Brain maturationists assume that the movement from globally undifferentiated perceptual to more and more hierarchically structured functioning is orchestrated by gene-based brain maturation and experiences in the environment that are species-relevant. For example, while a child is genetically programmed with the capability to learn any language in the world, the language of the environment in which she or he is reared is the language that is learned.

Gazzaniga (1992), a more recent theorist, has gone much further. He proposes that the brain contains, in various modules important for language, cognition, and so forth, mechanisms by which the child constructs experience. Infants draw on prelinguistic mechanisms, programmed for all humans in a sequence, moving from cries, coos, and babbling, to protowords (mama, dada), and then words in the first year of life (Bates, 1979). Drawing on the work of Pinker (1991), Gazzaniga (1992) notes that very young children have the ability to interpret syntactic structures of their language with very few examples and without negative examples. Like Pinker, Gazzaniga contends that the mechanisms for such learnings are genetically programmed. Thus, infants not only possess self-regulating abilities, but they also are able to choose relevant areas of the environment to master.

Fischer's Skill Theory

Fischer (1980; Fischer & Canfield, 1986) postulates that all knowledge is stored as skills. Like Piaget, Fischer believes that the complexity of knowledge stored over time is acquired in a hierarchical fashion, through environmental interactions with an adult or knowledgable peer, much as Vygotsky (1978, 1987) postulated. Unlike Piaget, Fischer believes that the process of moving into higher and higher skill levels is related to brain maturation. Thus, as an individual's thinking processes become more sophisticated, the advances are attributed to environmental influences, especially the support of adults and more advanced peers, in interaction with brain maturation. In the course of maturation, the brain takes in information and builds structures for processing it (Greenough et al., 1992). The learnings must occur before the brain areas serving the functions are mature, hence the importance, for children with disabilities, of early intervention (Anastasiow, 1982). To Fischer, the level of subsequent functioning is greatly dependent on the nature and quality of early experience and intervention.

According to Fischer, development is characterized by the progression of skills through ever-increasing hierarchical levels into the fourth year of life. The child matures as the brain matures, and through the teaching of others, the child's skills gradually increase in complexity through the process of combining and integrating lower-level skills into new structures. While maturation plays a role, this process does not occur in a social vacuum.

Psychobiological Theories of Affect

Contemporary theories of affect owe much to earlier formulations of Freud, Spitz, Erikson, and other psychoanalytic theorists (Emde, Gaensbauer, & Harmon, 1976). However, these theorists have also drawn heavily on recent work in the area of brain development and have employed a more behavioral approach in their research with children. They too are transactionists, emphasizing the importance of transactions occurring between brain development as an affective system and the environment in which the infant develops a sense of self, as well as feelings of autonomy and competence, most of which is mastered in the first four years of life (Emde, 1991a, 1991b). Emde's (1983) basic assumption, after Izard (1977), is that emotions are biologically programmed and become "affect" as the child develops strong feelings, the consequences of which lead to actions. It is through the expression of affects in transaction with information from the environment (i.e., the caregiver's responses) that the self is developed, similar to what occurs as an outcome of the process of *attachment* (Sroufe, 1983). The psychobiological position thus includes the important caregiver–child transactions that influence the development of the secure or insecure self, feelings of self-esteem, and the moral rules of a given culture (Emde, 1991a). While biology has prepared the child with the mechanisms for learning, the ability to regulate oneself, gained through transactions with the caregiver, affects monitoring and goal orientation. The latter refers to the task of the development of the self, a continuing process through which all behavior is related and integrated throughout a person's life (Emde, 1989, Emde & Buchsbaum, 1989).

To support the universality and importance of goal orientation, Emde uses examples of children with disabilities drawn from research, such as Fraiberg's (1977) with congenitally blind infants. They, as well as infants with congenital deafness, cerebral palsy, or without limbs, "have different sensorimotor experiences but . . . typically develop object permanence, representational intelligence and self awareness in early childhood" (Emde, 1983, p. 170). Generally, these recent theoretical developments concerned with social and affective areas of young children's development appear to offer important implications for work with infants with disabilities, congruent with the *family-focused* emphasis in early intervention.

Summary

As we have seen, there is no overall consensus among psychological theorists concerning the nature of children's development or the salience of factors that influence its course. However, one can abstract from the various theoretical perspectives, and from research they have generated, the following basic scientific principles:

1. The brain is only partially (30 percent) mature at birth and continues to develop over the first five years of life (Lecours, 1975).
2. The incompleteness of brain development makes it very open to the influence of experiences (Greenough et al., 1992; Plomin, 1986).
3. Experiences of all types are recorded in the brain (Greenough et al., 1992).
4. Experience does not write on the brain as if it were a "blank slate"; there are species-specific biological tendencies to develop some forms of behavior, such as language (Gazzaniga, 1992; Hebb, 1949, 1980).
5. These potentials direct the organism toward behavior potentials that every member will develop if reared in species-typical environments (Kuo, 1967).
6. Culture is an organizing influence, the impact of which begins early

and which affects every domain (Hebb, 1949, 1980; Kuo, 1967; Vygotsky, 1987).

7. Development is a process of continuous change, an open biological system that is self-maintaining, self-restoring, and self-regulating (von Bertalanffy, 1968, 1978).

8. Human beings are, from infancy, active organisms exploring the environment, whose innate abilities and dispositions help them to select what is relevant and adaptive (Emde, 1983; Plomin, 1986).

9. While reinforcement (Bijou & Baer, 1961; Skinner, 1938) and social learning (Bandura, 1977) theorists consider behavioral laws involving external influences to be the mechanisms of all behavioral change, they are mechanisms of learning and teaching, not of development. Change in the course of children's development results from reciprocal transactions of the biologically maturing organism with the social and physical environment (Emde et al., 1976; Fischer, 1980; Sameroff & Fiese, 1990).

CONCLUSION

The emergence and rapid growth of the field of early childhood special education has been influenced by a combination of social–historical and political developments, advocacy on the part of parents, and scientific influences. A core belief underlying the field is that early intervention can positively influence the course of development of infants and young children with or at risk for disabilities. The research that has been and continues to be conducted, both to test that fundamental hypothesis and to identify the components of optimally effective intervention, has been to varying degrees guided by theory. Conversely, research findings concerning early intervention with young children with disabilities also suggest implications for emerging theoretical perspectives on the nature of human development itself. The affect theory of Emde and the skill theory of Fischer, in particular, reflect promising current efforts to integrate diverse research findings and provide a coherent, comprehensive view of early development as a foundation for early intervention.

REFERENCES

Aiello, B. (1976). Especially for special educators: A sense of our own history. In J. B. Jordan (Ed.), *Exceptional child education at the bicentennial: A parade of progress* (pp. 16–25). Reston, VA: Council for Exceptional Children.

Anastasiow, N. J. (1982). *Development and disability.* Baltimore: Paul H. Brookes.

Bandura, A. (1977). *Social learning theory.* Englewood Cliffs, NJ: Prentice-Hall.

Bates, E. (1979). The emergence of symbols. In E. Bates (Ed.), *Symbol formation* (pp. 1–32). Orlando, FL: Academic Press.

Batshaw, M. L., & Perret, Y. M. (1986). *Children with handicaps: A medical primer* (2nd ed.). Baltimore: Paul H. Brookes.

Bijou, S., & Baer, D. M. (1961). *Child development.* New York: Appleton-Century-Crofts.

Bloom, B. S. (1964). *Stability and change in human characteristics.* New York: Wiley.

Bradley, R. H., & Caldwell, B. M. (1977). Home observation for measurement of the environment: A validation study of screening efficiency. *American Journal of Mental Deficiency, 81,* 417–420.

Bredekamp, S. (1987). *Developmentally appropriate practice in early childhood programs serving children from birth through age 8* (Expanded ed.). Washington, DC: National Association for the Education of Young Children.

Cairns, R. B. (1983). The emergence of developmental psychology. In P. H. Mussen (Ed.), *Handbook of child psychology* (Vol. 1, 4th ed., pp. 41–102). New York: Macmillan.

Clarke, A. M., & Clarke, A. D. (1976). *Early experience: Myth and evidence.* New York: Macmillan.

Emde, R. N. (1983). The prerepresentational self and its affective core. In A. Solnit (Ed.), *The psychoanalytic study of the child* (Vol. 38, pp. 165–192). Washington, DC: National Institute of Mental Health.

Emde, R. N. (1989). Toward a psychoanalytic theory of affect: I. The organizational model and its propositions. In S. Greenspan & H. Pollack (Eds.), *Infancy* (pp. 165–191). Madison, CT: International Universities Press.

Emde, R. N. (1991a). Amae: Intimacy and early moral self. *Infant Mental Health Journal, 13*(1), 34–42.

Emde, R. N. (1991b). The wonder of our complex enterprise: Steps enabled by attachment in the effects of relationships. *Infant Mental Health Journal, 12*(3), 164–172.

Emde, R. N., & Buchsbaum, H. K. (1989). Toward a psychoanalytic theory of affect: II. Emotional development and signaling in infancy. In S. Greenspan & H. Pollack (Eds.), *Infancy* (pp. 193–227). Madison, CT: International Universities Press.

Emde, R. N., Gaensbauer, T. J., & Harmon, R. J. (1976). *Emotional expression in infancy.* New York: International Universities Press.

Fischer, K. W. (1980). A theory of cognitive development: The control and construction of hierarchies of skills. *Psychological Review, 87*(6), 477–531.

Fischer, K. W., & Canfield, R. L. (1986). The ambiguity of stage and structure in behavior: Person and environment in the development of psychological structures. In I. Levin (Ed.), *Stage and structure: Reopening the debate* (pp. 246–267). Norwood, NJ: Ablex.

Fraiberg, S. (1977). *Insights from the blind: Comparative studies of blind and sighted infants*. New York: Basic Books.

Furuno, S. (1990). *HELP*. Palo Alto, CA: VOIT.

Gazzaniga, M. (1992). *Nature's mind*. New York: Basic Books.

Greenough, W., Wallace, C., Alcanta, B., Hawrylak, A., Weiler, I., & Withers, G. (1992). Development of the brain: Experience affects the structure of neurons, gila, and blood vessels. In N. Anastasiow & S. Harel (Eds.), *The at-risk infant: Vol. 3, Intervention, families, and research*. Baltimore: Paul H. Brookes.

Gullo, D. (1992). *Developmentally appropriate teaching in early childhood*. Washington, DC: National Education Association.

Hebb, D. O. (1949). *The organization of behavior*. New York: Wiley.

Hebb, D. O. (1980). *Essay on mind*. Hillsdale, NJ: Erlbaum.

Horowitz, F. D. (1987). *Exploring developmental theories*. Hillsdale, NJ: Erlbaum.

Hunt, J. M. (1961). *Intelligence and experience*. New York: Ronald Press.

Izard, C. E. (1977). The emergence of emotion and the development of consciousness in infancy. In J. Davidson & R. Davidson (Eds.), *Human consciousness and its transformation* (pp. 193–216). New York: Plenum.

Kirk, S. (1972). *Presidential address*. Presented at the meeting of the Division of Early Childhood, Council for Exceptional Children, Washington, DC.

Kirk, S., Gallagher, J., & Anastasiow, N. (1993). *Educating exceptional children*. Boston: Houghton Mifflin.

Kuo, Z. Y. (1967). *The dynamics of behavior development*. New York: Random House.

Lecours, A. R. (1975). Myelogenetic correlates of the development of speech and language. In E. H. Lenneberg & E. Lenneberg (Eds.), *Foundations of language development* (Vol. 1, pp. 121–135). New York: Academic Press.

Mead, G. H. (1934). *Mind, self, society*. Chicago: University of Chicago Press.

Miller, P. H. (1983). *Theories of developmental psychology*. San Francisco: Freeman.

Osofsky, J. D. (1979). *Handbook of infant development*. New York: Wiley-Interscience.

Piaget, J. (1983). Piaget's theory. In P. H. Mussen (Ed.), *Handbook of child psychology* (Vol. I, pp. 703–732). New York: Wiley.

Pinker, S. (1991). Role of language. *Science, 253*(3), 530–535.

Plomin, R. (1986). *Development, genetics, and psychology*. Hillsdale, NJ: Erlbaum.

Rockefeller, S. (1991). *John Dewey*. New York: Columbia University Press.

Sameroff, A. J., & Fiese, B. H. (1990). Transactional regulation and early intervention. In S. J. Meisels & J. P. Shonkoff (Eds.), *Handbook of early childhood intervention* (pp. 119–149). New York: Cambridge University Press.

Scheerenberger, R. C. (1983). *History of mental retardation*. Baltimore: Paul H. Brookes.

Sears, R. R. (1975). Your ancients revisited. In E. M. Hetherington (Ed.), *Handbook of research in child development* (Vol. 5, pp. 1–28). Chicago: University of Chicago Press.

Skeels, H. M. (1966). Adult status of children with contrasting early life experiences: A follow-up study. *Monographs of the Society for Research in Child Development, 31* (Serial No. 105).

Skinner, B. F. (1938). *The behavior of organisms*. New York: Appleton-Century-Crofts.

Sroufe, L. A. (1983). Infant-caregiver attachment patterns of adaptation in preschool. In M. Perlmutter (Ed.), *Minnesota symposia in child psychology* (Vol. 16, pp. 41–81). Hillsdale, NJ: Erlbaum.

Vaillant, G. E., & Vaillant, C. O. (1981). Natural history of male psychological health. *American Journal of Psychiatry, 138*, 1433–1440.

von Bertalanffy, L. (1968). *General systems theory*. New York: George Braziller.

von Bertalanffy, L. (1978). *Perspectives on general systems theory*. Cambridge: Harvard University Press.

Vygotsky, L. S. (1978). *Mind in society*. Cambridge: Harvard University Press.

Vygotsky, L. S. (1987). *Thought and language*. Cambridge: MIT Press.

Werner, E., & Smith, R. (1992). *Overcoming all odds*. Ithaca, NY: Cornell University Press.

Ziron, T. J. (1990). Physical abuse. *Intervention in School and Clinic, 26*(1), 6–10.

CHAPTER 2

Family and Professional Collaboration: Issues in Early Childhood Special Education

Judy I. Stahlman

While educators have long pondered, discussed, and researched the importance in a child's education of effective relationships between professionals and families, the quality of these relationships has been highly variable (Gallagher & Vietze, 1986). Parents have been viewed as individuals to be ignored, as sources of problems, as resources, and as teachers in relationship to their children's educational programs (Turnbull & Turnbull, 1990). Although parent involvement has been a key focus of services for children with disabilities, such variability and ambivalence have especially characterized parent-professional relationships in special education (Shea & Bauer, 1991). Parents do not always report positive or supportive relationships on the part of professionals (American Association for the Care of Children's Health, 1987), nor is the level and quality of parental involvement in children's educational planning always commensurate with legal requirements, let alone best practice guidelines.

Like societal views of families in general, our conceptions of family and professional involvement in the education of children with special needs have evolved over time. As family structures themselves have changed and become more diverse, the diversity of family resources, styles, and priorities has been increasingly recognized. Moreover, needs and potential contributions of brothers and sisters of children enrolled in special education programs have been explored, as have those of extended family members.

The special emphasis on working with families that has developed in programs for infants, toddlers, and preschoolers with or at risk for disabilities (Peterson, 1987) has been influenced by a variety of factors.

First, the field of early childhood in general has recognized the importance of positive relationships with parents of the children served in early childhood programs. Second, the concept of *normalization* for individuals with disabilities has played a strong role in this evolutionary process (Kaiser & Hemmeter, 1989; Nirje, 1985; Wolfensberger, 1972), both because of the centrality of parents in the lives of all young children and because parents want their child with a disability, to the extent possible, to have life opportunities experienced by other children. Finally, legal mandates have been established that give a far more fundamental role to parents and families in determining and providing services for infants and toddlers who have or are at-risk for having disabilities. These mandates encourage continued opportunities for meaningful parent involvement during the preschool years, for children age 3 to 5.

The issues of concern to early childhood specialists working with families of children with special needs include those relating to all family and professional collaborations, as well as some that are unique to families of children with disabilities. Variables such as geographic location, population density, parents' and teachers' cultural backgrounds, parents' previous experiences with education and educational professionals, and educators' previous experiences with parents influence all relationships between educational staffs and families (Turnbull & Turnbull, 1990). The unique issues that are specific to parents of children with disabilities include the affective consequences for the family when a child has a disability, influences associated with the specific nature and severity of the child's disability and the resulting demands on parents' energy and time, financial issues brought about by such things as the child's medical and treatment needs, and other factors (Bailey & McWilliam, 1990; Frey, Greenberg, & Fewell, 1989; Gallagher, Beckman, & Cross, 1983; Lambie & Daniels-Mohring, 1993; Minnes, 1988; Stewart, 1986).

Early childhood educators must understand and consider these issues when working with families of young children with developmental delays or disabilities. This is not an easy task and it requires skills that, for most teachers, also must evolve over time. Bailey and McWilliam (1990) identified two basic guidelines for facilitating a "normalized family focus":

(1) families of children with [disabilities] should be accorded the same respect given to parents of normally developing children with a particular emphasis on promoting family choice; and
(2) a primary goal of early intervention should be to engage in activities designed to promote normalized community adaptation. (p. 41)

Understanding complex attitudinal issues and using specific interaction and intervention strategies can contribute to more successful
collaboration. This chapter considers such issues and examines ways in
which early childhood educators can build more positive relationships
with families and thus enhance their work with young children, including those with disabilities.

LEGISLATIVE INFLUENCES ON
FAMILY/PROFESSIONAL RELATIONSHIPS

A significant factor in promoting increased involvement of families
of children with disabilities in their youngsters' educational programs
has been the passage of specific legislation to mandate such opportunities. Prior to the passage of P.L. 94-142 in 1975 (now entitled the
Individuals with Disabilities Education Act—IDEA), parents of children with disabilities were often excluded from participating in their
child's school program (Washington & Gallagher, 1986). Children were
at times placed in special education classrooms and labeled as having a
disability without the informed consent of their parents. P.L. 94-142
put a halt to such practices and, moreover, required that parents be
treated as "equal partners" in the development of their child's education
program. The mechanisms to ensure this were informed consent for a
process of multifactored evaluation to determine a child's eligibility
and, if the child were determined eligible, participation in the development of, and formal agreement to, a child's Individual Education Program (IEP).

Although the initial legislation did not mandate that states provide
educational services to preschool-age children with disabilities, enactment in 1986 of its subsequent amendment, P.L. 99-457, extended all
the rights and privileges afforded to parents of school-age children receiving special education services to parents of children from 3 to 5
years of age who had disabilities. Parents were to be involved in the
development of their child's educational program after they had given
their consent for a multifactored assessment and for their child to receive special education services. Parents of preschool-age children were
also provided with the same procedural safeguards, such as due-process
rights, as parents of school-age children with suspected disabilities.
Moreover, the amended law suggested that parents of preschoolers be
given additional opportunities to become involved in their child's school
program.

P.L. 99-457 also provided incentives for serving eligible infants and toddlers, from birth to age 3, mandating that if services were provided, programs must maintain a *family-centered* focus (Kaiser & Hemmeter, 1989). Regulations were established requiring that Individualized Family Services Plans (IFSP) be designed for infants and toddlers up to age 3 instead of Individual Education Programs. This mandate indirectly set a requirement for *family assessment*, since the IFSP must be based on family concerns, priorities, and resources (Winton & Bailey, 1990). In addition, parents are to be treated as *primary decision makers* for their child's program rather than "equal partners" in the development of the IFSP. These mandates moved the emphasis from parents to *families*. They reflected the growing awareness that young children are not only individuals but are members of a family unit; decisions made about educational services for young children affect not only them, but most often the entire family.

VARIABLES INFLUENCING FAMILY AND PROFESSIONAL COLLABORATION

As stated previously, in addition to issues that are unique to families of young children with disabilities, parent-professional relationships are also affected by more general issues. As noted by Leonard in an interview with *Newsweek* (Seligmann, 1990) "family has become a fluid concept" (p. 38). Both the composition of the family and the responsibilities of its members are changing. One main factor that influences parents' ability to collaborate with educators and other professionals is the number of other roles they play as adults, in addition to that of parent. This may be greatly influenced by the changing configuration of the family in today's culture. If children today live in a two-parent family, both parents may be working outside the home. If one adult has the main responsibility for the children, as is true in many single-parent families, that parent often provides sole financial support.

Another family issue that influences home–school collaboration is the number of other children in the family (Barber, Turnbull, Behr, & Kerns, 1988). Parents may have several children for whom they must provide support for basic (i.e., physical and emotional) and educational needs (Lambie & Daniels-Mohring, 1993). In addition, parents may have responsibilities for extended family members such as their own parents, who may live with their children or may require extra support with daily living. Work responsibilities that require extended hours or day and evening work hours may also put extra demands on parents.

Another issue related to diversity among families is that of cultural background. This factor may influence not only the type of day-care or preschool program parents seek for their young child, but the way in which they view their role in collaborating with professionals (Lynch & Hanson, 1992). Interactions may also be influenced by parents' own experiences as children with teachers, as well as by previous experiences they have had as adults with educators. Similarly, educators bring their own set of values to each interaction they have with families. In addition to the skills they have learned in the course of their own general education and professional training, they are also influenced by their cultural backgrounds, their previous experiences with parents, and the attitudes and values conveyed in the policies established for the programs in which they work. Although these variables are not conscious parts of the interactions between families and professionals, they need to be recognized by all educators as ones that affect their contacts with parents, as well as their children.

Issues Related to Having a Child with a Disability

In addition to these common issues, there are a number of factors that are unique to families of children with disabilities, most basically that parents must deal with the fact their child has a disability (Bromwich, 1984; Gargiulo, 1985). This has been compared to the loss of the "perfect child" (Turnbull & Turnbull, 1990). All parents build expectations during a pregnancy relating to the unborn child and how this new arrival will change their lives. Prospective parents, however, generally do not plan for a child with a disability. Therefore, when their child is diagnosed as having special needs, parents often experience feelings that are part of a grieving cycle. Such feelings are experienced not only by parents of children with disabilities, but by most people when confronted with a loss in their lives (Kubler-Ross, 1969). As with all feelings, they change over time, both in type and in intensity.

Gargiulo (1985) has outlined several common phases of feelings experienced by parents when they find out that their child has a disability. In the primary phase, parents may experience shock, grief, and depression. These feelings are characteristic reactions when one is trying to relate to the fact that a problem exists. The secondary phase, represented by such feelings as ambivalence, guilt, anger, sadness, shame, and embarrassment, reflects the fact that the parent has recognized the problem and is trying to figure out what this means in his or her life. The tertiary phase, which may include bargaining, adaptation and reorganization, and acceptance, represents the individual's adjust-

ment to this new situation. Although this grieving cycle has been repeatedly identified as a common reaction experienced by parents, it is critical to recognize that each parent's response is unique (Hunt, Cornelius,
Leventhal, Miller, Murray, & Stoner, 1989). The amount of time it takes
for parents to work through these feelings varies, as do the actual emotions experienced. In fact, some parents report that they never experienced any of the emotions considered part of this grieving process.

Adjustment to having a child with a disability does not mean that
parents can then respond to all situations with equanimity. Turnbull
and Turnbull (1990) have reported that parents often reexperience some
of these emotions when significant events occur for their child, or when
significant events are occurring for their child's peers but not for their
son or daughter. This pattern has been described as "recapitulation."
Recapitulation in music occurs when a particular phrase of the score
that was presented previously is later repeated. This is not necessarily
the first line of the music, but may be found at any point in the piece.
Just as musicians repeat phrases of music, parents repeat feelings that
they have experienced previously in relationship to their child's disability. Sadness may resurface when they first encounter other three-year-
olds who are "talking up a storm" while their child remains nonverbal.
A suggestion by a physical therapist that their child use a walker to
assist with ambulation may cause parents to feel angry again that their
child has a disability. It is natural and appropriate for these feelings to
reoccur.

Acceptance, therefore, does not mean that parents are happy or
unemotional about the fact that their child has a disability. Instead,
perhaps acceptance means that parents no longer try to change the fact
that their child has a disability. They are able to adjust to this fact and
continue with their lives. It is always appropriate, however, for parents
to continue to advocate for their child, to seek appropriate services, and
to promote as typical a life as possible for their child. Families learn to
cope in spite of the fact that they experience great stress with the recognition that their child has a disability. In fact, these families may become closer and stronger as a result of dealing with this challenge than
they would have without it (Kneedler, Hallahan, & Kauffman, 1984).
Professionals must be willing to recognize this fact and to give families
the respect they deserve.

Another issue that families of children with disabilities face at
times is that of extensive demands on resources, both physical and financial (Boyce, Behl, Mortensen, & Akers, 1991; Innocenti, Kwisun, &
Boyce, 1992). Erickson and Upshur (1989) compared the caretaking

burden and social support for mothers of infants with disabilities with those for mothers of typically developing infants. Significant differences in overall caretaking time were reported by both mothers of children with Down syndrome and children with motor disabilities, as compared with mothers of children who were typically developing. Interestingly, mothers of children with disabilities tended to be more satisfied with the support they received from family, friends, and community support groups than were mothers of infants without disabilities.

In a longitudinal study of parent stress, Hanson and Hanline (1990) found a positive relationship between maternal stress and the "demandingness" of a child with disabilities. This was particularly true for children with neurological disorders. These studies exemplify the fact that children with disabilities often require additional attention and physical care from parents. Activities such as feeding, bathing, and dressing may take longer as a result of the child's disability. In addition, parents may be responsible for completing these self-care tasks for a longer period of time than are most parents. For example, individuals with severe multiple disabilities, such as may be associated with cerebral palsy, may need assistance with these tasks throughout their lives. These types of needs result in extended energy demands on many parents during their sons' and daughters' preschool years and sometimes throughout childhood and into adulthood.

Financial concerns are also often exacerbated for a family by a child's needs associated with a disability. Children with disabilities often have a higher incidence of medical problems along with need for various medical treatments (Batshaw & Perret, 1992). Added visits to the doctor, surgeries to correct disability-related problems (e.g., tendon lengthening or shunt revision), chronic needs for medication (e.g., seizure-control drugs), and adaptive equipment and braces all can add up to extensive financial demands on some parents. In addition, parents may have to pay more for baby sitters, since trained individuals may be needed to care for their child's medical needs.

Bailey and McWilliam (1990) noted that "families of children with [disabilities] inevitably must assume 'nonnormal roles' and engage in activities not expected of other parents" (p. 41). Parents of children with disabilities are often involved in working with medical and community agency professionals from a very early point in their child's life. They may be asked to plan intervention programs, attend training sessions, and follow through on and provide educational and therapeutic intervention at home. These demands can be quite taxing, depending on the many other variables with which parents have to cope and on the sensitivity with which professionals approach parents about such issues.

Family issues centering around siblings of children with disabilities must also be considered. A variety of research findings have been identified concerning siblings of children with disabilities — some negative, others positive. On the negative side, researchers have found that siblings of children with disabilities may receive less attention from their parents as a result of the care requirements of their brother or sister with a disability (Fisher & Roberts, 1983). Some, especially oldest female children, may themselves have had to assume extensive and demanding responsibilities (Fowle, 1968). In addition, Lobata (1991) found that mothers were more likely to reprimand siblings of individuals with disabilities and to provide more directives to these children. Consequently, some siblings may feel angry, although many tend to keep these feelings to themselves.

On the other hand, studies have shown that having a brother or sister who has a disability can also have a positive or neutral effect on siblings. Lobata (1991) also found that young siblings of children with disabilities demonstrated more parallel and social play than did siblings of typically developing children. These siblings were also found to be more nurturing. Mates (1990) conducted research on 33 siblings of individuals with autism in which he examined the children's academic achievement, self-concept, school adjustment, and home adjustment. No significant differences were found on any of the variables as compared with normative samples for each measure. Grossman (1972), on the other hand, found that college-age siblings reported that their sensitivity to diversity had been enhanced by their relationship with their brothers and sisters who were disabled. Ferrari (1984) reported that the adjustment of siblings appears to be strongly connected to the level of adjustment parents are able to attain.

Finally, families of children with disabilities may have been involved in seeking services and advocating for appropriate programs for their young child since the time of their son or daughter's birth. In fact, enactment of public policies and provision of services for children with disabilities have in many instances resulted directly from parent advocacy (Turnbull & Turnbull, 1990). This type of action often requires assertive and sometimes aggressive behavior on the part of parents. Whether or not parents have had to "fight" to secure service, for many, their involvement with educators and early interventions began shortly after their child's birth. These varied experiences with service providers all influence the ways in which parents continue to deal with early childhood professionals.

STRATEGIES FOR ENHANCING FAMILY
AND PROFESSIONAL COLLABORATION

There are a number of strategies that professionals in the field of early childhood education can use to facilitate the development of enhanced relationships with parents of children with disabilities. First, it is critical to respond to each family on an individual basis. Barber et al. (1988) stress the importance of taking a "family systems" approach to working with young children. This requires knowing not only the needs of the child, but also the needs and resources of the family in relationship to meeting the child's needs and the expectations set by service providers for family involvement. Just as all children are unique, all families have their own strengths and styles. Professionals must be sensitive to this fact and work *with* parents to meet the needs of their child.

In some cases, informal discussion with parents may provide the needed information to allow for this type of communication and relationship. At other times, more formal needs assessment may be required (Bailey & Simeonsson, 1988; Dunst & Leet, 1987). Such types of assessment may range from merely collecting information on parents' preferences for methods to communicate their child's behavior at preschool to asking parents to complete surveys on the types of social supports they have and financial needs in relationship to their child's disability (Dunst, Trivette, & Deal, 1988). Regardless of the information that is sought, it is critical for professionals to be sensitive to the intrusive nature of needs assessments and to work with families on this activity in a way that best meets each family's individual style and needs.

A variety of methods have been designed to accomplish the goal of family assessment while maintaining respect for family needs and diversity. Dunst et al. (1988) published a series of rating forms that could be used in a selective fashion to secure such information. A more general family-focused ecological assessment tool, the *Inventory of Parent Experiences Scale* (IPE), was designed by Crnic and Greenberg (1981). Although a study completed by Sexton, Thompson, Scott, and Wood (1990) questioned the validity of the subscale data, results showed that the total IPE scores were acceptable.

Winton (1988) designed the *Family Planning Guide*, which provides professionals with a method for using referral information, medical records, and other information often received initially on a child to determine appropriate family interview topics. This approach promotes face-to-face discussions with multiple family members in the assessment process, which has been found advantageous in developing positive relationships with parents (Winton & Bailey, 1990).

Meeting Diverse Needs

Because of the emphasis on family assessment and involvement in early intervention and early childhood special education, sensitivity to cultural diversity is particularly important. Hanson, Lynch, and Wayman (1990) suggest that professionals must first examine their own values in relationship to "fundamental issues, such as personal development, family relationships, and the relationships between the family and the community" (p. 126). They must also analyze ethnographic information relevant to the families that they serve. Focus should be given to the following aspects:

1. Describe the ethnic group with which the family identifies;
2. Identify the social organization of the ethnic community;
3. [Identify] the prevailing belief system within the particular ethnic community;
4. Become informed about the history of a particular ethnic group;
5. Determine how members of the community gain access to and utilize social services; and
6. [Identify] the attitudes of the ethnic community toward help seeking. (p. 127)

Teachers who take the time to follow these suggestions will gain a better understanding of the families with whom they work and be better prepared to reflect respect for and sensitivity to the family diversity. This type of heightened sensitivity can only help to enhance the relationships between educators and all parents, including those who have children with disabilities.

It is also important for professionals to reflect an understanding of the fact that a knowledge of the full reality of what a particular disability means in a child's life and in the lives of his or her family members can only be known over time. Carney (1986) found, for example, that parents of children with severe disabilities perceived themselves as "survivors" by the time their children reached adolescence. During the early years of their child's life, parents may be struggling with the need to adjust emotionally, physically, and financially to the situation. Successive "developmental tasks," stages, and life events experienced by all children and youth in the course of growing up may be influenced in different ways by a disability (Dieterich-Miller & Safford, 1992), and such changes involve corresponding needs on the part of parents. It is important for educators to reflect an understanding of these factors and to provide support, when possible and as appropriate, for parents.

One way to accomplish this is simply to let parents know that their feelings are valid, whatever they may be (Gargiulo, 1985). Professionals often need to adopt a "helping model" as good listeners. Educators can then gently explore the meanings behind statements made by parents and give support and guidance when appropriate.

Another way to support families is to offer a variety of options for family participation in their child's program that match the families' needs. There may be a few basic requirements that are important for all parents to meet (e.g., sending a lunch for their child), but typically options can be established based on the varying needs and resources of families. Early childhood educators have traditionally understood this issue, as is reflected in the flexible ways in which day care is often provided. Examples of options for family involvement could include: sending a notebook back and forth between school and home to communicate or calling the parents weekly to briefly discuss their child's participation in the program if parents do not transport their child to the program; asking parents for their preferences for meeting days and times within the confines of the staff's schedules when conferences are to be held; and asking parents to share whether they need information on any topics related to their child's program or disability, plus requesting information on how they would like to receive that information (e.g., written form, guest speakers, informal discussion with staff, etc.). Providing options gives parents a message that you are sensitive to their needs.

This type of approach may not only support the development of a more positive relationship between parents and professionals, but can also have an impact on how parents feel about themselves. For example, Affleck, Tennen, Rowe, Roscher, and Walker (1989) found that when services were provided to mothers of infants who were at-risk that were *not* recognized by the parents as needed supports, these women reacted with feelings of reduced competence. They also perceived that they had less control as parents.

Similarly, educators' respect for diversity among families implies recognizing and providing for the need for parents to participate in different ways in their children's programs. It is not appropriate to expect all parents to "fit the mold" of what we set as "good" parent involvement. Professionals must develop and maintain attitudes that reflect an understanding of the complex issues that influence family collaboration and convey this sensitivity to parents.

Showing sensitivity to parents' needs could be interpreted as providing social support, which has been shown to be correlated with various positive aspects of family status. In a study conducted with 137 parents of preschool children with mental retardation or physical disabilities, or who were developmentally at-risk, Dunst, Trivette, and Cross (1986) found that parent satisfaction with sources of support and the number of supports correlated positively with a variety of family issues. These included parents' personal well-being, attitudes toward their child, child functioning, parent–child play opportunities, and child behavior and developmental gains (pp. 409–412). In particular, satisfaction with support was linked to less overprotection on the part of parents, a critical issue in promoting a typical life for children with special needs. Satisfaction also had a positive correlation with children's growth and parents' physical and emotional health. Moreover, separation from their sons and daughters can be difficult for parents of children with disabilities (Vincent, 1992), just as for parents of typically developing children. Parents' knowledge that early childhood educators are supportive of them, as well as of their children, may help to ease this discomfort.

Respect for and valuing of diversity among families requires professionals to collaborate with parents to mediate differing values and views of service priorities. Bailey (1987) noted that this process is often difficult for early childhood educators since their focus has historically been on "the child." Basic abilities he identified as important for successful collaboration were the abilities to view a family from a systems perspective; to systematically assess from a systems perspective; to use effective listening and interviewing techniques; to negotiate values and priorities to reach a joint solution; and to act as "case managers" in helping families match needs with available community resources (p. 64).

Facilitating Parent Advocacy

In addition to accepting differences among families, it is important to provide support that will help some parents gain new skill in working with early childhood professionals. Just as children come to programs with varying talents and needs, so do parents. Early childhood educators must be willing to meet parents where they are and, where appropriate, provide caring guidance concerning ways for parents to collaborate more successfully. This is not to say that all parents need this type of support, however. Part of professionals' acceptance of family differences is their understanding that many parents are quite skilled at working successfully with educators. As mentioned previously, some families have had years of experience in attempting to work collaboratively with professionals by the time their children with special needs reach age 3.

The philosophy and focus of the Liaison Infant Family Team (LIFT) Project (Thurman, Cornwell, & Korteland, 1990) exemplifies this type of approach. "In order to foster independence and empower families LIFT encourages families to use and develop their own resources" (p. 78). Four guiding principles are promoted as critical to this type of model: adaptive fit (promotion of mutual acceptance); family-driven services; family empowerment in which families develop skills to acquire resources to meet their own needs; and family dynamism that recognizes that family systems are vulnerable to and responsive to events in the environment.

Recognizing Educators' Fears and Biases

It is also important for early educators to understand their own fears and biases in regard to working with families in general, and with families of children with disabilities in particular (Combs, Avila, & Purkey, 1971). It is not uncommon for early childhood educators to experience feelings of fear and inadequacy when they are first asked to work with a child who is disabled (Volk & Stahlman, 1994). As teachers have a chance to deal with their initial fears and an opportunity to interact with the child they typically regain their confidence and begin to see the child as just another member of the class. These same issues extend to interacting with parents of children with disabilities. If professionals feel unprepared to work with a child, they may also feel unprepared to collaborate with that child's parents. Recognizing that parents are invaluable sources of information concerning the child's abilities and needs, and that they are generally happy to share this information, may help to ease these feelings. Also, relationships with parents, like relationships with children, develop over time. Often parents of children with disabilities are thrilled to have their child participate in a "regular" early childhood education program and are eager to support the program's staff in whatever ways are necessary.

Recognizing that negative reactions from parents may actually result from reasons other than dissatisfaction with a program may also help to depersonalize situations that might otherwise become conflictual. Professionals need to keep in mind that parents sometimes experience a "recapitulation" of emotions associated with adjusting to having a child with a disability. The responses that parents give in certain situations that might appear to be directed toward program staff may in reality come from a reminder that their child has special needs.

Supporting Inclusion

Although many parents look forward to enrolling their child with disabilities in a regular preschool program, the child's inclusion may also precipitate certain concerns. A significant issue for parents is whether their child will receive the special support needed to be successful. Parents may also worry that both they and their child may experience rejection in the integrated setting, that safety issues may surface, or that programs may not be fully committed to inclusion (Winton, 1983; Winton, Turnbull, & Blacher, 1985). Bailey and Winton (1987) examined the feelings of parents prior to enrollment of their children with disabilities in a regular preschool program and again nine months later. Their findings indicated that even though such expectations and fears were not actualized, parents continued to express similar concerns. This suggests the need for professionals to be particularly sensitive to continuing concerns of parents.

Turnbull, Winton, Blacher, and Salkind (1982) found that parents of young children with disabilities had feelings similar to those of parents of typically developing children in regard to integration. Both groups of parents perceived extensive social benefits in integrated programs, for both typical children and those with disabilities. Parents of typically developing children believed that their sons and daughters would develop greater "sensitivity" as a result of their early relationships with young children who have disabilities. Parents of children with disabilities felt that participation in inclusive programs could encourage their children to "try harder."

Parents of typically developing children may have a variety of other fears, however. Such concerns may be based on inaccurate cultural stereotypes of persons with disabilities (e.g., the belief that individuals with mental retardation tend to be violent). They may also express concern about integration because it is new to them and an "unknown." The attitudes and values conveyed by a program's staff can facilitate the alleviation of such concerns. Safford (1989) advised early childhood educators to:

1. Respect the individual needs of all children;
2. Convey uniformly positive attitudes toward each child in the group, not singling out one or two as sources of potential concern;
3. Convey a sense of self confidence in their ability to work with all children in the group;
4. Refrain from speaking negatively to any parent about the characteristics of behavior of another child; and
5. Respond directly and factually to questions raised by a parent, whether of a [child with a disability] or a typical child. (p. 336)

Supporting Siblings

Just as educators need to provide the appropriate supports for parents, professionals can also encourage parents to provide appropriate support for siblings of children with disabilities. They can recommend that parents deal with their other children in a direct and honest fashion in regard to the child who has a disability. Programs can also sponsor support groups or workshop series for siblings that can assist both the children and parents with this issue (Lobata, 1990; Meyer, Vadasy, & Fewell, 1985; Summers, Bridge, & Summers, 1991). In addition, Swenson-Pierce, Kohl, and Egel (1987) found that siblings could be trained to use special strategies to facilitate skill development among children with severe disabilities. Some brothers and sisters may wish to participate more formally in facilitating their sibling's growth.

CONCLUSION

The variables that influence collaboration between early childhood professionals and families are extensive and complex. These issues are even more complex when the child who is served has a disability. Positive relationships are most enhanced when professionals reflect an understanding of and sensitivity to the unique concerns of families whose young child has a disability, in addition to those shared by most families. This is not an easy task given the many direct service responsibilities of most early childhood educators. The benefits of such an approach to working with families can be great, however. Parents can prove to be tremendous resources by providing information on their children's abilities and needs, as well as a significant support for program staff in their work with the child. In a reciprocal fashion, parents respond to this sensitive treatment and are likely to be eager to assist staff members in meeting the needs of their child when strong collaborative relationships are established. The efforts on both sides result in greater satisfaction for all and better services for children.

REFERENCES

Affleck, G., Tennen, H., Rowe, J., Roscher, B., & Walker, L. (1989). Effects of formal support on mothers' adaptation to hospital to home transition of high risk infants: The benefits and costs of helping. *Child Development, 60*, 488–501.

American Association for the Care of Children's Health (1987). *Family-centered care for children with special health needs.* Washington, DC: Author.

Bailey, D. B. (1987). Collaborative goal-setting with families: Resolving differences in values and priorities for services. *Topics in Early Childhood Special Education, 7*(2), 59–71.

Bailey, D. B., & McWilliam, R. A. (1990). Normalizing early intervention. *Topics in Early Childhood Special Education, 10*, 33–47.

Bailey, D. B., & Simeonsson, R. J. (1988). *Family assessment in early intervention*. Columbus, OH: Merrill.

Bailey, D. B., & Winton, P. J. (1987). Stability and change in parents' expectations about mainstreaming. *Topics in Early Childhood Special Education, 7*(1), 73–88.

Barber, P. A., Turnbull, A. P., Behr, S. K., & Kerns, G. M. (1988). A family systems perspective on early childhood special education. In S. L. Odom & M. B. Karnes (Eds.), *Early intervention for infants and children with handicaps*. Baltimore: Paul H. Brookes.

Batshaw, M. L., & Perret, Y. M. (1992). *Children with handicaps: A medical primer*. Baltimore: Paul H. Brookes.

Boyce, G. C., Behl, D., Mortensen, L., & Akers, J. (1991). Child characteristics, family demographics, and family process: What are their effects on the stress of families of children with disabilities? *Counseling Psychology Quarterly, 4*, 273–288.

Bromwich, R. (1984). *Working with parents and infants*. Baltimore: University Park Press.

Carney, I. H. (1986). Raising a child with a handicap: A comparison of parents' and professionals' beliefs. *Dissertation Abstracts International, 48*, 103A. (University Microfilms No. DA8705721)

Combs, A. W., Avila, D. L., & Purkey, W. W. (1971). *Helping relationships: Basic concepts for the helping profession*. Boston: Allyn and Bacon.

Crnic, K. A., & Greenberg, M. T. (1981). *Inventory of parent experiences: Manual*. Seattle: University of Washington.

Dieterich-Miller, C. A., & Safford, P. L. (1992). Psychosocial development of children with hemangiomas: Home, school, health care collaboration. *Children's Health Care, 21*(2), 84–89.

Dunst, C. J., & Leet, H. E. (1987). Measuring the adequacy of resources in households with young children. *Child: Care, Health and Development, 13*, 111–125.

Dunst, C. J., Trivette, C. M., & Cross, A. H. (1986). Mediating influences of social support: Personal, family, and child outcomes. *American Journal of Mental Deficiency, 90*, 403–417.

Dunst, C. J., Trivette, C., & Deal, A. (1988). *Enabling and empowering families*. Cambridge, MA: Brookline Books.

Erickson, M., & Upshur, C. C. (1989). Caretaking burden and social support: Comparison of mothers of infants with and without disabilities. *American Journal on Mental Retardation, 94*, 250–258.

Ferrari, M. (1984). Chronic illness: Psychosocial effects on siblings. *Journal of Child Psychology and Psychiatry, 25*, 459–476.

Fisher, J., & Roberts, S. C. (1983). The effects of the mentally retarded child on his siblings. *Education, 103*, 399–401.

Fowle, C. M. (1968). The effect of the severely mentally retarded child on his family. *American Journal of Mental Deficiency, 73*, 468–473.

Frey, K. S., Greenberg, M. T., & Fewell, R. R. (1989). Stress and coping among parents of handicapped children: A multidimensional approach. *American Journal on Mental Retardation, 94*, 240–249.

Gallagher, J. J., Beckman, P., & Cross, A. H. (1983). Families of handicapped children: Sources of stress and its amelioration. *Exceptional Children, 50*, 10–19.

Gallagher, J. J., & Vietze, P. M. (Eds.). (1986). *Families of handicapped persons.* Baltimore: Paul H. Brookes.

Gargiulo, R. M. (1985). *Working with parents of exceptional children: A guide for professionals.* Boston: Houghton Mifflin.

Grossman, F. (1972). *Brothers and sisters of retarded children: An exploratory study.* Syracuse, NY: Syracuse University Press.

Hanson, M. J., & Hanline, M. F. (1990). Parenting a child with a disability: A longitudinal study of parental stress and adaptation. *Journal of Early Intervention, 14*, 234–248.

Hanson, M. J., Lynch, E. W., & Wayman, K. I. (1990). Honoring the cultural diversity of families when gathering data. *Topics in Early Childhood Special Education, 10*(1), 112–131.

Hunt, M., Cornelius, P., Leventhal, P., Miller, P., Murray, T., & Stoner, G. (1989). *Into our lives.* Tallmadge, OH: Family Child Learning Center.

Innocenti, M. S., Kwisun, H., & Boyce, G. C. (1992). Families of children with disabilities: Normative data and other considerations on parenting stress. *Topics in Early Childhood Special Education, 12*, 403–427.

Kaiser, A. P., & Hemmeter, M. L. (1989). Value-based approach to family intervention. *Topics in Early Childhood Special Education, 8*(4), 72–86.

Kneedler, R. D., Hallahan, D. P., & Kauffman, J. M. (1984). *Special education for today.* Englewood Cliffs, NJ: Prentice-Hall.

Kubler-Ross, E. (1969). *On death and dying.* New York: Macmillan.

Lambie, R., & Daniels-Mohring, D. (1993). *Family systems within educational contexts: Understanding students with special needs.* Denver: Love Publishing Company.

Lobata, D. J. (1990). *Brothers, sisters, and special needs.* Baltimore: Paul H. Brookes.

Lobata, D. J. (1991). Preschool siblings of handicapped children: Interactions with mothers, brothers and sisters. *Research in Developmental Disabilities, 12*, 387–399.

Lynch, E. W., & Hanson, M. J. (1992). *Developing cross-cultural competence: A guide for working with young children and their families.* Baltimore: Paul H. Brookes.

Mates, T. E. (1990). Siblings of autistic children: Their adjustment and performance at home and at school. *Journal of Autism and Developmental Disorders, 20*, 545–553.

Meyer, D. J., Vadasy, P. F., & Fewell, R. R. (1985). *Sibshops.* Seattle: University of Washington Press.

Minnes, P. M. (1988). Family resources and stress associated with having a mentally retarded child. *American Journal on Mental Retardation, 93,* 184–192.

Nirje, B. (1985). The basis and logic of the normalization principle. *Australia and New Zealand Journal of Developmental Disabilities, 11*(2), 65–68.

Peterson, N. L. (1987). *Early intervention for handicapped and at-risk children: An introduction to early childhood special education.* Denver: Love.

Safford, P. L. (1989). *Integrated teaching in early childhood: Starting in the mainstream.* White Plains, NY: Longman.

Seligmann, J. (1990). Variations on a theme. *Newsweek, 114*(27), 38–46.

Sexton, D., Thompson, B., Scott, R. L., & Wood, T. A. (1990). Measurement characteristics of the Inventory of Parent Experience Scales. *Topics in Early Childhood Special Education, 10*(1), 36–49.

Shea, T. M., & Bauer, A. M. (1991). *Parents and teachers of children with exceptionalities: A handbook for collaboration* (2nd ed.). Boston: Allyn and Bacon.

Stewart, J. C. (1986). *Counseling parents of exceptional children* (2nd ed.). Columbus, OH: Merrill.

Summers, M., Bridge, J., & Summers, C. R. (1991). Sibling support groups. *Teaching Exceptional Children, 23*(4), 20–23.

Swenson-Pierce, A., Kohl, F. L., & Egel, A. L. (1987). Siblings as home trainers: A strategy for teaching domestic skills to children. *JASH, 12,* 53–60.

Thurman, S. K., Cornwell, J. R., & Korteland, C. (1990). The Liaison Infant Family Team (LIFT) Project: An example of case study evaluation. *Infants and Young Children: An Interdisciplinary Journal of Special Care Practices, 2*(2), 74–82.

Turnbull, A. P., & Turnbull, H. R. (1990). *Families, professionals, and exceptionality: A special partnership* (2nd ed.). Columbus, OH: Merrill.

Turnbull, A. P., Winton, P. J., Blacher, J., & Salkind, N. (1982). Mainstreaming in the kindergarten classroom: Perspectives of parents of handicapped and nonhandicapped children. *Journal of the Division for Early Childhood, 6,* 14–20.

Vincent, L. J. (1992). Families and early intervention: Diversity and competence. *Journal of Early Intervention, 16,* 166–172.

Volk, D., & Stahlman, J. (1994). I think everyone is afraid of the unknown: Early childhood teachers prepare for mainstreaming. *Day Care and Early Education, 21*(3), 13–17.

Washington, V., & Gallagher, J. J. (1986). Family roles, preschool handicapped children, and social policy. In J. J. Gallagher & P. M. Vietze (Eds.), *Families of Handicapped Persons* (pp. 261–272). Baltimore: Paul H. Brookes.

Winton, P. J. (1983). The consequences of mainstreaming for families of young children. In S. J. Meisels (Ed.), *Mainstreamed handicapped children: Outcomes, controversies, and new directions* (pp. 129–149). Hillsdale, NJ: Erlbaum.

Winton, P. J. (1988). The family-focused interview: An assessment measure and goal setting mechanism. In D. B. Bailey & R. J. Simeonsson (Eds.), *Family assessment in early intervention* (pp. 185–206). Columbus, OH: Merrill.

Winton, P. J., & Bailey, D. B. (1990). Early intervention training related to family interviewing. *Topics in Early Childhood Special Education, 10*(1), 50–62.

Winton, P. J., Turnbull, A. P., & Blacher, J. (1985). Expectations for satisfaction with public school kindergarten: Perspectives of parents of handicapped and nonhandicapped children. *Journal of the Division of Early Childhood, 9*, 116–124.

Wolfensberger, W. (1972). *The principle of normalization in human services.* Toronto: National Institute on Mental Retardation.

CHAPTER 3

Social Competence with Peers: Outcome and Process in Early Childhood Special Education

Michael J. Guralnick

The excitement, tension, and high drama that characterize the social play of young children with their peers serve to focus our attention on what is now regarded as a vital developmental process. Even during the infant and toddler periods, children strive to establish meaningful and productive relationships with their peers. This process continues throughout the life cycle, but it is during the preschool years that peer relations and the beginnings of friendship become so central to young children's daily activities.

The ebb and flow of peer interactions reveal that young children are, in fact, struggling to solve a series of important problems of a social nature. For example, children must figure out how to initiate play with another child or to enter into a group in which many peers are already participating in an activity with a well-developed theme. They must resolve conflicts precipitated by ownership surrounding toys and materials or the "truth" of the assertions of others; they must learn how to defend their own domain yet allow others access; and they must somehow manage the dynamics of sustained social play with its repeated intrusions and demands. The ability of young children to accomplish their interpersonal goals in these and other social problem-solving contexts in an appropriate and effective manner constitutes the core of what is referred to as peer-related social competence (Guralnick, 1990c). Moreover, as will be discussed, the outcomes and processes associated with peer-related social competence appear to apply equally well to children with and without special needs (Guralnick, 1992a; in preparation).

Even casual observations of children's social play with their peers reveal its complexity. In the context of important social tasks such as entering into a peer group, young children must set and maintain over-arching goals, continually judge the intentions of others, rapidly adapt to changing circumstances, deal with their own fears and anxieties, particularly around issues of rejection, and manage their emotional reactions to incursions into their space or to attacks on their possessions. It is evident that to achieve outcomes that are considered to be socially competent, children must continually rely on virtually their entire array of relevant skills and abilities, and must invoke a variety of pro-cesses to integrate, organize, and sequence effective and appropriate social strategies during interactions with their peers.

The importance of peer-related social competence to development is based in part on the fact that competent peer interactions enable access to critical experiences in a child's life. Gaining entry into estab-lished playgroups, and later finding a role in the peer structure, is related to a child's evolving sense of self. Preferences for specific peers also emerge and, if reciprocated, allow friendships to flourish with all the advantages of support and intimacy that characterize these special relationships (Ginsberg, Gottman, & Parker, 1986; Rubin, 1980). Simi-larly, competent peer interactions enable young children to gain access to interesting materials and to adventures with peers, thereby establish-ing the potential for engaging in creative and novel forms of play. In view of this, it is not surprising that many researchers and theorists have indicated that interactions with one's peers promote a young child's language and communicative development, contribute to moral development and the socialization of aggression, and facilitate overall prosocial behaviors and social–cognitive processes (Bates, 1975; Gar-vey, 1986; Hartup, 1978, 1983; Rubin & Lollis, 1988). In contrast, failure to establish competent interactions with peers during the pre-school years, particularly manifested by peer rejection, tends to be a stable feature of development and is predictive of later adjustment problems (Parker & Asher, 1987).

In this chapter, both the outcomes and the processes of peer-related social competence will be examined. First, key features in the develop-ment of young children's peer interactions will be discussed, with a special emphasis on the strategies children use to solve the social tasks of peer-group entry, resolving conflicts, and maintaining play. This analy-sis of outcomes will be followed by a description of the processes in-volved in generating strategies considered socially competent. The third section will begin with a brief discussion of the problems children expe-rience in establishing relationships with their peers and then address assessment and intervention issues. The final section will discuss how an understanding of the underlying processes governing peer-related social competence is applicable to children both with and without special needs.

OUTCOMES

Assessing Social Competence

How can young children's peer-related social competence be characterized? Put another way, what constitutes reasonable assessment of outcomes for this important aspect of development? Researchers and theorists have grappled with this issue repeatedly with only limited success (Anderson & Messick, 1974; Foster & Ritchey, 1979; O'Malley, 1977), and it is apparent that observational data as well as the perspectives of teachers, parents, and peers must be considered (Connolly & Doyle, 1981; Ladd & Mars, 1986). We can expect, of course, that children's developmental patterns in connection with their associations with peers would reflect increasingly sophisticated degrees of social competence. In fact, the broad developmental changes that characterize children's interactions with their peers from the toddler period through the preschool years have been investigated extensively (Bakeman & Brownlee, 1980; Parten, 1932; Rubin, Watson, & Jambor, 1978). As might be anticipated, a pattern of increasing participation with peers is observed as children tend to engage in progressively greater amounts of group play with their peers across the preschool years. Increased activities with peers occur in conjunction with a corresponding decline in nonsocial play, particularly solitary activities and being unoccupied. Parallel play, however, remains quite variable across children and tends not to decline appreciably over the years. Apparently, children move freely within each developmental period between the safer haven of parallel play and the more demanding requirements of group play (Bakeman & Brownlee, 1980; Howes & Matheson, 1992).

Increased levels of group play are, in fact, correlated with greater degrees of peer-related social competence, particularly when social competence is assessed by one's peers (e.g., Goldman, Corsini, & DeUrioste, 1980; Howes, 1988). Nevertheless, the correspondence is relatively modest and does not account for the findings that many children who tend to prefer solitary play appear to be highly socially competent (e.g., Rubin, 1982). Consequently, a child's tendency to associate with peers in group activities is a reasonable but clearly imperfect index of peer-related social competence.

An alternative developmental perspective is to focus primarily on the structural complexity of children's play as an index of the growth of peer-related social competence. This approach has been adopted by Howes and Matheson (1992) in a recent longitudinal study that began when children were between 13 and 24 months of age and extended for 3 years. The developmental scale applied to children across the extensive age range was especially interesting. The scale's lowest level consisted of parallel play, and then an awareness of others during parallel play, followed by simple social play (talking, offering, and receiving toys). Complementary and reciprocal play was the next highest level and focused on the importance of role reversals in shared activities (e.g., run and chase games). The final two levels of the scale focused on pretend play, initially when children simply enacted complementary roles and, at the highest level of complexity, when children communicated about the pretend activities and roles in order to plan and sustain the play.

This developmental sequence did hold generally across time, these various organized levels of complexity emerging as children became older. Of importance to the issue of social competence was the finding that, for the most part, the emergence of or greater proportion of complex play manifested by individual children in earlier developmental periods was associated with higher levels of peer-related social competence in later developmental periods based on a wide array of measures of social competence (Howes & Matheson, 1992). However, once again the magnitude of these relationships was relatively modest.

Consequently, these overall developmental sequences focusing on children's associations with one another and the structural complexity of their play provide important sources of information about young children's emerging social competence with their peers, and establish an essential developmental framework. Nevertheless, a more complete understanding of peer-related social competence will require an approach that can incorporate the patterns of actual interactive skills and strategies that can be drawn on by individual children to meet the increasing demands that accompany more sophisticated forms of peer interaction. For example, we must be able not only to determine the extent to which children engage in group or complex social pretend play but also to account for the skills and abilities that enable them to do so when social play with peers is of interest to them. This is, in fact, the approach I adopted (Guralnick, 1990c) along with others who view social competence with peers as the "*ability of young children to successfully and appropriately carry out their interpersonal goals*" (p. 4; emphasis in original). These goals are best framed as social tasks, and the social strategies children employ can be evaluated in terms of their effectiveness and appropriateness. In essence, it is the selection and implementation of these strategies in the context of social tasks that enable children to engage in group or complex social pretend play when they choose to do so. We turn now to a discussion of social tasks and social strategies as indices of peer-related social competence.

Social Tasks and Social Strategies

The notion that young children establish social tasks for themselves is an important concept in the field of peer relations (Dodge, Pettit, McClaskey, & Brown, 1986). It suggests that children determine their interpersonal goals, consider the complexities of the existing social situation, and then utilize an array of social strategies to achieve those goals. It is this framework provided by social tasks that appears to create the psychological meaning for the child and allows observers to more readily interpret the effectiveness and appropriateness of social strategies (i.e., peer-related social competence). In addition, as discussed shortly, a strong correspondence exists between children's abilities to carry out these social tasks and measures of peer-related social competence.

The three social tasks to be discussed are (1) peer group entry, (2) conflict resolution, and (3) maintaining play. Each of these social tasks has been thoroughly investigated and linked directly to children's peer-related social competence (see Guralnick, 1992a, 1992b). In the following sections, social strategies correlated with peer-related social competence for each social task will be discussed.

Peer Group Entry. Children are frequently confronted with the task of entering into already existing groups of children in order to participate in ongoing activities. This ability is not only important for newcomers (Fox & Field, 1989; Shea, 1981), but is a circumstance that occurs repeatedly in preschools as children shift from one activity to another. The importance of this task is also apparent as it is the key to subsequent opportunities for extended social contact with peers.

The complexity of the entry task should not be underestimated. In fact, as many as half of all entry attempts are rejected or ignored by host children (Corsaro, 1981). Consequently, young children must persist in their efforts utilizing strategies that somehow "persuade" their peers to allow them entry into the ongoing play activities. In view of the complexity and importance of the task to children's peer relations, it comes as little surprise that social strategies employed during peer-group entry are strongly associated with overall measures of peer-related social competence, particularly peer sociometric status (Dodge et al., 1986; Putallaz, 1983; Putallaz & Wasserman, 1990). In fact, the associations with overall measures of peer-related social competence are much greater for strategies utilized during social tasks than for children's global participation in groups or in social pretend play with peers, again highlighting the significance of strategies that are part of key social tasks.

Based on extensive research, it is now clear which strategies are most effective and appropriate for the peer-group entry task (Black & Hazen, 1990; Corsaro, 1981; Dodge, Schlundt, Schocken, & Delugach, 1983; Hazen & Black, 1989; Putallaz, 1983; Putallaz & Gottman, 1981; Putallaz & Wasserman, 1989). Specifically, the child must somehow communicate initially to the host children that he or she is seeking to join the existing flow of activities and is not interested in redirecting those activities. To accomplish this, strategies relevant to and harmonious with the hosts and hosts' activities are essential. Successful specific strategies typically include maintaining proximity to the hosts, gaining attention through eye contact or gesture, imitating aspects of the hosts' play, producing some variation of their activities, or showing or offering a toy related to the hosts' game or project. Nondemanding requests for access, sharing information relevant to the play theme, and even reasonable direct requests for entry are often effective.

A similar set of strategies can be developed for successive efforts should initial failure occur. The ability of the child to vary the intrusiveness of strategies is important here, as these strategies should differ depending on the nature of the hosts' responses to the initial social bid (e.g., rejecting, ignoring, or postponing). Beyond variations in intrusiveness, successful children refrain from redirecting the activities, from making self-statements that are not relevant, and from utilizing disagreeable or negative strategies. In general, relevance and connectedness characterize the behavior of children rated high in peer-related social competence as they interact with their peers during the entry task.

Conflict Resolution. Conflicts and their resolution are ubiquitous and essential features of social relationships and a central aspect of children's evolving peer-related social competence (Hay, 1984; Shantz, 1987). Disputes over possessions or space are dominant during the toddler and early preschool period (Hay & Ross, 1982), and are gradually supplemented by conflicts arising from disagreements over assertions, ideas, rule violations, or general social control (Dawe, 1934; Eisenberg & Garvey, 1981; Killen & Turiel, 1991). Conflicts can arise in any context, including those associated with other social tasks. Strategies within the conflict-resolution social task often are analyzed in the context of directive episodes in which one child fails to obtain some goods or services from another child and then persists in order to achieve this interpersonal goal (Guralnick & Paul-Brown, 1984; Levin & Rubin, 1983). In essence, conflicts preempt other activities and must be resolved in some manner prior to proceeding with other tasks.

Observers of conflicts among preschool-age children have been able to identify those strategies (outcomes) that are closely associated with peer-related social competence (Eisenberg & Garvey, 1981; Genishi & Di Paolo, 1982; Hartup, Laursen, Stewart, & Eastonson, 1988; Phinney, 1986). As will be discussed in a later section, the key to competent conflict resolution appears to hinge on the ability of children to recognize the rights, obligations, and needs of their companions and to consider those factors when selecting a strategy. As Garvey (1975) points out so well, young children are clearly aware of these factors, and they frequently comment on violations of these presumed shared understandings or rules. Consequently, as we would expect, simple insistence (or slight modifications of the original request), although by far the most frequently used strategy, is least effective in ending a conflict episode successfully (Eisenberg & Garvey, 1981). Insistence provides no new information (Eisenberg & Garvey, 1981) and fails to communicate that the companion's perspective through a shared understanding has been recognized. Without this occurring, children easily fall into a cycle of repetitive exchanges often resulting in an escalation of the conflict or complete disengagement.

Conciliatory strategies — that is, ones that do consider the perspective of others — are difficult for preschool-age children. However, as Eisenberg and Garvey (1981) note, though they occur at a modest rate, success in resolving the conflict is quite high. Providing a reason for a specific request, again reflecting consideration of the other child's perspective, also contributes to a higher rate of success. In general, offering an alternative, even with conditions attached, is an essential feature of competent strategies in resolving conflicts. Similarly, maintaining connectedness (Asher, 1983), such as responding to a companion's proposal or request for clarification, constitutes another important dimension associated with successful and appropriate resolutions of conflicts. Outright rejections of others' suggestions without any further efforts are certain to lead to failure (Hazen & Black, 1989).

Maintaining Play. Our understanding of the strategies associated with the ability of young children to maintain play with peers has less of an empirical basis than other social tasks. Nevertheless research by Gottman (1983), Hartup et al. (1988), and Howes (1988) focusing on friendship development provides important insights into the strategies likely to maintain play. One cluster of strategies relates to the ability of children to conform to role and activity structures during play situations by remaining within the theme or role. In essence, as was the case for the other two social tasks, strategies that consist of a general agreeableness to the suggestions of others and a responsiveness to information requests within the play context are key elements for sustaining play. Strategies that reflect connectedness are typically those that are judged to be socially competent.

The second cluster of strategies associated with maintaining play is best referred to as management strategies. Dynamic changes in intensity characterize children's play, especially social pretend play. Demands placed on the players increase, roles and activities become more defined and even restrictive, and rules tend to become more complex. Sometimes conflicts arise from these increasing demands, temporarily preventing play from continuing. Consequently, children who are able to maintain play successfully have been able to develop a series of strategies in which they either de-escalate the play prior to conflict or disengage momentarily when conflicts or intrusions reach a critical point. However, they remain in proximity to the play area and peers. Similarly, children who are able to maintain play can also escalate play to increase its interest value. Accordingly, repairing a play sequence by matching one's behavior to that of the peer in order to reestablish interest or otherwise maintain the association constitutes an important strategy.

PROCESSES

As we have seen, an array of strategies can be identified for each of three psychologically meaningful social tasks that are closely associated with children's peer-related social competence. Strategies that were relevant to the ongoing activity of the host children and that varied appropriately in intrusiveness over the course of the episode were associated with success in the peer-group entry task. For conflict resolution, strategies that considered the rights, obligations, and needs of one's peers were found to be most appropriate and effective. Finally, strategies that conformed to the role and activity structure of play and that could manage variations in intrusiveness were found to be of value in maintaining play. Consequently, it is important to consider how children can be encouraged to use those strategies as they interact with their peers.

We can, of course, simply attempt to teach the strategies that have been identified through direct or indirect methods, framed within the context of a social task. This approach, focusing on the strategies themselves, can be and has been extremely helpful (McEvoy, Odom, & McConnell, 1992), but it is uncertain what children actually learn beyond the context-specific social skills that are selected to be taught. A somewhat different framework that can guide the assessment and intervention approach to be discussed in a subsequent section of this chapter may be of even greater value. Specifically, as has been suggested, peer-related social competence can best be conceptualized as a problem-solving task in the social domain. Consequently, as is the case for nonsocial problem-solving situations, this suggests that children utilize a series of *processes* to generate strategies when faced with a particular task that requires problem solving of a social nature. If those processes can be identified and intervention techniques developed that consider specific processes of concern, it is possible that children will learn to generate competent strategies that will generalize to the myriad of situations they will inevitably confront even within the context of specific social tasks.

Recent research and theoretical developments have suggested that four interrelated processes are involved in the generation of strategies (see Guralnick, 1992a, 1992b, 1993). Two processes are referred to as *foundation processes* — processes that form the essential bases for peer-related social competence. The first foundation process is the ability of the child to maintain a "shared understanding" of events, activities, rules, and so forth, with their peers. Without a shared understanding, connectedness and therefore competent social exchanges are not possible. The second foundation process involves the way in which children regulate their emotions during a social task. Anxiety, anger, or unusually rapid (impulsive) responding can interfere with the appropriate and effective selection of strategies even when children have well-developed social–cognitive processes. Third, social–cognitive processes themselves are vital, especially during specific social exchanges with peers, as they govern the way that children think about the social problem they are confronting in a manner that ultimately leads to the selection of a specific strategy. Finally, a series of higher-order processes are involved that serve to guide and integrate the operation of the other processes as well as provide the mechanism for integrating, organizing, and sequencing social strategies over the various cycles of exchange within a social task. Figure 3.1 illustrates these relationships, and additional details are presented below.

Shared Understanding

This foundation process is composed of a series of separate "understandings" that together constitute a necessary circumstance for the connectedness of social/communicative exchanges. Among the components of shared understanding are mutually agreed on social rules such as ownership (Newman, 1978) and turn-taking, as well as a recognition of the rights and obligations of others (Garvey, 1975). Sharing a common cognitive structure for everyday experiences and events (e.g., birthday parties, baking) is also essential for establishing roles and expectations during pretend and nonpretend play sequences. Representa-

Figure 3.1. A Model Illustrating Processes Associated with the Selection of Social Strategies

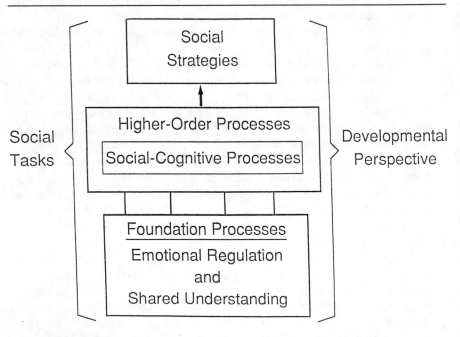

tions of these everyday experiences appear to organize conceptually in terms of "scripts" (Nelson, 1986; Schank & Abelson, 1977), a fact that has important implications for both assessment and intervention (Guralnick, 1993). In any case, shared understanding of the social context with peers provides a foundation for the selection of effective and appropriate social strategies during social tasks.

Emotional Regulation Processes

Social tasks are often stressful events for young children. Many children become uncomfortable, even anxious, in play situations, tending to withdraw especially in circumstances involving unfamiliar peers (Kagan, Reznick, & Snidman, 1990). Others react to the slightest rejection or provocation with upset or anger and have difficulty returning to some equilibrium point (Campbell, 1990). It is these reactions as well as positive responses, including warm and exuberant expressions, that provide the affective and energetic quality so evident and vital in children's peer relations.

Children's ability to regulate their emotional reactions during play with peers is an essential feature of the development of inhibition of action that helps organize one's behavior. The importance of emotional regulation processes to peer-related social competence is clearly captured in Gottman and Katz's (1989) description of emotional regulation as the ability of children to "(a) inhibit inappropriate behavior related to the strong negative or positive affect, (b) self-soothe any physiological arousal that the strong affect has induced, (c) refocus attention, and (4) organize themselves for coordinated action in the service of an external goal" (p. 373). As Figure 3.1 implies, failure to properly regulate one's emotions can also directly alter higher-order processes by affecting the integration, organization, and sequencing of social strategies (related to an external goal), and can also influence each of the component social–cognitive processes.

Social–Cognitive Processes

As suggested in Figure 3.1, once children elect to engage in a particular social task they proceed to generate strategies based on available information. From the perspective of social–cognitive processes, Dodge et al. (1986) suggest that at least four component processes are involved. First, children must encode information that is relevant to the social task. In the peer-group entry task, for example, this means that attending to and encoding cues related to the play themes that the hosts are engaged in is especially important (Putallaz, 1983), as this component of the social–cognitive process is essential for establishing a shared frame of reference. Second, the encoded cues must be properly interpreted. In a situation in which play is being maintained, for example, children who have had a history of using aggressive strategies frequently interpret rather benign acts (e.g., accidentally knocking over blocks) as purposeful attacks (see Dodge et al., 1986). Another example from the peer-group entry task would be a child interpreting a host's cues of postponement in response to an initial entry strategy as a flat rejection. These interpretations then give rise to the third component social–cognitive process in which a number of alternative strategies are generated. To a substantial degree, the strategies that arise at this point are connected to prior interpretations of encoded cues, but typically consist of an array of alternatives. The range of possible strategies for each social task, especially those judged to be competent, was discussed in the previous section of this chapter. Finally, and perhaps most important, children must then evaluate the situation and select a specific strategy.

This last component process, evaluation, is in fact most critical because it is here that children must consider the understanding that is shared among interacting children and recognize the impact of existing social relationships (e.g., friend vs. nonfriend or older vs. younger) in selecting a strategy. This is one important way in which shared understanding affects other processes. As noted, shared understanding can include a mutual understanding of the activities engaged in as well as the underlying rule structures, particularly those associated with turn-taking and ownership. For example, the selection of a strategy will vary depending on whether the child believes he or she "owns" an object in a possession dispute (i.e., ownership confers a special status and implies a corresponding set of appropriate strategies). Similarly, unless the interactors share a common understanding of the roles as part of a theme, a disconnected (and therefore likely to be considered less competent) strategy may well emerge. Dodge et al. (1986) suggest that these processes operate in a rapid fashion, often without the awareness of the individual. However, a variety of creative experimental techniques using videotaped vignettes of social task situations have enabled these investigators to tease out the individual contributions of each of these components and relate them to children's peer-related social competence.

The foundation process of emotional regulation also exerts considerable influence on social–cognitive processes. For example, children unable to inhibit inappropriate behavior fail to properly evaluate which strategies might be most effective and appropriate and have difficulty refocusing their attention; they are often judged to be responding impulsively. Moreover, those who cannot right themselves emotionally often selectively bias the encoding and interpretation components of social–cognitive processes so that certain cues, especially ambiguous ones, are more likely to be detected and interpreted in a manner consistent with their (often negative) emotional reaction. Consequently, less competent strategies may become preeminent, and emotional arousal may increase as the social exchange proceeds.

Higher-Order Processes

For the most part strategies generated through the operation of social–cognitive and emotional regulation processes have been discussed in terms of a specific cycle occurring within the context of an extended social task. But, of course, peer-related social competence requires the long view, as Asher (1983) has pointed out. Consequently, it is essential that some process be postulated in which the ultimate goal is kept in perspective while the episode unfolds. This requires not only planning but monitoring of one's own and others' behavior. It is particularly important, as illustrated in Figure 3.1, that children first recognize that they are, in fact, challenged by a social task. It is this framework, then, that guides the subsequent series of exchanges. So-called executive processes have been identified in the literature on cognitive development in recent years and provide the structure for integrating component processes (Sternberg, 1985). Although conceptualized primarily for nonsocial tasks, these processes appear to be highly relevant as mechanisms for guiding social tasks.

PEER INTERACTION PROBLEMS: ASSESSMENT AND INTERVENTION

In view of the complexity of the strategies that are the substance of peer-related social competence, and particularly the underlying processes governing the appropriate and effective selection of those strategies, it is not surprising that so many young children experience difficulties interacting with peers. It has been estimated that as many as 10 percent of children without disabilities enrolled in regular early childhood programs manifest substantial problems in terms of their peer-related social competence (Asher, 1990). In view of the dependence of peer-related social competence on virtually every aspect of development, one can anticipate that biologically and/or environmentally based problems will filter their way through the peer interaction system to adversely influence one or more of the underlying processes that have been discussed. There are, of course, numerous self-righting tendencies that can compensate for factors that threaten the integrity of the child, but the increase in emotional and economic stressors on family life associated with significant adverse biological and environmental influences will eventually have an impact. These factors include family-child interaction patterns (Booth, Rose-Krasnor, & Rubin, 1991), child maltreatment (Alessandri, 1991), prenatal exposure to alcohol and drugs (Zuckerman & Bresnahan, 1991), and prematurity and low birth-weight (Bennett & Guralnick, 1991; Ross, Lipper, & Auld, 1990). Of equal importance is that difficulties in children's peer relations are often the first consistent signs observed by teachers suggesting that significant problems lie ahead. It appears that the unpredictability of the peer situation and its typically unstructured nature create special challenges for young children who have been compromised in some manner.

For children with established disabilities, this peer-relations problem appears to be even more severe, involving far more children than the 10 percent estimated for children without established disabilities. It has now been well established that young children with disabilities manifest deficits or lags in the peer domain that extend *beyond* those that would be expected simply based on the child's overall developmental level. This is particularly the case for young children with general cognitive delays (see Guralnick & Bricker, 1987, for definition of this population), a finding that has been demonstrated repeatedly in a range of settings (Guralnick & Groom, 1985, 1987a, 1987b, 1988a). These special difficulties hold for other groups of children with established disabilities as well (see Guralnick, 1986).

Assessment

Accordingly, in consideration of the importance of peer-related social competence to so many aspects of a child's development, it is essential that a systematic assessment and intervention program be available to teachers and clinicians working with young children. With regard to assessment, we must recognize that an evaluation of a child's peer-related social competence is highly subjective, situationally specific, and culturally determined. Attempts to quantify this domain have been notably unsuccessful, and developmental checklists provide only minimal confidence that reliable and valid measures are being employed (see Bailey & Wolery, 1989; Guralnick & Weinhouse, 1984).

Nevertheless, sufficient observational methods and developmental check-lists are available to teachers, parents, and service personnel to enable them to at least reach a reasonable consensus that indicates a concern about a particular child's peer-related social competence. Once this decision has been reached, a more systematic assessment can follow.

The recently developed *Assessment of Peer Relations* (APR; Gural-nick, 1992b) is designed to provide an assessment approach consistent with the model of peer-related social competence described above that views social strategies and their underlying processes within the context of critical social tasks as the central focus. In the APR, observations of children's social play are, in fact, structured within the social tasks of peer-group entry, resolving conflicts, and maintaining play. The assessment first leads the teacher or clinician to arrive at a perspective of the child's ability to use the array of strategies associated with each social task. Those carrying out the assessment are then guided to blend their knowledge of the special characteristics of each child with their observations of peer play to arrive at an identification of processes that may be interfering with the focal child's peer-related social compe-tence. Knowledge of the unique developmental characteristics of the focal child and their influence on underlying processes related to peer relations constitutes a separate segment of the APR. It is here that the impact of special cognitive, language, motor, or affective problems are considered. Although each analysis must be based on the individual characteristics of the child being considered, an example of assessment based on the general features of children with Down syndrome has been described elsewhere in connection with the APR (Guralnick, 1993). It is within this framework of special considerations that teachers and clinicians identify those processes associated with children's peer-related social competence that are most likely to be affected.

Included among the possible processes are the social–cognitive components of encoding, interpreting, generating alternative strategies, and the role of a shared understanding in evaluating which strategies to select. Of course, shared understanding in relation to everyday events, social rules and pretend play, themes, roles, and complexity are assessed separately. Emotional regulation processes focus on reacting too quick-ly, thereby short-circuiting consideration of alternative (presumably more appropriate) strategies, delayed responding to peers, angry or negative reactions compounded by difficulties reestablishing equilib-rium, and social withdrawal (often related to disorganization of behav-ior). Higher-order processes related to social task recognition and plan-ful behavior are also identified.

Finally, a related aspect of the APR includes its "Inventory of

Resources," a mechanism that serves to help bridge assessment and intervention. The inventory is designed to identify those social (e.g., preferred or most responsive playmates) and environmental (e.g., preferred play times or materials) factors that will maximize peer interactions, and to establish which play opportunities within the early childhood program's format might best be utilized when interventions are initiated.

Intervention

Interventions ultimately intended to improve children's peer-related social competence through enhancing their ability to solve social tasks are best implemented by organizing programs at two separate levels: involvement and enhancement. Within the APR approach, information for involvement is first summarized into three areas:

1. Special considerations that must be addressed based on information from the child's developmental profile
2. The nature of any emotional regulation issues that require intervention
3. Specific areas in which a shared understanding must be established or enhanced

Relying on the Inventory of Resources, activities are designed to address concerns in one or more of these areas. Interventions at this level are characterized by considerable teacher or clinician structuring, efforts to maximize the interest value and responsiveness of the social and physical environment in relation to interactions with peers, experimentation with techniques to foster social play, and designing adaptations in the play situation that address directly the child's special considerations (e.g., greater use of pantomime in play for children with severe expressive language disorders).

No attempt is made at the level of involvement to address the focal child's ability to utilize appropriate and effective strategies in the context of social tasks through process-guided interventions. However, many of the level-of-involvement interventions are likely to influence processes of concern in related contexts, and help prepare the teacher or clinician for focused efforts in the second level.

For second-level interventions, referred to as enhancement, intervention approaches based on the assessment of strategies and processes related to specific social tasks become the primary area of interest. It is at this stage that strategies are encouraged that foster the child's ability to solve particular social tasks. By both adapting to special considerations related to the underlying processes and developing techniques to directly enhance those processes of concern whenever possible (e.g., strategies for anger management), a long-term approach designed to improve a child's peer-related social competence is established.

Involvement. Fortunately, an array of techniques that can increase the peer-related social interactions of young children are available to teachers and clinicians. Utilized in conjunction with the APR Inventory of Resources to determine the preferences of the child, specific toys and materials that encourage and invite interactive play can be selected (Quilitch & Risley, 1973; Rubin, Fein, & Vandenberg, 1983; Stoneman, Cantrell, & Hoover-Dempsey, 1983). Similarly, capitalizing on certain activity structures, maximizing the familiarity and responsivity of peers available, and arranging for smaller predictable social groups can yield important beneficial effects on children's overall interactions with their peers (Doyle, Connolly, & Rivest, 1980; Harper & Huie, 1985; Kohl & Beckman, 1984; Sainato & Carta, 1992). Techniques related to emotional regulation issues can be addressed in this context as well. For example, anger control and coping mechanisms (Guevrement, 1990) as well as relaxation and calming techniques (see Hinshaw, Henker, & Whalen, 1984) may be needed as problems arise in these play situations.

Particularly during the early phases of the first level, it may be advisable to implement more structured activities for the child that are teacher-mediated. In fact, for many youngsters these activities provide the structure necessary to expand the shared context between themselves and others in the preschool. The use of scripts associated with play activities can be especially valuable (Furman & Walden, 1990; Nelson & Gruendel, 1979; Nelson & Seidman, 1984), and have been successfully applied to children with disabilities (e.g., Goldstein, Wickstrom, Hoyson, Jamieson, & Odom, 1988). Often these techniques are used in conjunction with the direct involvement of peers whose assistance has been solicited by the teacher. With prior training of peers, these peer-mediated techniques are capable of increasing the responsivity of those peers and providing the child with many opportunities to respond to the social bids of others (Strain & Odom, 1986).

The use of peers as agents of change to facilitate a child's social/communicative interactions (see Guralnick, 1984) suggests a more general principle. Specifically, we can expect that by arranging highly responsive social environments for young children, substantial increases should be observed in their level of social/communicative interactions.

This may be particularly the case for children with disabilities, especially because peer-mediated techniques usually involve children without disabilities as the agents of change. Assuming that higher levels of social stimulation and responsivity are associated with children without disabilities (see Guralnick, 1990b), benefits to children with disabilities should be evident as a result of their participation with these more socially and communicatively active children. This is precisely what is obtained when the social/communicative interactions of children with disabilities placed in inclusive preschool programs (mainstreamed settings containing primarily children without disabilities) are compared with those of children placed in segregated settings (Guralnick, 1990a; Guralnick & Groom, 1988b; Strain, 1983). In many respects, then, the involvement of children with disabilities in inclusive programs constitutes a valuable first-level intervention.

Despite the well-established validity of these techniques, the fact remains that greater degrees of involvement that result tend to have limited generalizability. This, of course, is to be expected because the changes that occur in children's social behavior utilizing these techniques are presumably externally driven and supported. Nevertheless, first-level interventions allow teachers and clinicians to gain a better understanding of the child's individual developmental characteristics and how they influence interactions with peers, enhance the shared context as needed, and generally focus on activities that will improve children's play with their peers. In essence, successful first-level interventions provide the initial framework for the challenging task of improving children's peer-related social competence by altering the child's ability to solve social tasks effectively and appropriately.

Enhancement. Interventions seeking to improve the selection of children's social strategies within the context of specific social tasks by utilizing process-related information have not been nearly as well documented as the level-of-involvement techniques. Nevertheless, encouraging information is emerging suggesting the value of this process-oriented approach (Mize & Ladd, 1990). Once the shared understanding, emotional regulation, social–cognitive, or higher-order processes of concern are identified, the complexity of this intervention effort becomes apparent. One challenge is that social problem-solving processes must be applied to numerous and generally unpredictable situations. The structure provided by social tasks, however, creates the opportunity for organizing intervention activities. As was the case for the first level, considerable adult involvement may be needed initially. Coaching, modeling, role playing, scripting activities, and the use of specially designed vignettes addressing problems of concern are all part of the structure. Often, however, numerous naturally occurring activities provide the context for interventions related to social tasks. Moreover, the information derived from the Inventory of Resources can be of value in identifying those contexts and events that conform to aspects of social tasks of concern.

After the social task context has been identified or arranged, teachers and clinicians can then implement techniques that take process information into consideration when designing ways to improve social strategy selection within social tasks. As was the case for level-of-involvement interventions, a range of techniques derived from various disciplines is available and should be applied in a manner adapted to the special characteristics of children. These techniques have been summarized elsewhere (Guralnick, in preparation), and detailed descriptions are well beyond the scope of this chapter. However, it should be noted that social task recognition is an essential element, as it provides the goal structure for the remaining social exchanges in the sequence, thereby encouraging direction by higher-order processes. The child's ability to encode and interpret relevant information, to generate alternative strategies, and to select one that is appropriate all must occur within that structure. In essence, scripting or scaffolding provides the essential structure within which these many processes operate.

The entry task can provide a sense for this general approach. For social–cognitive processes, the ability of the focal child to encode relevant information can be facilitated through helping the child label specific activities or select toys that match hosts' activities before proceeding with an entry attempt. This practice can then be applied to less familiar play themes. Similarly, attempts to correct faulty bias in interpreting cues might focus on teaching the focal child that only specific facial expressions and related statements or gestures are associated with rejection, with a more benign interpretation provided for other responses of peers. It may be necessary to teach a series of alternative positive strategies directly in the peer-group entry context using modeling and demonstration and then linking possession rules or other shared context issues to the choice of those strategies.

As noted, a variety of techniques are available to help children regulate their emotions, particularly anger (Guevrement, 1990; Hinshaw et al., 1984). Techniques that may have been used in the first level of interventions in more general circumstances can now be applied directly in the context of specific social tasks. In the peer-group entry situation, rejection or even postponement of social bids for entry may generate inappropriate strategies as a consequence of negative emotional arousal. Vignettes based on a child's actual experiences invoking relaxation and calming techniques can be of value.

INTEGRATION OF EARLY CHILDHOOD AND SPECIAL EDUCATION

A major theme of the preceding discussion is that both the outcomes and the processes associated with children's peer-related social competence apply equally well to children with and without disabilities. The approach described in this chapter emphasizing social tasks, social strategies, and underlying processes was clearly rooted within a developmental framework, fully expecting that general developmental principles, processes, and the means by which environmental and biological factors influence development would provide the necessary framework for all children. In fact, research continues to confirm the applicability of the developmental model for widely heterogenous groups of children, particularly those with general (cognitive) delays (Cicchetti & Beeghly, 1990; Hodapp, Burack, & Zigler, 1990). In terms of peer relations, the organization and general course of development appear similar (though delayed) for children with a range of disabilities (see Guralnick & Groom, 1987a, 1987b; Guralnick & Weinhouse, 1984). In general, although the extent, number, and configuration of processes that may be affected will certainly vary between children with and without disabilities, these differences are essentially quantitative, not qualitative.

It is further anticipated that educational/developmental practices and techniques that emerge from this framework would be of value to children with and without disabilities. It can be argued that contemporary approaches designed to facilitate the peer-related social competence of young children are consistent with developmentally appropriate practices (Bredekamp, 1987). The goals and priorities, approaches to assessment and planning, and techniques for intervention and structuring of situations to foster peer-related social competence seem to fit well within early childhood practices based on developmental principles (Guralnick, in preparation). Some concerns exist regarding the degree of structure that may be needed for some children under some circumstances, but the integrity of practices that are developmentally appropriate remains intact.

Moreover, the focus on processes and strategies within the context of social tasks provides a framework for considering how children's special characteristics may affect their interactions with peers. This approach can accommodate the relatively mild but important articulation problems experienced by many young children, as well as the severe expressive language problems that are common to children with Down syndrome (Fowler, 1990); it can accommodate highly prevalent attentional problems that cause many children to fail to recognize accurately the intent of their peers (Barkley, 1990), as well as the unusual difficulties experienced by children with autism in recognizing that others can actually hold intentions that are different from their own (Baron-Cohen, Leslie, & Frith, 1985); and it can accommodate the wide variations in planning, sequencing, and organization often found in preschool children (Casey, Bronson, Tivnan, Riley, & Spenciner, 1991), as well as the unusual higher-order processing problems experienced by children with early treated phenylketonuria (Welsh, Pennington, Ozonoff, Rouse, & McCabe, 1990).

REFERENCES

Alessandri, S. M. (1991). Play and social behavior in maltreated preschoolers. *Development and Psychopathology, 3*, 191–205.

Anderson, S., & Messick, S. (1974). Social competency in young children. *Developmental Psychology, 10*, 282–293.

Asher, S. R. (1983). Social competence and peer status: Recent advances and future directions. *Child Development, 54*, 1427–1434.

Asher, S. R. (1990). Recent advances in the study of peer rejection. In S. R. Asher & J. D. Coie (Eds.), *Peer rejection in childhood* (pp. 3–14). Cambridge: Cambridge University Press.

Bailey, D. B., Jr., & Wolery, M. (Eds.). (1989). *Assessing infants and preschoolers with handicaps.* Columbus, OH: Merrill.

Bakeman, R., & Brownlee, J. R. (1980). The strategic use of parallel play: A sequential analysis. *Child Development, 51*, 873–878.

Barkley, R. A. (1990). *Attention-Deficit Hyperactivity Disorder: A handbook for diagnosis and treatment.* New York: Guilford Press.

Baron-Cohen, S., Leslie, A. M., & Frith, U. (1985). Does the autistic child have a "theory of mind"? *Cognition, 21*, 37–46.

Bates, E. (1975). Peer relations and the acquisition of language. In M. Lewis & L. A. Rosenblum (Eds.), *The origins of behavior: Vol. 4. Friendship and peer relations* (pp. 259–292). New York: Wiley.

Bennett, F. C., & Guralnick, M. J. (1991). Effectiveness of developmental intervention in the first five years of life. *The Pediatric Clinics of North America, 38*, 1513–1528.

Black, B., & Hazen, N. L. (1990). Social status and patterns of communication in acquainted and unacquainted preschool children. *Developmental Psychology, 26*, 379–387.

Booth, C. L., Rose-Krasnor, L., & Rubin, K. H. (1991). Relating preschoolers' social competence and their mothers' parenting behaviors to early attachment security and high-risk status. *Journal of Social and Personal Relationships, 8*, 363–382.

Bredekamp, S. (Ed.). (1987). *Developmentally appropriate practice in early childhood programs serving children from birth through age 8*. Washington, DC: National Association for the Education of Young Children.

Campbell, S. B. (1990). The socialization and social development of hyperactive children. In M. Lewis & S. M. Miller (Eds.), *Handbook of developmental psychopathology* (pp. 77–91). New York: Plenum Press.

Casey, M. B., Bronson, M. B., Tivnan, T., Riley, E., & Spenciner, L. (1991). Differentiating preschoolers' sequential planning ability from their general intelligence: A study of organization, systematic responding, and efficiency in young children. *Journal of Applied Developmental Psychology, 12*, 19–32.

Cicchetti, D., & Beeghly, M. (Eds.). (1990). *Children with Down syndrome: A developmental perspective*. Cambridge: Cambridge University Press.

Connolly, J. A., & Doyle, A. (1981). Assessment of social competence in preschoolers: Teachers versus peers. *Developmental Psychology, 17*, 454–462.

Corsaro, W. A. (1981). Friendship in the nursery school: Social organization in a peer environment. In S. R. Asher & J. M. Gottman (Eds.), *The development of children's friendships* (pp. 207–241). New York: Cambridge University Press.

Dawe, H. C. (1934). An analysis of two hundred quarrels of preschool children. *Child Development, 5*, 139–157.

Dodge, K. A., Pettit, G. S., McClaskey, C. L., & Brown, M. M. (1986). Social competence in children. *Monographs of the Society for Research in Child Development, 51*(2, Serial No. 213).

Dodge, K. A., Schlundt, D. C., Schocken, I., & Delugach, J. D. (1983). Social competence and children's sociometric status: The role of peer group entry strategies. *Merrill-Palmer Quarterly, 29*(3), 309–336.

Doyle, A., Connolly, J., & Rivest, L. (1980). The effect of playmate familiarity on the social interactions of young children. *Child Development, 51*, 217–223.

Eisenberg, A. R., & Garvey, C. (1981). Children's use of verbal strategies in resolving conflicts. *Discourse Processes, 4*, 149–170.

Foster, S. L., & Ritchey, W. L. (1979). Issues in the assessment of social competence in children. *Journal of Applied Behavior Analysis, 12*, 625–638.

Fowler, A. E. (1990). Language abilities in children with Down syndrome: Evidence for a specific syntactic delay. In D. Cicchetti & M. Beeghly (Eds.), *Children with Down syndrome: A developmental perspective* (pp. 302–328). Cambridge: Cambridge University Press.

Fox, N. A., & Field, T. M. (1989). Individual differences in preschool entry behavior. *Journal of Applied Developmental Psychology, 10*, 527–540.

Furman, L. N., & Walden, T. A. (1990). Effect of script knowledge on pre-school children's communicative interactions. *Developmental Psychology, 26*, 227–233.

Garvey, C. (1975). Requests and responses in children's speech. *Journal of Child Language, 2*, 41–63.

Garvey, C. (1986). Peer relations and the growth of communication. In E. C. Mueller & C.R. Cooper (Eds.), *Process and outcome in peer relationships* (pp. 329–345). Orlando, FL: Academic Press.

Genishi, C., & Di Paolo, M. (1982). Learning through argument in a pre-school. In L. C. Wilkinson (Ed.), *Communicating in the classroom* (pp. 49–84). New York: Academic Press.

Ginsberg, D., Gottman, J. M., & Parker, J. G. (1986). The importance of friendship. In J. M. Gottman & J. G. Parker (Eds.), *Conversations of friends: Speculations on affective development* (pp. 3–48). New York: Cambridge University Press.

Goldman, J. A., Corsini, D. A., & DeUrioste, R. (1980). Implications of posi-tive and negative sociometric status for assessing the social competence of young children. *Journal of Applied Developmental Psychology, 1*, 209–220.

Goldstein, H., Wickstrom, S., Hoyson, M., Jamieson, B., & Odom, S. L. (1988). Effects of script training on social and communicative interac-tions. *Education and Treatment of Children, 11*, 97–177.

Gottman, J. M. (1983). How children become friends. *Monographs of the Society for Research in Child Development, 48*(3, Serial No. 201).

Gottman, J. M., & Katz, L. (1989). Effects of marital discord on young children's peer interaction and health. *Developmental Psychology, 25*, 373–381.

Guevrement, D. (1990). Social skills and peer relationship training. In R. Bark-ley (Ed.), *Attention Deficit Hyperactivity Disorder: A handbook for diag-nosis and treatment* (pp. 541–572). New York: Guilford Press.

Guralnick, M. J. (1984). The peer interactions of young developmentally de-layed children in specialized and integrated settings. In T. Field, J. Roopnarine, & M. Segal (Eds.), *Friendships in normal and handicapped children* (pp. 139–152). Norwood, NJ: Ablex.

Guralnick, M. J. (1986). The peer relations of young handicapped and non-handicapped children. In P. S. Strain, M. J. Guralnick, & H. M. Walker (Eds.), *Children's social behavior: Development, assessment, and modifi-cation* (pp. 93–140). New York: Academic Press.

Guralnick, M. J. (1990a). Major accomplishments and future directions in early childhood mainstreaming. *Topics in Early Childhood Special Edu-cation, 10*(2), 1–17.

Guralnick, M. J. (1990b). Peer interactions and the development of handi-capped children's social and communicative competence. In H. Foot, M. Morgan, & R. Shute (Eds.), *Children helping children* (pp. 275–305). Sussex, England: Wiley.

Guralnick, M. J. (1990c). Social competence and early intervention. *Journal of Early Intervention, 14*, 3–14.

Guralnick, M. J. (1992a). A hierarchical model for understanding children's peer-related social competence. In S. L. Odom, S. R. McConnell, & M. A. McEvoy (Eds.), *Social competence of young children with disabilities: Issues and strategies for intervention* (pp. 37–64). Baltimore: Paul H. Brookes.

Guralnick, M. J. (1992b). *Assessment of peer relations.* Seattle: University of Washington, Child Development and Mental Retardation Center.

Guralnick, M. J. (1993). Developmentally appropriate practice in the assessment and intervention of children's peer relations. *Topics in Early Childhood Special Education, 13*(2), 344–371.

Guralnick, M. J. (in preparation). *Peer relations and early childhood mainstreaming: A developmental and systems approach.*

Guralnick, M. J., & Bricker, D. (1987). The effectiveness of early intervention for children with cognitive and general developmental delays. In M. J. Guralnick & F. C. Bennett (Eds.), *The effectiveness of early intervention for at-risk and handicapped children* (pp. 115–173). New York: Academic Press.

Guralnick, M. J., & Groom, J. M. (1985). Correlates of peer-related social competence of developmentally delayed preschool children. *American Journal of Mental Deficiency, 90*, 140–150.

Guralnick, M. J., & Groom, J. M. (1987a). Dyadic peer interactions of mildly delayed and nonhandicapped preschool children. *American Journal of Mental Deficiency, 92*, 178–193.

Guralnick, M. J., & Groom, J. M. (1987b). The peer relations of mildly delayed and nonhandicapped preschool children in mainstreamed playgroups. *Child Development, 58*, 1556–1572.

Guralnick, M. J., & Groom, J. M. (1988a). Friendships of preschool children in mainstreamed playgroups. *Developmental Psychology, 24*, 595–604.

Guralnick, M. J., & Groom, J. M. (1988b). Peer interactions in mainstreamed and specialized classrooms: A comparative analysis. *Exceptional Children, 54*, 415–425.

Guralnick, M. J., & Paul-Brown, D. (1984). Communicative adjustments during behavior-request episodes among children at different developmental levels. *Child Development, 55*, 911–919.

Guralnick, M. J., & Weinhouse, E. M. (1984). Peer-related social interactions of developmentally delayed young children: Development and characteristics. *Developmental Psychology, 20*, 815–827.

Harper, L. V., & Huie, K. S. (1985). The effects of prior group experience, age, and familiarity on the quality and organization of preschoolers' social relationships. *Child Development, 56*, 704–717.

Hartup, W. W. (1978). Peer interaction and the processes of socialization. In M. J. Guralnick (Ed.), *Early intervention and the integration of handicapped and nonhandicapped children* (pp. 27–51). Baltimore: University Park Press.

Hartup, W. W. (1983). Peer relations. In E. M. Hetherington (Ed.), *Handbook of child psychology: Vol. 4. Socialization, personality, and social develop-ment* (pp. 103–196). New York: Wiley.

Hartup, W. W., Laursen, B., Stewart, M. I., & Eastonson, A. (1988). Conflict and the friendship relations of young children. *Child Development, 59,* 1590–1600.

Hay, D. F. (1984). Social conflict in early childhood. In G. Whitehurst (Ed.), *Annals of child development* (Vol. 1, pp. 1–44). Greenwich, CT: JAI.

Hay, D. F., & Ross, H. S. (1982). The social nature of early conflict. *Child Development, 54,* 557–562.

Hazen, N. L., & Black, B. (1989). Preschool peer communication skills: The role of social status and interaction context. *Child Development, 60,* 867–876.

Hinshaw, S. P., Henker, B., & Whalen, C. K. (1984). Self-control in hyperac-tive boys in anger-inducing situations: Effects of cognitive-behavioral training and of methylphenidate. *Journal of Abnormal Child Psychology, 12,* 55–77.

Hodapp, R. M., Burack, J. A., & Zigler, E. (Eds.). (1990). *Issues in the devel-opmental approach to mental retardation.* Cambridge: Cambridge Uni-versity Press.

Howes, C. (1988). Peer interaction of young children. *Monographs of the Soci-ety for Research in Child Development, 53*(1, Serial No. 217).

Howes, C., & Matheson, C. (1992). Sequences in the development of compe-tent play with peers: Social and social pretend play. *Developmental Psy-chology, 28,* 961–974.

Kagan, J., Reznick, J. S., & Snidman, N. (1990). The temperamental qualities of inhibition and lack of inhibition. In M. Lewis & S. M. Miller (Eds.), *Handbook of developmental psychopathology* (pp. 219–226). New York: Plenum Press.

Killen, M., & Turiel, E. (1991). Conflict resolution in preschool social interac-tions. *Early Education and Development, 2,* 240–255.

Kohl, F. L., & Beckman, P. J. (1984). A comparison of handicapped and nonhandicapped preschoolers' interactions across classroom activities. *Journal of the Division for Early Childhood, 8,* 49–56.

Ladd, G. W., & Mars, K. T. (1986). Reliability and validity of preschoolers' perceptions of peer behavior. *Journal of Clinical Child Psychology, 15,* 16–25.

Levin, E. A., & Rubin, K. H. (1983). Getting others to do what you want them to do: The development of children's requestive strategies. In K. E. Nelson (Ed.), *Children's language* (Vol. 4, pp. 157–186). Hillsdale, NJ: Erlbaum.

McEvoy, M. A., Odom, S. L., & McConnell, S. R. (1992). Peer social compe-tence intervention for young children with disabilities. In S. L. Odom, S. R. McConnell, & M. A. McEvoy (Eds.), *Social competence of young children with disabilities: Issues and strategies for intervention* (pp. 113–133). Baltimore: Paul H. Brookes.

Mize, J., & Ladd, G. W. (1990). A cognitive-social learning approach to social skill training with low-status preschool children. *Developmental Psychology, 26,* 388–397.

Nelson, K. (Ed.). (1986). *Event knowledge: Structure and function in development.* Hillsdale, NJ: Erlbaum.

Nelson, K., & Gruendel, J. (1979). At morning it's lunchtime: A scriptal view of children's dialogues. *Discourse Processes, 2,* 73–94.

Nelson, K., & Seidman, S. (1984). Playing with scripts. In I. Bretherton (Ed.), *Symbolic play: The development of social understanding* (pp. 45–71). New York: Academic Press.

Newman, D. (1978). Ownership and permission among nursery school children. In J. Glick & K. A. Clarke-Stewart (Eds.), *The development of social understanding* (pp. 213–249). New York: Gardner Press.

O'Malley, J. M. (1977). Research perspective on social competence. *Merrill-Palmer Quarterly, 23,* 29–44.

Parker, J. G., & Asher, S. R. (1987). Peer relations and later personal adjustment: Are low-accepted children at risk? *Psychological Bulletin, 102,* 357–389.

Parten, M. B. (1932). Social participation among preschool children. *Journal of Abnormal Social Psychology, 27,* 243–269.

Phinney, J. S. (1986). The structure of 5-year-olds' verbal quarrels with peers and siblings. *Journal of Genetic Psychology, 147*(1), 47–60.

Putallaz, M. (1983). Predicting children's sociometric status from their behavior. *Child Development, 54,* 1417–1426.

Putallaz, M., & Gottman, J. M. (1981). Social skills and group acceptance. In S. R. Asher & J. M. Gottman (Eds.), *The development of children's friendships* (pp. 116–149). Cambridge: Cambridge University Press.

Putallaz, M., & Wasserman, A. (1989). Children's naturalistic entry behavior and sociometric status: A developmental perspective. *Developmental Psychology, 25,* 297–305.

Putallaz, M., & Wasserman, A. (1990). Children's entry behavior. In S. R. Asher & J. D. Coie (Eds.), *Peer rejection in childhood* (pp. 60–89). Cambridge: Cambridge University Press.

Quilitch, H. R., & Risley, T. R. (1973). The effects of play materials on social play. *Journal of Applied Behavior Analysis, 6,* 573–578.

Ross, G., Lipper, E. G., & Auld, P. A. M. (1990). Social competence and behavior problems in premature children at school age. *Pediatrics, 86,* 391–397.

Rubin, K. H. (1982). Nonsocial play in preschoolers: Necessarily evil? *Child Development, 53,* 651–657.

Rubin, K. H., Fein, G. G., & Vandenberg, B. (1983). Play. In E. M. Hetherington (Ed.), *Handbook of child psychology: Vol. 4. Socialization, personality, and social development* (pp. 693–774). New York: Wiley.

Rubin, K. H., & Lollis, S. P. (1988). Origins and consequences of social withdrawal. In J. Belsky & T. Nezworski (Eds.), *Clinical implications of attachment* (pp. 219–252). Hillsdale, NJ: Erlbaum.

Rubin, K. H., Watson, K. S., & Jambor, T. W. (1978). Free-play behaviors in preschool and kindergarten children. *Child Development, 49*, 534–536.

Rubin, Z. (1980). *Children's friendships*. Cambridge: Harvard University Press.

Sainato, D. M., & Carta, J. J. (1992). Classroom influences on the development of social competence in young children with disabilities. In S. L. Odom, S. R. McConnell, & M. A. McEvoy (Eds.), *Social competence of young children with disabilities: Issues and strategies for intervention* (pp. 93–109). Baltimore: Paul H. Brookes.

Schank, R. C., & Abelson, R. P. (1977). *Scripts, plans, goals and understanding: An inquiry into human knowledge structures*. Hillsdale, NJ: Erlbaum.

Shantz, C. U. (1987). Conflicts between children. *Child Development, 58*, 283–305.

Shea, J. D. C. (1981). Changes in interpersonal distances and categories of play behavior in the early weeks of preschool. *Developmental Psychology, 17*, 417–425.

Sternberg, R. J. (1985). *Beyond I.Q.* New York: Cambridge University Press.

Stoneman, Z., Cantrell, M. L., & Hoover-Dempsey, K. (1983). The association between play materials and social behavior in a mainstreamed preschool: A naturalistic investigation. *Journal of Applied Developmental Psychology, 4*, 163–174.

Strain, P. S. (1983). Generalization of autistic children's social behavior change: Effects of developmentally integrated and segregated settings. *Analysis and Intervention in Developmental Disabilities, 3*, 23–24.

Strain, P. S., & Odom, S. L. (1986). Peer social initiations: Effective intervention for social skills development of exceptional children. *Exceptional Children, 52*, 543–551.

Welsh, M. C., Pennington, B. F., Ozonoff, S., Rouse, B., & McCabe, E. R. B. (1990). Neuropsychology of early-treated phenylketonuria: Specific executive function deficits. *Child Development, 61*, 1697–1713.

Zuckerman, B., & Bresnahan, K. (1991). Developmental and behavioral consequences of prenatal drug and alcohol exposure. *The Pediatric Clinics of North America, 38*, 1387–1406.

CHAPTER 4

The Role of Play in
Early Childhood Special Education

Toni Linder

Jessica sits with her mother on the floor in her living room. Next to her are a bucket full of plastic shapes and a pop-up toy activated when various knobs, buttons, or levers are manipulated. In her right hand she holds a cylindrical shape. She places her weight on her left arm, reaches over with her right arm, and pounds with the shape on a button of the pop-up toy. A chicken head pops up. Jessica smiles and vocalizes "ah." Her mother imitates her sound. Jessica pushes the lid down over the chicken, but it pops back up. Mother helps to push so it stays down. Jessica repeats her actions with the button, then drops the cylinder and tries to manipulate the lever. She vocalizes "bah." Mother says "bah-bah." Jessica repeats, "bah-bah." Mother says, "bye-bye, doggie." Jessica crawls over to the bucket, takes out a shape, and throws it. She looks at her mother, laughs, and takes another shape out and throws it. This is repeated several times. Mother smiles and says, "You sure can throw! Let's put them *in* the bucket now." Mother picks up a shape and drops it in the bucket. Jessica looks in the bucket, looks at her mother, takes out another block, throws it, and laughs.

In this brief play episode, the significance of play can be demonstrated. Perhaps the most important aspect is that Jessica is having fun investigating the toys in her environment. She enjoys the engagement with toys and her mother. Her pleasure is seen both in her positive affect and in her sustained attention to the activities. Although Jessica is actually 2 years old, her play skills reveal that she is functioning at about the 8- to 11-month level. While her play skills are delayed for her age, they are positively influencing the course of her development. She is practicing established skills and learning new skills, confirming patterns of interaction, and discovering limits and expectations. Cognitively, she is exploring cause-and-effect associations, learning about spatial relationships, discovering the use of a tool, and making efforts at problem solving. Socially, Jessica is acknowledging the importance of others, learning to read social cues, and discovering behavioral limits. In communication, Jessica is imitating the adult's sounds, practicing taking turns, and using her vocalizations to communicate her intentions. Motorically, she is practicing playing in different positions, and in doing so she rotates her body, supports her weight on one arm, shifts her weight from one side of her body to another, uses varying grasp patterns, and practices releasing an object.

All these efforts positively influence Jessica's growth and development. Play, then, is of value to children for many reasons. In this chapter various aspects of play are explored, including the impact of play on children whose development follows a typical developmental progression as well as the influence of disabilities on play behaviors. Relatively little research exists on the play of children with disabilities, and much of it, according to Quinn and Rubin (1984), is of poor quality and suggests inconsistent results. This may be due in part to the heterogeneous nature of the population, but it is also due to the virtual omission of play from the skill-focused assessment and intervention approaches typically used with these children (Fewell & Kaminski, 1988). This trend is beginning to shift as play becomes a more acceptable approach for assessing and working with young children (Linder, 1990).

Given the limitations of the research, there is considerable evidence that the play of children with disabilities is qualitatively and quantitatively different from the play of children without disabilities. Overall, it is less sophisticated, less organized, and more isolated, and involves more functional and ritualistic use of objects. Greatest discrepancies are reported in the areas of symbolic play and social interaction (Quinn & Rubin, 1984). Moreover, children with disabilities engage in less group play and often have low social status as assessed by sociometric measures, indicating that they are perceived by peers as less appealing play partners (Odom, McConnell, & McEvoy, 1992). If it is true that play skills facilitate developmental growth, then the characteristics of the play of children with disabilities may inhibit their cognitive, language, motor, and social–emotional development. It follows that if these play skills can be improved, developmental progress should be enhanced.

This has, in fact, been shown to be the case through play training studies (e.g., Christie, 1983). The importance of play to the development of the child underlines the need to incorporate play facilitation in infant and preschool settings that include children with disabilities. Play as an intervention mode holds great promise as a functional, intrinsically motivating approach to working with young children with special needs (Linder, 1993).

DEFINITION OF PLAY

Play is not easily defined in the academic sense. Affectively, we recognize play when we see it or are involved in activities that we would describe as play. Our fondest memories of childhood, and even adulthood, may be associated with play. Scholars' descriptions (e.g., Garvey, 1977; Hutt, 1971; Rubin, Fein, & Vandenberg, 1983) note numerous elements that seem important. Play is voluntary, spontaneous, and pleasurable, and requires active engagement of the participants. The motivation for play is intrinsic, with the players valuing the activity. Neumann (1971) describes play as a continuum of lesser-to-greater degrees of expression with three elements — locus of control (freedom to choose), internal determination of reality, and intrinsic motivation — which combine to determine where on the play-nonplay continuum a specific behavior falls. Bettelheim (1987) states, "Play refers to the young child's activities characterized by freedom from all but personally imposed rules (which are changed at will), by free-wheeling fantasy involvement, and by the absence of any goals outside the activity itself" (p. 37). The types of play that are pleasurable shift as the child develops. In fact, play and development are intricately interrelated, with play seeming to "lead" development (Fromberg, 1992).

PLAY AND COGNITIVE DEVELOPMENT

Theories concerning the relationship between play and cognitive development have been influenced by Piaget's (1962) emphasis on the importance of the child's actions on the environment and Vygotsky's (1967) emphasis on the importance of the child's social interactions. From the earliest days of infancy, children have an impact on their environment, first through interactions with people and then through interactions with objects and events in the environment. As the child's cognitive understanding of the world expands, as motoric skills become refined, as social understandings mature, and as communication abilities become more sophisticated, the child's play skills undergo a corresponding advancement. The reciprocal nature of these changes is important to understand.

During play the child has control over the content and processes employed and can decide whether to engage in exploration of the familiar or modify and expand into novel behaviors (Almy, Monighan, Scales, & VanHoorn, 1984). In order to play with objects, the child needs to examine them using the various sensory systems, the development of which, in tandem with cognitive understanding, enables discriminatory skills. Discrimination and classification skills and spatial understanding have been shown to be associated with higher levels of play (Rubin & Maioni, 1975), which in turn has been found to be related to language and prereading achievement among preschool children (Pellegrini, 1980). Manipulation of objects in play also provides opportunities for the child to experiment with different approaches to problem solving. Through trial and error the child acquires a greater ability to discriminate between relevant and irrelevant information (Athey, 1984). As problem-solving skills develop, the child establishes relationships between objects, words, and ideas, which can then be applied to novel situations (Dansky & Silverman, 1975; Pellegrini, 1980; Pellegrini & Greene, 1980). Persistence in problem solving, or mastery motivation, is also promoted through play as the child practices a new skill until it can easily be accomplished (Morgan & Harmon, 1984). Play provides a safe arena for the child to derive pleasure from completing a task and solving a problem posed by play materials, independent of adult praise and approval.

Play also facilitates the ability to solve different types of problems. Convergent thinking, or coming up with one "right" answer to a problem, is promoted through play with toys that require a specific approach, such as puzzles. Divergent thinking, or solving problems that have numerous solutions, is facilitated through more open-ended play, such as with blocks or in dramatic play (Pepler & Ross, 1981), and creativity, which involves divergent thinking, has been found to be correlated with play proficiency (e.g., Dansky & Silverman, 1975). In promoting the ability to use objects in atypical and representational ways, symbolic play contributes to the child's ability to plan, employ hypothetical reasoning, and understand abstract symbols and logical transformations (Almy et al., 1984). Symbolic play also appears to enhance recognition of numbers and understanding of set theory (Yawkey, Jones, & Hrncir, 1979), sequential memory performance (Saltz,

Dixon, & Johnson, 1977), and decentration and "reversible" thinking (Rubin et al., 1983). The latter skills are necessary, according to Piaget (1962), for the development of such cognitive abilities as conservation, while the former are consistent with Vygotsky's (1967) view that play fosters the internal mental processes of association, logical memory, and abstract thinking, abilities needed in the elementary grades. Since such abilities are measured by intelligence tests, there is also evidence that play may increase IQ. Johnson, Ershler, and Lawton (1982) found a correlation between group make-believe (or sociodramatic) play and constructive play and IQ scores, and increasing sociodramatic play skills through play training has been found to result in IQ gains (Saltz, Dixon, & Johnson, 1977). Moreover, such gains appear to be lasting (Christie, 1983).

Children with Cognitive Delays

Children with cognitive delays appear to progress through the same play sequences as typical children (Hill & McCune-Nicholich, 1981; Mahoney, Glover, & Finger, 1981; Motti, Cichetti, & Sroufe, 1983; Rogers, 1977; Sigman & Ungerer, 1984). Their level of play has generally been found to be related to their assessed developmental age equivalent, with several areas of deficiency. In a review of literature, Li (1981) noted that the play of children identified as having mental retardation is characterized by a restricted repertoire of play skills, including less language during play, less sophisticated representational play, and limited selection of play materials. Mindes (1982) found that preschool children with developmental delays exhibited more nonplay behaviors, more solitary play behaviors, and less cooperative play than typical preschoolers. Their play may be lower level, with functional, manipulative play predominating; more ritualistic; and less organized (Hulme & Lunzer, 1966). Riquet and Taylor (1981) examined the play of children with Down syndrome, children diagnosed as autistic, and typical children (equated on developmental status), concluding that the children with disabilities tended to elaborate the same idea repeatedly throughout the play period.

Cognitive delays are similarly related to play-related social skills involved in cognitive development. Imitation, critical for learning cognitive, language, social, and motor skills, is often difficult for children with cognitive delays (Cooke & Apolloni, 1976). In addition, children functioning at lower cognitive-developmental levels may not achieve the symbolic play level (Hill & McCune-Nicholich, 1981), remaining focused on object or functional role play. They may have difficulty recognizing the intention of play companions, initiating play with peers, integrating the objects of play with the events in which peers are engaged, and understanding how to enter a play group (Guralnick, 1992; Chapter 3, this volume), tasks that require both cognitive and social communicative skills, and the ability to coordinate pretend play with peers (Lieber & Beckman, 1991).

Play in infancy, characterized by social play with the parent, is also noticeably different among children with cognitive delays. Infants with Down syndrome have been found to engage in less vocal imitation than typical infants (Mahoney et al., 1981) and to have difficulty with state control, to be more passive, to use less eye-gaze, and to have less positive affect (Richard, 1986), all of which tend negatively to influence play interaction with caregivers. Delayed infants who are verbal have been reported to demonstrate less frequency of speech and shorter mean length of utterance (MLU) (Hulme & Lunzer, 1966) which, together with the above-noted characteristics, have a dampening effect on social play interactions between parent and child. Attentional differences also affect the play of children with developmental delays, who appear to monitor the environment less, engage their mothers less in social play, and spend more time in unoccupied behavior than children without disabilities (Krakow & Kopp, 1983). Stereotyped behaviors in some children with severe and profound delays also mitigates their play, since repetitive behaviors not only preclude exploration and engagement in diverse play activities, but also tend to isolate the child and keep others from engaging the child in play.

Play Intervention

Play interactions are a natural part of the parent-infant relationship, providing a scaffold for the child's emerging skills (Bruner, 1977). For the child with cognitive deficits, this scaffold is particularly important. The parent or professional can facilitate higher levels of play through imitation of the child, shifting activities into turn-taking games, and modeling a modification or higher-level behavior (Mahoney & Powell, 1986). The repetitive verbalizations and pauses used to signal the end of the adult's turn (Bruner, 1977) must be emphasized with the child with developmental delays. In addition, the adult can help the child orient and maintain attention (Carlson & Bricker, 1982); initiate play interchanges; respond to play overtures and imitate higher-level play behaviors of others (Cooke & Apolloni, 1976); and organize, direct, and expand play sequences (Guralnick & Groom, 1987). Guralnick (1992) also emphasizes the importance of integrating skills from all developmental areas, with an emphasis on social communicative skills and tasks. Modeling within playful interactions, suggesting an alternative course of action, and structuring the play to encourage higher-level strategies stimulate the child to engage the materials in the environment through more creative means (Linder, 1993). Provision of toys and materials that promote comprehension of cause-effect relationships, spatial understanding, representational thinking, and problem solving is also important. Allowing the child to initiate and select activities fosters mastery motivation, the role of the adult being to observe and then facilitate the child's engagement, as shown in the following example:

> Lana, a 4-year-old child with Down syndrome, played in the water table with a baby doll, repeatedly washing it with her hand and then holding it up to watch the water run off. After observing her for a few minutes, the teacher knelt beside Lana at the water table with her own doll. She took a bar of soap, put some on a wash cloth, and washed her baby, saying, "My baby's dirty, too." Lana watched the teacher, then took another cloth and the bar of soap, washed the doll, and said, "Baby dirty." The teacher progressed through drying the baby and putting lotion on it. At each step Lana observed, imitated, and commented on the action. In subsequent play at the water table, Lana was observed to increase her play sequence with the doll spontaneously. If the soap, wash cloth, and towel were present, Lana would use one or more in her play. After several days, she would even search for the props if they were absent.

In this episode, the teacher was able to incorporate social interaction, lengthening of play sequences, higher-level representational play, cause-and-effect understanding, problem solving, and language production. It illustrates that, while imitation does not necessarily occur spontaneously in many children with developmental delays, it can be fostered by building on behavior in which the child is engaged.

PLAY AND LANGUAGE DEVELOPMENT

Play with language is a conventional aspect of children's play. As Garvey (1977) has pointed out, "almost all the levels . . . of language . . . and most phenomena of speech and talking, such as expressive

noises, variation in timing and intensity, the distribution of talk between participants, the objectives of speech . . . are potential resources
for play" (p. 59). Children from 2 to 6 are fascinated by language and
can freely experiment with its various nuances within play. They may
play with sounds by repeating a succession of vocalizations of vowels
and/or consonants, substituting words in a syntactical sequence, or intentionally playing with words to make others laugh (Garvey, 1977).
As children learn to represent objects, actions, and feelings in symbolic
play, a corresponding ability to represent them through language also
develops (Westby, 1980). In the same way that children master cognitive problems through experimentation, play provides a medium for
increasing their conscious awareness of linguistic rules (Cazden, 1974)
and then mastering the phonological, syntactical, and semantic rules of
language (Athey, 1984). Social play with language allows the child to
practice sounds, intonations, spontaneous rhyming and word play; play
with fantasy and nonsense; and play with speech acts and discourse
(Garvey, 1977).

As children begin to develop play skills with others, social communicative acts become more important (Guralnick, 1992). The interrela-
tionships among language, cognition, and social development are complex, and not completely understood, but need to be considered as a
whole. In sociodramatic play, the child is expressing cognitive understandings in a social situation and using language to define a situation
and location, assign roles and props, carry out an action plan, correct or
refine the script, monitor others' performance, invoke rules, terminate a
theme or transition to another, and comment on the interpersonal cli-
mate in the group (Garvey, 1977). Although some studies of the efficacy
of sociodramatic play training have had methodological problems, such
training has been found to result in increased language skills (Smith &
Syddall, 1978). Smilansky (1968) reported that training in sociodramatic play resulted in increased play-related speech, vocabulary,
number of words spoken, and length of sentences in disadvantaged
preschool children. Sociodramatic play, in particular, provides a motivating context for "literate behaviors" (Heath & Mangiola, 1991), or
forms of expression of needs, interests, and desires that form the basis
for later literacy. In dramatic play, children learn to grasp the concept
of a story and the sequencing of events expressed through actions and
communication, thus building a foundation for reading and writing.

In play, children also learn to distinguish the effects that deviant or
unconventional language patterns produce in interaction, thus enabling
them to establish and practice the social conventions of language. The
development of social cognition, or understanding of social rules, inter-

actions, and consequences, is also enhanced through language use in play. Language and communication are central to social interactions in play, as children plan, manage, solve problems, and sustain play through verbal explanations, discussions, or commands. Nonlinguistic communication through eye contact and eye-gaze, gesture, and physical manipulation is also an important facet of social play (Spodek & Saracho, 1988). Delays in verbal and nonverbal communication skills therefore impair children's ability to engage in play interactions.

Children with Communication Disorders and Hearing Impairments

The literature concerning children with language-related delays and impairments is confusing, as various types of problems are often not clearly differentiated, diagnostic labels are often not consistent across studies, and children with language delays are sometimes included under the broad rubric of "developmental delays." For purposes of this discussion, language delay, specific language impairment (SLI), and hearing impairment are addressed. Language disorders in young children are difficulties or delays in "language, oral speech, and the functional-practical use of communication as a social tool" (Peterson, 1987, p. 242). Language impairments can be seen in children who demonstrate no other impairments, as well as in those who have hearing, cognitive, motor, and/or social impairments. Since language delays are frequently associated with other disabilities, few studies have involved children experiencing only language delays. As with other types of disabilities, however, they have been found to engage in symbolic play less often and solitary play more often, to make fewer social contacts, and to have less organized play than typical age peers (e.g., Lovell, Hoyle, & Siddall, 1968). Participation in dramatic play is likely to be impaired by its social demands, which require language, and the more severe the language delay, the greater is the deficit in play skills.

Specific language impairment, a developmental language disorder, is distinguished from general language delay. SLI has been defined (Fey & Leonard, 1983) as "a pronounced deficit in the comprehension and/or expression of language in the relative absence of impairments in other areas of development" (p. 65). Such deficits may include linguistic nonfluency, continuous revising of language, delays before responding, nonspecific vocabulary, inappropriate (out of context) responses, and need for repetition (without increased comprehension). Children with SLI often have unusual language patterns and consequently are avoided by other children in play. They may initiate play in inappropriate

ways, lack problem-solving skills in interactions, and demonstrate negative behaviors to avoid difficult situations or to gain attention (Goldstein & Gallagher, 1992). While peer interactions among children
between 3 and 7 years of age are characterized by coordination of
interactive/temporal play sequences with a maximum of excitement,
entertainment, and affect, children with SLI may demonstrate a limited coordinated play partner code, with consequent diminished enthusiasm.

Impaired hearing does not appear to affect play during infancy,
for children with hearing impairments observe, explore, and imitate
the actions of others similarly to typical infants. However, mother–
child interactions differ from interactions between hearing infants and
their mothers in that interaction occurs in multiple but briefer sequences. Moreover, mothers initiate most interactions, making the infant primarily a responder. These interaction patterns, in conjunction
with developing language delays, may have an impact on play skills.
After 2 years of age, when symbolic use of words appears, the deaf child
begins to show delays in representational play (Gregory, 1976). As the
child moves into the preschool years, studies (e.g., Antia & Kreimeyer,
1992) suggest that children with impaired hearing initiate play with
others less than do hearing peers, spend more time in isolated or parallel
play, and prefer constructive rather than dramatic play, which requires
social interaction. Interactions are typically nonlinguistic and of brief
duration. Children with more severe hearing loss and who are less
linguistically proficient interact less frequently than those with mild
impairment (e.g., Brackett & Henniges, 1976). Lederberg, Ryan, and
Robbins (1986) found that nonlinguistic communication skills are important in play interactions where both partners are hearing impaired,
while in hearing/hearing-impaired dyads the abilities and motivation
of the hearing partner were important factors in successful play interactions.

Play Intervention

In her review of approaches to language intervention over the past
three decades, Bricker (1993) observed that interventions for children
with language delays have evolved, as have interventions for children
with other delays, from a highly structured, behavioral, isolated therapy model to one involving multiple disciplines and natural, functional
settings. Interventionists now recognize the need to integrate cognitive,
social, and motor goals with communication goals within natural social
contexts, which, for young children, involve play. Initiating interven-

tion with prelinguistic infants with or at-risk for communication delays
has been reported to ameliorate later delays (Yoder & Warren, 1993),
and an ecological approach to intervention involves parents, siblings,
and other family members, peers, and professionals (Bricker, 1993).
Current approaches focus on *pragmatics*, or the communicative intent
of language, while also addressing the traditional areas of phonology,
morphology, syntax, and semantics. Models for language intervention
involving following the child's lead and encouraging the child's initiation to build on natural motivation and give the child control include
milieu teaching (Kaiser, Hendrickson, & Alpert, 1991), which expands
the child's language through structured prompts within everyday social/
communicative exchanges; *play-based intervention* (Linder, 1993),
which emphasizes child-directed play activities as a medium for facilitating communicative competence; and *activity-based intervention*
(Bricker & Cripe, 1992), which also emphasizes intervention in child-
initiated play, as well as routine activities, and uses naturally occurring
antecedents and consequences to develop skills.

In providing a context within which to build on a child's current
skills and enhance the quantity and quality of communicative output,
play is a natural medium through which to address language delays in
young children. Specific strategies suggested (e.g., Linder, 1990; Yoder
& Warren, 1993) include

1. Imitating the child's nonverbal and verbal behaviors
2. Commenting on the child's actions
3. Commenting on the adult's actions
4. Expanding the child's utterance
5. Elaborating on a comment
6. Modeling new sounds and words
7. Saying correctly what the child has attempted to say
8. Asking questions
9. Manipulating the play environment to elicit language initiations
10. Building turn-taking
11. Shaping responses

Peer-mediated approaches have also proven successful with children with SLI or with language delays. In one such approach (Goldstein & Gallagher, 1992), peers are taught to establish eye contact,
establish a joint focus of attention, initiate joint play, prompt requests,
describe their own play, repeat or expand children's utterances, and
request clarification. Rehearsal of skills through role-play and script

training has increased communication in children with SLI, language delays, and hearing impairment, as well as other types of disability (Antia & Kreimeyer, 1992; Goldstein & Gallagher, 1992).

PLAY AND MOTOR DEVELOPMENT

The exploratory and play behaviors of the early years contribute to the growth and control of the sensory and muscular systems. "It appears that repetition of movements, or sequences of movements, has the effect of establishing neural pathways that facilitate performance and make these sequences readily available for future use" (Athey, 1984, p. 12). Repetition of actions or behaviors in play is typical, and with each playful repetition, the child reproduces fine and gross motor movements. Such practice of motor responses in play activities results in motor skills that are swift, fluid, and accurate (Bundy, 1991). In play, children learn about the influence and control their own bodies can exert on the world. As stability, strength, and coordination develop, children gain greater self-control and an increased desire to use their motoric abilities in play. In gross motor play the child learns mastery over larger and more mobile objects and tools and an understanding of how the body moves through space, while fine motor skills and eye-hand coordination are developed through play with smaller objects (Athey, 1984). Motor abilities are related to perceived self-competence, as aspects of confidence derive from the child's perception of his or her body image and physical abilities.

Children with Motor Disabilities

Children's fine and gross motor skills have an impact not only on their ability to move in the environment, but also on their cognitive, language, and social skills. Motor abilities are needed to perform many cognitive tasks, to make the lip and tongue movements necessary for speech, or the hand movements necessary for signing, as well as to interact with peers. Consequently, the child with physical disabilities may be restricted in any or all of a variety of areas and, depending on the nature of the impairment, play will similarly be affected in different ways (Bundy, 1991). Poor head control affects the child's ability to anticipate an object's appearance, to identify an object, to examine it, to track its movements, and to judge distances between objects in the environment. Limited mobility affects the child's capacity to explore, to find objects to combine, or to summon someone to help accomplish a difficult task. Impaired control of limbs affects the accuracy of reaching, grasping, and releasing objects. Motor disabilities that negatively influence play behaviors may also affect mastery motivation, as the child may be dependent on others to assist and consequently may become increasingly passive in play and in self-help skills (Jennings, Connors, Stegman, Sankaranarayan, & Medolsohn, 1985). Inability to seek social interaction with peers may also result in reduced social play. Those children with physical disabilities who can move about the environment have been found to be less involved in their play, to spend more time wandering aimlessly, and to engage in more solitary play and less social play with peers (Jennings et al., 1985).

Play Intervention

Ensuring that the child's body is positioned to enable the child to play with toys and materials in the environment is critical. The child needs to be supported to allow good trunk stability, with arms and hands free to be able to manipulate toys. Placing objects within reach and at the optimal visual level for the child is also important. All of the positioning, however, should be done in an unobtrusive way that enhances rather than inhibits the child's desire to play. Consider the following example:

> Lonny, a 2½ year old with Down syndrome, was observed playing with puzzles at a table. His feet stuck out on either side of the chair, "braced" against the air, his back was curved, his arms rested on the table, his head protruded forward, and his neck was extended. His manipulations of objects was awkward. His low tone and lack of postural stability were impeding his ability to play. With a shorter chair that had back and side support, Lonny was able to plant his feet firmly on the floor and, consequently, sit straighter and move his head more freely. This minor positioning adjustment let him use his hands more freely and concentrate on the puzzle without worrying about his stability.

Children with motor problems are often seen in therapeutic settings where the therapist controls activities and movements and provides external rewards for performance. All of these conditions are in opposition to learning through play. When children are intrinsically motivated to move, controlling the interactions with the environment, and free from constraints of objective reality, they are more likely to become absorbed in their play, repeating and practicing movements until they demonstrate acquisition of adaptive behaviors. This is what occurs in fantasy play, which can readily become a context for integrating physical management and motor programming within an enjoyable activity. A play sequence can be an alternative to the traditional obstacle course. For example, the preschooler who is hunting lions on a jungle safari can climb "mountains" (a jungle gym), cross "rivers" (a wading pool), get momentarily stuck in "quicksand" (sticky oatmeal), throw "weapons" (bean bags) at "lions" (targets), swing on "vines" (ropes), and so on. With the addition of a few props and the help of children to create the story line, the play will incorporate motor activities that address balance, strength, coordination, sensory exploration, and numerous other motor components.

PLAY AND VISUAL DEVELOPMENT

Vision, we now know, is an ability newborns come into the world ready to use. While an overview of the revolutionary research findings concerning vision in the first days and weeks of life is beyond the scope of this chapter, suffice it here to note that infants focus, exhibit preference for certain forms, visually track, and even demonstrate imitative behavior much, much earlier than had been supposed. Then, over the first year of life, infants demonstrate awareness of discrepancies from the familiar, precipitating the evidence of distress we identify as "stranger anxiety." Vision clearly is a very important element in the ongoing transactional involvement with familiar caregivers that is the basis of communicative and social development. Moreover, visual abilities and motor skills are also interrelated from earliest infancy. Babies are inspired to move and reach by what they see. During the first 18–24 months of life, the *sensorimotor schemata* that become increasingly coordinated and purposeful form the building blocks of intelligence, including awareness of the permanent object, intentionality, imitation, and recognition of relationships of objects in space. The coordination of movement with visual information is a critical element in building that foundation.

Thus, development in the use of vision is integrated with and a vital element in motor, cognitive, social, and language development, as was evident in the foregoing discussions of these areas. As we saw, play has a vital role in all of these areas, in the early years of life, and many references were made in those discussions to information about the environment that the young child accesses through vision. So important is the role of vision that we might well expect congenitally blind infants to have a virtually impossible task in achieving the milestones of motor, social, language, and cognitive development. However, in spite of early delays, development in these areas can be facilitated through effective intervention.

Children with Visual Impairments

Infants who are blind or who have severe visual impairments may be unaware of objects in the environment. Due to their inability to see the toys in front of them, they are not motivated to reach out or move to attain objects (Campos, Svejda, Campos, & Berternthal, 1982). Insecurity about the location of toys affects their play in other ways as well. Once toys are placed in their hands, they may not want to let go of them, as they may not be able to retrieve them. Their means of exploration typically involves keeping the objects close to the body and often biting, licking, or rubbing the objects against their face or eyes (Fraiberg & Adelson, 1977). While it is functional, such stereotyped behavior can impede positive social interaction.

Children with visual impairments are often delayed in exploration of toys and the environment (Fewell, 1983; Fraiberg & Adelson, 1977). They often do not engage in complex social play routines (Sandler & Wills, 1965) and imitation of actions and role playing is delayed (Rogers & Puchalski, 1984). Blindness or severe visual impairment results in inability to observe others in play, thus reducing the child's ability to imitate higher-level skills. Children with visual impairments are more likely to engage in solitary play and, when they do play with other children, have fewer social exchanges (Fewell & Kaminski, 1988).

Play Intervention

Play behaviors can be enhanced for visually impaired children by the selection of appropriate toys and materials, use of adult facilitation techniques, and environmental modifications. Toys that combine visual elements with auditory or tactile elements enable the visually impaired child to identify objects or key attributes of objects. At the sensorimotor level, helping the child to track, scan, and explore objects is critical. These skills help the child to make play choices and to use play skills differentially. For instance, auditory scanning can assist the visually impaired child to determine what play activities are taking place throughout the room so a decision can be made about which to choose. The addition of tactile materials or fluorescent colors to the activating mechanisms on toys will help the child search for and differentiate the key element on cause-and-effect toys. Using larger toys and materials or enlarging symbols on the toys or in the environment may support the child in using existing vision. Lighting can also make a difference in the child's ability to play with toys. Depending on the individual child's impairment, more or less light may be required. The adult will also need to observe the child and carefully read cues so as to respond to the child's desires. Too often, the child with impaired sight is directed by the adult. If the child is not intrinsically motivated to play, the adult may stimulate interest by showing excitement, modeling interesting effects, or incorporating movement, music, or peer play.

PLAY AND SOCIAL–EMOTIONAL DEVELOPMENT

A major developmental task for young children is to acquire the knowledge, skills, and values needed to function well in society. This process of socialization begins in infancy and continues throughout the school years. Play serves as a medium for learning many social skills. Piaget (1962) noted that play is the practice ground for the social skills needed in adult life. This is particularly true of sociodramatic play, which requires children to cooperate, share, take turns, see another's perspective, and participate in social problem solving. Among its other values noted previously, dramatic play has been shown to enhance children's perspective-taking skills (Burns & Brainerd, 1979). Children develop social understanding through having to take the role of others into account; thus, play is a vehicle for broadening empathy for others and lessening egocentrism (Curry & Arnaud, 1984). Connolly and Doyle (1984) found a relationship between sociodramatic play in preschoolers and measures of social competence. Social competence, including play skills, influences the cognitive and language development of children with and without disabilities (Odom et al., 1992).

Emotional development is also influenced by play. As the child explores fantasy in an emotionally safe environment, feelings can be freely expressed. Children use play to work through and master the perplexing psychological complications of past and present. In dramatic play the child can create a "situation in which aspects of the past are relived, the present represented and renewed, and the future antici-pated" (Erikson, 1977, p. 44). Much representational play is motivated by inner conflicts, desires, and anxieties (Bettelheim, 1987). Through the choice of themes children choose to enact, they can work through traumatic experiences, act out fantasies, or become engrossed in the joy of self-expression (Erikson, 1977). Thus, play is a means of ego-building and self-realization. Dramatizing fears and anxieties enables children to understand themselves and gives them a source of control over obstacles and dilemmas. At the same time, play gives children the opportunity to create or recreate the joys and pleasures in life. As a self-enabling medium, play allows the child to be powerful and masterful (Sutton-Smith, 1980). The child's sense of identity emerges in play. Preferences for objects versus people, playfulness, fantasy-making predispositions, temperament, and play styles are expressed (Linder, 1990). The elaborateness of a child's play, organizational complexity, and persistence are also individual differences observed in play that may reflect the child's emerging identity.

Through play the child also learns that to enjoy continuous interactions with others, aggression must be controlled and various rules must be followed. Symbolic play with peers increases control over impulsivity (Saltz et al., 1977). High fantasy-making tendencies are associated with being able to entertain oneself, being able to delay gratification, being less disruptive, and interfering less with others (Singer, 1973). Fantasy and role-playing allow the child to practice the roles and rules of society (Erikson, 1977). While young children may manifest delays or problems in social–emotional development in many ways, and for many reasons, children with autism, although their disability is now generally considered to have biogenic rather than psychogenic causes, provide effective illustrations of disability involving social development.

Children with Autism

Childhood autism represents an extreme form of social dysfunction. Formerly thought to be a psychiatric disturbance, autism is now associated with neurological impairment; however, children with autism do demonstrate behaviors that impede emotional development and social interaction. Many demonstrate behaviors, such as rocking, head banging or shaking, finger flicking, hand flapping, and flicking or spinning objects close to the face, that are antithetical to typical play behavior. These behaviors have the effect of precluding engagement in meaningful play with objects and interaction with others. Some children demonstrate unusual responses to sensory input, either overreacting or underreacting to stimuli (Ayers & Tickle, 1980). Children with autism also demonstrate specific deficits in imitation skills, especially those requiring symbolic substitution of objects (Hammes & Langdell, 1981; Sigman & Ungerer, 1984). Qualitatively, the play of children with autism has been reported to involve fewer play sequences, less diversity, less time in advanced play skills, and less symbolic play with dolls or other persons (Ricks & Wing, 1975; Sigman & Ungerer, 1984). To varying degrees, the play behavior of young children who do not have autism but who do present significant delays or problems in social–emotional development may involve some of the foregoing characteristics. However, the problems of most of these children resemble more closely those of typically developing children.

Play Intervention

Play facilitation for children with autism may differ from that provided for children with emotional problems. For the child with autism, the adult may use imitation of the child in an attempt to capture attention and engage the child in turn-taking. Modifications of the child's actions may then lead to higher-level play skills. Use of sensory and vestibular play may be effective with some children, depending on sensory input needs (Bundy, 1991). With guidance, peers may also be effective play partners and tutors (Odom et al., 1992).

The child who has emotional difficulties, resulting from either a traumatic event or ongoing internal conflicts, can also benefit from support through play interventions. The adult facilitates play by providing toys and materials that allow the child to dramatize or reenact issues of concern in an emotionally safe environment. Various models of *play therapy* described in the literature, including psychoanalytic, structure, and relationship approaches, are used in treatment of disturbed children. Children who have undergone trauma, for instance, may find it necessary to repeatedly reenact the event; to work-through, or problem-solve different endings or resolutions to the event; and to experience mastery over thoughts and feeling associated with the event. The adult helps the child to identify feelings, interprets actions, and assists the child in identifying ways to gain mastery over the situation.

Sociodramatic play is a natural arena for supporting children's social interactions and social problem-solving skills. By making comments and suggestions and structuring play situations that encourage associative and cooperative efforts, the adult can lead children to play together. Using peer pairing, peer tutoring, and other peer-support strategies within play also promotes social interaction (McEvoy et al., 1992).

Emily, 4 years old, had already been in numerous foster homes. She frequently bit and hit her peers, called them

names, and played mostly in isolation. She had little eye contact with the teacher and, in fact, avoided being near her. She
seemed to fear getting emotionally close to anyone. The
teacher wanted to build a positive, nurturing relationship with
Emily, help her find appropriate outlets for her anger, and
support her in making friendships. She spent time each day
playing with Emily. In the housekeeping area, she would play
the child and Emily the mother. The teacher would respond
to Emily's anger, expressed in play, by stating how sad it made
her feel when someone yelled at her. She also modeled nurturing care of the "baby." With the zoo animals, they played
doctor and put bandages on all the animals to make them feel
better. In time, Emily was able to accept inclusion of a peer in
these schemes, allowing the teacher to fade out of the play.
Emily was then encouraged to participate in the group rough-
and-tumble activities and expend energy in large motor play.
Every day, the teacher watched for opportunities to react to
Emily's feelings, find outlets for them, and help her take the
risk of caring for others and having others care for her.

CONCLUSION

Although the play behaviors of many young children with special
needs are quantitatively and qualitatively different from those of children without disabilities, those differences can be used to pinpoint areas
to be addressed in intervention. The processes used in play are powerful
promoters of development, and with thoughtful use of play-facilitation
strategies, both play behaviors and developmental skills may be enhanced.

REFERENCES

Almy, M., Monighan, P., Scales, B., & VanHoorn, J. (1984). Recent research
on play: The teacher's perspective. In L. G. Katz (Ed.), *Current topics in
early childhood education*, 5 (pp. 1–25). Norwood, NJ: Ablex.
Antia, S. D., & Kreimeyer, K. H. (1992). Social competence intervention for
young children with hearing impairments. In S. L. Odom, S. R. McConnell, & M. A. McEvoy (Eds.), *Social competence of young children with
disabilities* (pp. 113–134). Baltimore: Paul H. Brookes.
Athey, I. (1984). Contributions of play to development. In T. D. Yawkey and

A. D. Pellegrini (Eds.), *Child's play: Developmental and applied* (pp. 9–28). Hillsdale, NJ: Erlbaum.

Ayers, A. J., & Tickle, L. S. (1980). Hyper-responsivity to touch and vestibular stimuli as a predictor of positive response to sensory integration procedures in autistic children. *American Journal of Occupational Therapy, 34,* 375–381.

Bettelheim, B. (1987, March). The importance of play. *Atlantic Monthly,* pp. 35–46.

Brackett, D., & Henniges, M. (1976). Communicative interactions of preschool hearing impaired children in the integrated setting. *The Volta Review, 778,* 276–290.

Bricker, D. (1993). Then, now, and the path between: A brief history of language intervention. In A. P. Kaiser & D. B. Gray (Eds.), *Enhancing children's communication: Research foundations for intervention* (pp. 11–34). Baltimore: Paul H. Brookes.

Bricker, D., & Cripe, J. W. (1992). *An activity-based approach to early intervention.* Baltimore: Paul H. Brookes.

Bruner, J. S. (1977). Early social interaction and language acquisition. In H. R. Schaffer (Ed.), *Studies in mother-infant interaction.* London: Academic Press.

Bundy, A. C. (1991). Play theory and sensory integration. In A. G. Fisher, E. A. Murray, & A. C. Bundy (Eds.), *Sensory integration: Theory and practice.* Philadelphia: F. A. Davis.

Burns, S. M., & Brainerd, C. J. (1979). Effects of constructive and dramatic play on perspective taking in very young children. *Developmental Psychology, 15,* 512–521.

Campos, J. J., Svejda, M. J., Campos, R. G., & Berternthal, B. (1982). The emergence of self-produced locomotion: Its importance for psychological development in infancy. In D. D. Bricker (Ed.), *Intervention with at-risk and handicapped infants: From research to application.* Baltimore: University Park Press.

Carlson, L., & Bricker, D. (1982). Dyadic and contingent aspects of early communicative intervention. In D. Bricker (Ed.), *Intervention with at-risk and handicapped infants* (pp. 291–308). Baltimore: University Park Press.

Cazden, C. (1974). Play with language and metalinguistic awareness: One dimension of language experience. *The Urban Review, 1,* 23–29.

Christie, J. F. (1983). The effects of play tutoring on young children's cognitive performance. *Journal of Educational Research, 76,* 326–330.

Connolly, J. A., & Doyle, A. (1984). Relation of social fantasy play to social competence in preschoolers. *Developmental Psychology, 20,* 797–806.

Cooke, T. P., & Apolloni, T. (1976). The development of positive social-emotional behaviors: A study of training and generalization effects. *The Journal of Applied Behavior Analysis, 9,* 65–78.

Curry, N. E., & Arnaud, S. H. (1984). Play in developmental preschool settings. In T. D. Yawkey & A. D. Pellegrini (Eds.), *Child's play: Developmental and applied* (pp. 273–290). Hillsdale, NJ: Erlbaum.

Dansky, J. L., & Silverman, I. W. (1975). Play: A general facilitator of associative fluency. *Developmental Psychology, 11*, 104.

Erikson, E. (1977). *Toys and reasons.* New York: Norton.

Fewell, R. R. (1983). Working with sensorily impaired children. In S. G. Garwood (Ed.), *Educating young handicapped children* (2nd ed., pp. 235–280). Rockville, MD: Aspen.

Fewell, R. R., & Kaminski, R. (1988). Play skills development and instruction for children with handicaps. In S. L. Odom & M. B. Karnes (Eds.), *Early intervention for infants and children with handicaps.* Baltimore: Paul H. Brookes.

Fey, M. E., & Leonard, L. G. (1983). Pragmatic skills of children with specific language impairment. In T. M. Gallagher & C. A. Prutting (Eds.), *Pragmatic assessment and intervention issues in language.* San Diego, CA: College Hill Press.

Fraiberg, S., & Adelson, E. (1977). Self-representation in language and play. In S. Fraiberg (Ed.), *Insights from the blind: Comparative studies of blind and sighted infants* (pp. 248–270). New York: Basic Books.

Fromberg, D. P. (1992). Play. In C. Seefeldt (Ed.), *The early childhood curriculum: A review of current research* (pp. 35–74). New York: Teachers College Press.

Garvey, C. (1977). *Play.* Cambridge, MA: Harvard University Press.

Goldstein, G., & Gallagher, T. M. (1992). Strategies for promoting the social-communicative competence of young children with specific language impairment. In S. L. Odom, S. R. McConnell, & M. A. McEvoy (Eds.), *Social competence of young children with disabilities* (pp. 189–214). Baltimore: Paul H. Brookes.

Gregory, F. (1976). *The deaf child and his family.* London: Allen and Unwin.

Guralnick, M. J. (1992). A hierarchical model for understanding children's peer-related social competence. In S. L. Odom, S. R. McConnell, & M. A. McEvoy (Eds.), *Social competence of young children with disabilities* (pp. 37–64). Baltimore: Paul H. Brookes.

Guralnick, M. J., & Groom, J. M. (1987). Dyadic peer interactions of mildly delayed and nonhandicapped preschool children. *American Journal of Mental Deficiency, 92*, 178–193.

Hammes, J., & Langdell, T. (1981). Precursors of symbolic formation and childhood autism. *Journal of Autism and Developmental Disorders, 11*(3), 331–346.

Heath, S. B., & Mangiola, L. (1991). *Children of promise: Literate activity in linguistically and culturally diverse classrooms.* Washington, DC: National Education Association.

Hill, P., & McCune-Nicholich, L. (1981). Pretend play and patterns of cognition in Down syndrome children. *Child Development, 52*, 611–617.

Hulme, I., & Lunzer, E. (1966). Play, language, and reasoning in subnormal children. *Journal of Child Psychology and Psychiatry, 7*, 107–123.

Hutt, C. (1971). Exploration and play in children. In R. E. Herron & B. Sutton-Smith (Eds.), *Child's play* (pp. 231–251). New York: Wiley.

Jennings, K. D., Connors, R. E., Stegman, C. E., Sankaranarayan, P., & Medolsohn, S. (1985). Mastery motivation in young preschoolers. *Journal of the Division of Early Childhood, 9*(2), 162–169.

Johnson, J. E., Ershler, J., & Lawton, J. T. (1982). Intellective correlates of preschoolers' spontaneous play. *Journal of General Psychology, 106,* 115–122.

Kaiser, A., Hendrickson, J., & Alpert, K. (1991). Milieu language teaching: A second look. In R. Gable (Ed.), *Advances in mental retardation and developmental disabilities* (Vol. 4, pp. 63–92). London: Jessica Kingsley Publisher.

Krakow, J., & Kopp, C. (1983). The effect of developmental delay on sustained attention in young children. *Child Development, 54,* 1143–1155.

Lederberg, A., Ryan, H. B., & Robbins, B. (1986). Peer interactions in young deaf children: The effect of partner hearing status and familiarity. *Developmental Psychology, 22,* 691–700.

Li, A. K. F. (1981). Play and the mentally retarded. *Mental Retardation, 19,* 121–126.

Lieber, J., & Beckman, P. J. (1991). The role of toys in individual and dyadic play among young children with handicaps. *Journal of Applied Developmental Psychology, 12,* 189–203.

Linder, T. (1990). *Transdisciplinary play-based assessment.* Baltimore: Paul H. Brookes.

Linder, T. (1993). *Transdisciplinary play-based intervention.* Baltimore: Paul H. Brookes.

Lovell, K., Hoyle, H. W., & Siddall, M. C. (1968). A study of some aspects of the play and language of young children in delayed speech. *Journal of Child Psychology and Psychiatry, 9,* 41–50.

Mahoney, G., Glover, A., & Finger, I. (1981). Relationship between language and sensorimotor development of Down syndrome and nonretarded children. *American Journal of Mental Deficiency, 86*(1), 21–27.

Mahoney, G., & Powell, A. (1986). *The Transactional Intervention Program: Teachers' Guide.* Farmington, CT: Pediatric Research and Training Center.

Mindes, G. (1982). Social and cognitive aspects of play in young handicapped children. *Topics in Early Childhood Special Education: Play and Development, 2*(3), 39–52.

Morgan, G. A., & Harmon, R. J. (1984). Developmental transformations in mastery motivation. In R. N. Ende & R. J. Harmon (Eds.), *Continuities and discontinuities in development.* New York: Plenum.

Motti, F., Cichetti, D., & Sroufe, L. A. (1983). From infant affect expression to symbolic play: The coherence of development in Down syndrome children. *Child Development, 54,* 1168–1175.

Neumann, E. A. (1971). *The elements of play.* New York: MSS Information.

Odom, S. L., McConnell, S. R., & McEvoy, M. A. (1992). Peer-related social competence and its significance for young children with disabilities. In S. L. Odom, S. R. McConnell, & M. A. McEvoy (Eds.), *Social competence of young children with disabilities: Issues and strategies for intervention* (pp. 3–35). Baltimore: Paul H. Brookes.

Pellegrini, A. (1980). The relationship between preschoolers' play and achievement in prereading, language, and writing. *Psychology in the Schools, 17,* 530–535.

Pellegrini, A., & Greene, H. (1980). The use of a sequenced questioning paradigm to facilitate associative fluency in preschoolers. *Journal of Applied Developmental Psychology, 1,* 189–200.

Pepler, D. J., & Ross, H. S. (1981). The effects of play on convergent and divergent problem-solving. *Child Development, 52,* 1202–1210.

Peterson, N. L. (1987). *Early intervention for handicapped and at-risk children: An introduction to early childhood special education.* Denver: Love.

Piaget, J. (1962). *Play, dreams, and imitation.* New York: Norton.

Quinn, J. M., & Rubin, K. H. (1984). The play of handicapped children. In T. D. Yawkey & A. D. Pellegrini (Eds.), *In child's play: Developmental and applied.* Hillsdale, NJ: Erlbaum.

Richard, N. B. (1986). Interactions between mothers and infants with Down syndrome: Infant characteristics. *Topics in Early Childhood Special Education, 6*(3), 57–71.

Ricks, D., & Wing, L. (1975). Language, communication and the use of symbols in normal and autistic children. *Journal of Autism and Childhood Schizophrenia, 5*(3), 191–221.

Riquet, C. B., & Taylor, N. D. (1981). Symbolic play in autistic, Down's syndrome, and normal children of equivalent mental age. *Journal of Autism and Developmental Disorders, 11,* 439–448.

Rogers, S. (1977). Characteristics of the cognitive development of profoundly retarded children. *Child Development, 48,* 837–843.

Rogers, S. J., & Puchalski, C. B. (1984). Development of symbolic play in visually impaired infants. *Topics in Early Childhood Special Education, 3*(4), 57–64.

Rubin, K. H., Fein, G. G., & Vandenberg, B. (1983). Play. In E. M. Hetherington (Ed.), *Handbook of child psychology: Socialization, personality, and social development* (pp. 693–774). New York: Wiley.

Rubin, K., & Maioni, T. (1975). Play preference and its relation to egocentrism, popularity, and classification skills in preschoolers. *Merrill-Palmer Quarterly, 21,* 171–179.

Saltz, E., Dixon, D., & Johnson, J. (1977). Training disadvantaged preschoolers on various fantasy activities: Effects on cognitive functioning and impulse control. *Child Development, 48,* 367–379.

Sandler & Wills. (1965). Preliminary rates on play and mastery in the blind child. *Journal of Child Psychotherapy, 1,* 7–19.

Sigman, M., & Ungerer, J. (1984). Cognitive and language skills in autistic, mentally retarded and normal children. *Developmental Psychology, 20*(2), 293–302.

Singer, J. L. (Ed.). (1973). *The child's world of make-believe: Experimental studies of imaginative play*. New York: Academic Press.

Smilansky, S. (1968). *The effects of sociodramatic play on disadvantaged preschool children*. New York: Wiley.

Smith, P. K., & Syddall, S. (1978). Play and non-play tutoring in preschool children: Is it play or tutoring which matters? *British Journal of Educational Psychology, 48*, 315–325.

Spodek, B., & Saracho, O. N. (1988). The challenge of educational play. In D. Bergen (Ed.), *Play as a medium for learning and development: A handbook of theory and practice* (pp. 9–22). Portsmouth, NH: Heinemann.

Sutton-Smith, B. (1980). Piaget, play and cognition revisited. In W. Overton (Ed.), *The relationship between social and cognitive development*. New York: Erlbaum.

Vygotsky, L. (1967). Play and its role in the mental development of the child. *Soviet Psychology, 12*, 62–76.

Westby, C. E. (1980). Assessment of cognitive and language abilities through play. *Language, Speech and Hearing Services in Schools, 11*, 154–168.

Yawkey, T. D., Jones, K. C., & Hrncir, E. J. (1979). The effects of imaginative play and sex differences on mathematics, playfulness, imaginativeness, creativity and reading capacity in five-year-old children. Paper presented at annual meeting on the North Eastern Educational Research Association, Boston.

Yoder, P. J., & Warren, S. F. (1993). Can developmentally delayed children's language be enhanced through prelinguistic intervention? In A. P. Kaiser & D. B. Gray (Eds.), *Enhancing children's communication: Research foundations for intervention* (pp. 35–62). Baltimore: Paul H. Brookes.

CHAPTER 5

Instructional Models in Early Childhood Special Education: Origins, Issues, and Trends

Philip L. Safford,
Maria Sargent, and Christine Cook

Little more than a decade ago, in an article provocatively subtitled "A Study in Conflict," Kaufman (1980) contrasted the traditions of early childhood education and special education. He concluded that, directed toward different purposes, informed by different models of human development, and employing different methods, the fields were inherently incompatible. Recently, however, there have been substantive moves to bring them together, even unified under the banners of inclusion and developmentally appropriate practice (DAP) (Burton, Hains, Hanline, McLean, & McCormick, 1992; Miller, 1992). Such discussions have aroused concerns on both sides, and debate within the field of early childhood special education (ECSE), but they have also stimulated curricular inquiry in a field dominated until recently more by clinical than by pedagogical influence (Widerstrom, 1986).

It is in fact its focus on impairment — defect, deviance, pathology — that, more than anything else, has given special education its identity, one arguably more closely linked to medicine, clinical psychology, and specialized therapies than to general pedagogy. Historically, disability inspired intervention, and thus experimentation with instructional "strategies," by clerics like Epee, Sicard, and Gallaudet and physicians like Itard, Seguin, Howe, and Montessori. Such a *deficit orientation* is reflected in Individual Education Programs (IEPs) mandated under federal law that address what children *cannot* do, as Mahoney and Wheatley note in Chapter 6.

While the common schools enrolled many children younger than 5 (Spodek, 1991), special education, mainly provided in residential schools, served older students, including adults. It was not an early childhood enterprise. That it became one was influenced by the later rapid growth of the kindergarten, although like such nursery education pioneers as Macmillan and Montessori, the first early childhood special educators had a *compensatory* purpose (Peterson, 1987). Since the instructional models they adopted were essentially extensions with young children of those used with older exceptional pupils, our discussion of the origins of ECSE curriculum and instruction describes certain features of those models.

CURRICULUM AND INSTRUCTION
IN SPECIAL EDUCATION

Although their paths diverged, ECSE's parent fields had common roots in the ideas of Locke, Rousseau, and Pestalozzi. Itard, Pereire, and Seguin were greatly influenced by such sense-realist philosophers as Condillac, as was Rousseau (Talbot, 1964). Moritz Hill, a major figure in the history of deaf education, adapted Pestalozzi's experiential learning approach and object lessons then being introduced in German schools. Edouard Seguin believed teachers should foster children's curiosity, exploration, and direct experience, as he himself did in teaching children with mental retardation. Montessori, who built upon Seguin's methods of sensory learning and direct experience, stands as a pioneer of both fields. In the United States, as in Britain, social settlements were important in furthering both early childhood education and provisions in schools for children with special needs. Through the persuasion of Lillian Wald, whose Henry Street Settlement provided both a nursery and a class for delayed children, the New York public schools began to employ her "district nurses" and, in 1889, established an "ungraded class," taught by Wald's 19-year-old friend, Elizabeth Farrell, later the first president of the Council for Exceptional Children.

Another "movement" at the turn of the century, G. S. Hall's Child Study, did not address childhood disability, although Arnold Gesell, Hall's student and intellectual heir and an extraordinarily important influence in early childhood education, was the first person formally identified as a "school psychologist," responsible for coordinating Connecticut's services for pupils with mental retardation (Fagan & Delugach, 1985). Though a strong advocate of special classes, Gesell

(1924) believed their more individualized approach and use of practical life activities would have "a beneficent, liberalizing effect upon the education of normal children," as well as those who were "intellectually inferior" (p. 272). Gesell (1923) also urged schools to address young children's physical and mental health, noting the key role of preschools and kindergartens in early identification of delays and prevention of subsequent school problems. But the first programs for young children with identified disabilities were "vertical" extensions of special education, rather than "horizontal" extensions of early childhood education.

Forerunners of ECSE

Until the 1880s, instruction of children with impaired hearing or vision usually began at about age 10, with enrollment in a residential school. In 1887, Michael Anagnos opened a kindergarten for blind children at the Perkins Institute, soon followed by day kindergartens in Europe. The next year, the Sarah Fuller Home for Little Children Who Cannot Hear opened, and in 1893 the "Union of Kindergartners for the Deaf" was formed with the goal of introducing such programs in all residential schools. Until A. G. Bell took up Howe's and Horace Mann's campaign for speech instruction, sign language had dominated American deaf education, and controversy continues, among hearing parents and educators, at any rate; American Sign Language (ASL) is now recognized as a wholly legitimate, rule-based alternative to English or other languages, a fact central to the cultural conception of deafness (Padden & Humphries, 1988). But oralism's hegemony heightened awareness of early language development, and by the 1920s, its advocates had achieved both a shift to day classes and establishment of preschool programs. Concerning *content*, Bell stressed the importance for young children of linguistic context for meaningful communication, a sound principle irrespective of method.

Similar trends occurred in the area of blindness, but later and much less extensively; by the 1930s there was a handful of nursery classes, established to begin mobility training and provide early socialization and communication experiences. In the 1940s and 1950s, the Society for Crippled Children and the United Cerebral Palsy Association established nursery classes for children with physical disabilities, also mainly to begin therapies earlier and to provide socialization opportunities for the children and support for parents. While some emphasized the need for early education of children with mental retardation, those of school age represented far more urgent concern.

Special Education Instructional Models

Special educators use diverse methods, but in principle, if not always in practice, a unifying principle is *individualized intervention* based on assessment. Such goals as *independence*, functional *communication*, and *social competence* have traditionally been emphasized, usually defined on the basis of instrumental skills. Concerns have been and continue to be expressed about the potentially limiting nature of specialized skill training (e.g., training blind pupils for a limited range of trades), especially in segregated settings. The concern of restricted alternatives, reflected today in arguments for the regular education initiative (REI) and full inclusion, is basic to any consideration of the context and content of instruction in ECSE.

The first American public school classes for children with hearing, vision, health, and intellectual impairments were formed around 1900, and by 1910, "speech teachers" recruited to assimilate immigrant children in "Steamer" classes were being assigned to work with articulation delays of "young stammerers" (Moore & Kester, 1953). By the 1920s, *ungraded classes*, like those Farrell pioneered in New York, were increasingly used for children who "did not fit" (Ysseldyke & Algozzine, 1982). While new ability tests provided a means to determine eligibility, teachers' referrals were based more on social behavior than on learning difficulties (Sarason & Doris, 1969). And while Farrell and W. E. W. Wallin stressed the need for individually tailored teaching, over time a separate curriculum emerged for students labeled "slow learners" or "educable mentally retarded," employing group lessons in skills thought practical to prepare pupils for a presumably quite limited range of opportunities in adult life. In the 1930s, states and local districts established policies to *exclude* from school many children thought mentally, physically, and socially deviant and, contrary to common belief, special education by no means served most of the exceptional students who were in school. Despite the proliferation of special classes from the late 1940s to the early 1970s, before P.L. 94-142, many pupils not excluded altogether were left, for better or worse, in the "mainstream," their special learning needs unaddressed. Those provided special education were often sorted into separate classes based on arbitrary and often discriminatory assessment practices (Mercer, 1973), with *placement* often a higher priority than instruction.

Excepting a few classes for "unrulies" formed in the 1870s, the first programs for children with emotional problems were, like those for children with physical impairments, ancillary to treatment. At first, instruction was mainly a context for the teacher-pupil relationship, and "curriculum" was whatever tasks were associated with a child's grade or achievement level. Newer theoretical perspectives implied a more important role for education in the "therapeutic milieu" in helping the child gain impulse control, a sense of mastery, and self-esteem. But while the curriculum was "therapeutic," it was distinguished only by a sort of affective curricular subtext. What differentiated instruction was its individualized approach, often simply "sequential tutoring," later complemented by more systematic psychoeducational (e.g., Life Space Interviewing) and behavioral (e.g., reinforcement schedule, token economy) techniques. The work of Anna Freud and Dorothy Burlingham in the Jackson Nursery in Vienna and the Hampstead War Nursery and Clinic in England inspired a few American specialized nursery programs (e.g., Furman & Katan, 1969), but there were few early intervention models (Wood, 1975) for young children identified as emotionally disturbed. Outside psychiatric settings and excepting studies such as Selma Fraiberg's (1977) with blind infants, psychoanalytic influence was more evident in early childhood (e.g., Bank Street [Shapiro & Biber, 1972]) than in special education.

The conception of specific learning disability as an inherently *educational* problem was a distinct departure. Initially, a variety of perceptual-motor and psycholinguistic goals were pursued, within highly structured classroom environments, but today it is usually not the curriculum that is differentiated but the means by which it is taught. Diagnostic-prescriptive teaching is more typically used to identify and improve deficient skills than to remediate underlying *process* deficits. Although this "category" accounts for about half the students who receive special education, it is difficult to apply to young children, who may present delays *predictive* of learning disabilities (Leigh & Riley, 1982).

While special communication and literacy needs of deaf and blind students imply certain specialized goals and methods, it is only in the area of mental retardation that we find a tradition of specialized curriculum per se. Earlier, the emphasis on work training and acquiring good work habits was based on the expectation of lifelong institutionalization. Preparation for work continued as a major focus in special classes, but it came to be interpreted more broadly in terms of *employability* skills, for maximally independent functioning in the community. Special education for all students considered exceptional has a *life-span* context. While individual transition plans are very important in ECSE, as Fowler and Ostroski emphasize in Chapter 7, they are also mandated for older students, for whom successful transition from school to work and community living is both essential and problematic. Generally, the future orientation of special education, its adult-directed and assessment-based approach to instruction, and its emphasis on functional skill training imply fundamental differences from what is considered "best practice" in early childhood education.

DEVELOPMENTALLY APPROPRIATE
PRACTICE AND ECSE

Publication of *Developmentally Appropriate Practice in Early Childhood Programs Serving Children from Birth Through Age 8* (Bredekamp, 1987), with its presumptively *constructivist* agenda, was a critical event in initiating dialogue concerning ECSE (Wolery, Strain, & Bailey, 1993), a field that, as Mallory (1992) observed, "has had to construct its own identity over the past 25 years" (p. 1). DAP is defined on the basis of two principles: age appropriateness and individual appropriateness, the former predicated on concerns about early academic skill instruction, artificial compartmentalization of curriculum, and the press for teachers to employ methods that denied young children's learning modes, especially excessive adult direction (Weikart, Rogers, Adcock, & McClelland, 1970). Age-inappropriate practices are those used rightly or wrongly with older learners. These were not new issues; they had been addressed by Comenius, Rousseau, and Pestalozzi; by Froebel and the "kindergartners"; and in the British Infant School movements of the 1830s and 1970s, both briefly tried and abandoned in the United States. But in the context of school reform, which seemed to be "pushing downward" on primary, kindergarten, and prekindergarten education, they had taken on new urgency. Whatever its other merits, or its limitations, DAP is clearly a manifesto of the uniqueness of the early years of life.

The issue of age appropriateness had also been increasingly addressed in special education, but in the opposite sense. Children and also adults, particularly those with severe or multiple disabilities, had typically been presented with learning tasks selected on the basis of such indices of normative developmental equivalence as mental age. This "bottom-up" approach, based on maturationist assumptions, came to be considered *inappropriate* since, given tasks typical for younger learners in the belief that their mastery must precede learning more complex skills, students were often relegated to permanent practice. Applications of an alternative "top-down" approach, based on a criterion of ultimate function, have served to invalidate many assumptions about

typical developmental sequence, especially for students with severe disabilities. Such demonstrations have had implications for the setting in
which instruction is provided, as well as for its content. In recent years,
emphasis has been placed on selecting *functional* skills the learner will
need to be maximally independent within current and anticipated future environments, based on a *community-referenced* curriculum, and
taught with *age-appropriate* instructional materials and methods (Snell
& Brown, 1993).

While the need for this shift was most evident with older students,
it has also affected ECSE. Age appropriateness, in special education
and in ECSE, implies an explicit rejection of maturationist assumptions
about learning. Special educators' reservations concerning DAP involve
a tendency to equate what Hymes (1955) famously termed "the child
development point of view" with *maturationism* and constructivism
with *laissez-faire* (Billingsley, 1993), anathema to special educators. In
the ECSE literature, the "developmental model" is often described as
assuming "that children acquire skills when they are physically and
mentally ready, and, for that reason, teaching is a passive process in
which the instructional environment is provided so that children can
acquire skills" (Fewell & Neisworth, 1991, p. xvi). Such a model, as
reflected in DAP, has been interpreted as defining instruction essentially as providing "well-planned, safe, and nurturing environments"
(Carta, Schwartz, Atwater, & McConnell, 1991, p. 8). If a "developmentally based curriculum" precludes planned, systematic intervention, it is believed ineffective even for young children with disabilities.
Thus, despite their shared concern for age appropriateness, there would
seem to be a mismatch between the skill-focused, future-oriented, and
often teacher-directed approach of ECSE and DAP's constructivist,
present-oriented, child-initiated philosophy.

There have been critical forces for rapprochement, however, especially in accumulating evidence of the benefits of integration of young
children with and without disabilities, as Guralnick reviews in Chapter
3. Even more fundamentally, the philosophy of *normalization* argues
against practices, for persons with disabilities of any age, that set them
apart or deprive them of experiences and opportunities afforded others.
That such deprivation occurred in early intervention programs for
young children was evidenced by reports of "deficiencies of environments . . . difficult to justify on the argument that handicapped children require something different in the absence of supporting data"
(Bailey, Clifford, & Harms, 1982, p. 98). Yet, there is considerable
evidence that many young children, if they are to benefit optimally

from interaction with the physico-social environment, no matter how nurturing, require something more than just "being there."

Individual Appropriateness and Systematic Instruction

Much of the ensuing debate has focused on the dimension of *individual appropriateness* and, consequently, on DAP's universality. Its critics include post-Piagetians and social reconstructionists (Swadener & Kessler, 1991) who argue that, in its reliance on a canon drawn from developmental psychology, DAP fails to consider the voices of multiple stakeholders (Jipson, 1991), societal values as sources of curriculum (Spodek, 1991), and poststructuralist philosophical (Kessler, 1991) and social science (Walsh, 1991) perspectives. With its few references to "special needs," DAP does not explicitly consider young children with disabilities (Mallory, 1992), although some (e.g., Kostelnick, 1992) maintain that, as long as children's individual interests are fostered within a natural context, addressing their individual needs does not violate DAP's basic principles. If DAP is in fact itself "developmental, . . . a dynamic document that will grow and change in response to changing needs and new knowledge" (Bredekamp, 1991, p. 203), such criticisms may be moot.

In its present form, DAP has been characterized as perhaps "necessary but not sufficient" as a guide for teaching young children with disabilities (Wolery et al., 1993). Carta, Schwartz, Atwater, and McConnell (1991) have noted its omission of specific techniques of systematic instruction that have been found effective with young children with disabilities. But a more fundamental issue is whether DAP is compatible with what they identify as the "basic premises" of ECSE: need for range and varying intensity of services; individualized teaching plans based on multisource assessment data that target "skills required for future school and nonschool environments," taught with methods that are "effective, efficient, functional, and normalized" that result in "high levels of active involvement and participation in activities" (Carta et al., 1991, pp. 5–6). Another key feature, reflected as policy under Part H of P.L. 99-457, is a "focus on strengthening the abilities of families to nurture their children's development and to promote normalized community adaptation" (p. 7). Overall, a core concern for ECSE, as for special education generally, is the need for "specific criteria, procedures, and timelines used to determine if individual children progress toward stated outcomes" (Carta et al., 1991, p. 7). Because of the fundamental importance, legally and ethically, of *accountability*, assessment and evaluation are especially critical components of ECSE (Wolery et al., 1993) that are less explicitly defined in DAP.

Four key elements are identified in Bricker's (1993) summary of the purpose of early education for children with disabilities as "the delivery to eligible children and their families of a broad range of quality services in integrated community-based settings by well trained professionals from an array of disciplines and fields . . . [that] enable children and families to reach established outcomes or goals" (pp. 91–92). In their synthesis of "best practices" in ECSE, McDonnell and Hardman (1988) state that programs should be integrated, adaptable, comprehensive, normalized, peer and family-referenced, and outcome-based, also implying a balance of accountability with normalization. While "the explicit mission of ECSE is to produce outcomes that would not occur in the absence of intervention or teaching" (p. 4), Carta et al. (1991) emphasize that this implies a "need not for specialized settings but for specialized instruction" (p. 12). Thus, integrating individualized interventions in "nonspecialized," integrated settings is the major challenge in ECSE (p. 12).

Wolery and Fleming (1993) described systematic strategies teachers can use within an integrated, developmentally appropriate program for young children for identifying specific skills, scheduling instruction, programming for generalization, and reinforcing children's engagement. However, both their reference to systematic reinforcement and the menu of alternative prompting techniques they recommend involve a degree of adult direction of questionable compatibility with DAP or its subsequent elaborations. Yet, there is well-documented evidence that systematic planning, intervention, and monitoring are effective in enabling young children with disabilities to acquire targeted skills (Carta et al., 1991) and of teachers' ability to reliably implement such specific strategies as Progressive Time Delay and Transition-Based Teaching (Wolery, Doyle, Gast, Ault, & Simpson, 1993) to enhance the efficiency of skill acquisition. We concur with Carta et al. (1991) that instructional procedures in ECSE "should be effective, efficient, functional, and normalized" (p. 5), and also with their observation that the first three, but less notably the last, have been defining attributes of ECSE, as of special education in general.

Influence of Behavioral Perspectives in ECSE

While early childhood education has been dominated by—some (e.g., Kessler, 1991) might say in thrall to—child-development theory, a major force in special education, as Mahoney and Wheatley (Chapter

6 in this volume) note, has been learning theory. Prior to the 1960s, early childhood education reflected the Child Study legacy, enriched by psychoanalytic notions, but defined mainly by an "ages and stages" maturationism based on Gesell's normative descriptions of development and reflected in the "child-centered" schools of the 1930s and 1940s. Special education, on the other hand, had, since Itard, been concerned with factors leading to *change* in the learner. Informed by empirical studies of learning and motivation, these concerns were systematized and, with Skinner's influence, the conditions of behavior maintenance and change were understood to involve relationships between events in the environment (antecedents and consequences) and observed behavior. While early childhood education grew in the tradition of child psychology and child study begun by Hall, advanced by Gesell, and influenced by psychoanalysis, special education grew in that of educational psychology begun by Thorndike and advanced by Skinner and behavior analysis.

By 1960, operant techniques had been demonstrated to be effective in enabling persons in institutions to reduce maladaptive behaviors and acquire functional skills. In the 1960s, the experimental analysis of behavior began to be used in single case interventions with children with significantly deviant behavior or delay (e.g., Homme, DeBaca, DeVine, Steinhorst, & Rickert, 1963) and adapted in structured classrooms for children manifesting maladaptive behavior. The pioneer demonstration projects with young children with disabilities in the 1960s and early 1970s were profoundly influenced by behavioral perspectives. Indeed, many of the early interventionists whose work established the field's initial knowledge base were themselves trained as behavioral psychologists and had used applied behavior analysis with institutionalized populations. It is not surprising that ECSE is characterized by language conventions—for example, "programming," "targets," "fading," "shaping," and so forth—that have tended to distinguish it, if not alienate it, from early childhood education. The language of early childhood education, by contrast, has become increasingly the language of *constructivism*: Learning is intrinsically motivated and self-initiated; the teacher guides and facilitates as children "construct" reality through spontaneous interaction with their environment.

Behavioral approaches are attractive to professionals working with persons with disabilities because they are grounded in empirical science and responsive to individual differences, and suggest specific objectives that can be efficiently accomplished and are amenable to measurement. A behavioral orientation is, moreover, inherently optimistic, rather than fatalistic, seeking always to find "what works." While often misunderstood or thought by some "nonhumanistic," behaviorism has been of fundamental importance in establishing a scientific basis for early intervention, in demonstrating its efficacy and in improving the quality of services for young children with disabilities (Strain, McConnell, Carta, Fowler, Neisworth, & Wolery, 1992). Applied behavioral analysis (ABA) provides an *instructional technology* for ascertaining an individual student's present skills, potential reinforcers, and reinforcement schedules (behavioral observation and reinforcer sampling); for analyzing the requirements of a given task (ecological and task analytic assessment); and for systematically monitoring the child's progress toward eventual achievement of task mastery (data recording and charting). But while it may imply that certain skills may be more functional than others, ABA does not, in itself, provide a "curriculum" for ECSE.

CURRICULUM MODELS AND CONCEPTS IN ECSE

In ECSE, the term *curriculum* is often used to refer to all facets of a program, including the "how" as well as the "why," "where," and "what" of instruction (Wolery et al., 1993). Individual programs for young children with disabilities may, like any other educational enterprise, be loosely constructed, lack an explicit philosophy or coherent organizational plan, or be eclectic to the point of promiscuity. But these are not considered to reflect "best practice." On the contrary, consistency of assessment practices, instructional procedures, group composition, arrangement of the environment, provision for special therapies, and, very importantly, provision for family involvement with a clearly articulated philosophy is considered essential in quality programs (Bailey & Wolery, 1992). While a program's philosophy and consequently the nature of each of its components may, and arguably should, be to some degree program-specific, within limits prescribed by federal and state policy, many programs adhere to, or are influenced by, one or another program *model*, a term often considered virtually synonymous with "curriculum" in ECSE.

This quality of consistency and coherence, while not unique to ECSE, is a distinctive characteristic of programs for young children with disabilities, mainly due to the leadership of the Handicapped Children's Early Education Program (HCEEP), renamed under the Individuals with Disabilities Education Act (IDEA) amendments Early Education Programs for Children with Disabilities (EEPCD). This federal agency was established through legislation enacted in 1968 to encourage development, validation, and dissemination of models for delivering quality services to young children with disabilities and their families. While the focus of model projects shifted to family services, infant intervention, and certain highly specific needs, many of the initial projects (e.g., the Portage Guide to Early Education, the Hawaii Early Learning Profile, etc.) were essentially assessment-based ECSE curricula (Suarez, Hurth, & Prestridge, 1988). Various curriculum models developed since have reflected the influence of Piaget and Vygotsky, as has "general" early childhood education. But they have been informed also by other theoretical constructs, such as *cognitive modifiability* (Feuerstein, Rand, Hoffman, & Miller, 1980), new understandings of the importance of communicative *context* in children's language acquisition, and *transactional* (Sameroff & Fiese, 1990) and *ecological* (Bronfenbrenner, 1979) views of development.

Early Cognitive-Learning Approaches

The American "discovery" of Piaget brought about major shifts in both fields, though far more visibly in early childhood educational theory and practice. By the early 1970s, as cognitive psychology gained ascendance, a few early interventionists (e.g., Bricker & Bricker, 1974) were attempting to synthesize Piagetian and behavioral perspectives. Piaget's description of the sensorimotor *schemata* of infancy, in particular, suggested a lattice structure for planning and monitoring interventions to foster such key "building blocks" of early development as imitation, means-end awareness, and purposive manipulation of objects, although an inherent danger pointed out (Bricker, Macke, Levin, & Campbell, 1982) in adapting Piaget's *structural* model is that of simply substituting one set of "milestones" for another. More importantly, this *cognitive-learning* approach (Anastasiow, 1981; Mallory, 1992) reflected a *process* orientation that stressed the importance of young children's active engagement with an environment responsive to their actions as a foundation for behavioral repertoires capable of adapting to new situations (Bricker & Cripe, 1992).

This work paralleled, yet was distinctly different from, the *cognitive-developmental* orientation endorsed in "regular" early childhood education (Kamii & DeVries, 1993) and reflected in a "Piaget-inspired" model (Spodek, 1991, p. 12) used extensively with young children at environmental risk. The latter, known as *High/Scope*, virtually alone among the compensatory "planned variations" to have survived more or less intact (Spodek, 1991), is purportedly able to provide for a wide range of individual differences among young children, including those of children with disabilities. *High/Scope* is intended to maintain a balance of child-initiated and adult-initiated activity but explicitly rejects adult-directed diagnostic-prescriptive and corrective teaching as inappropriate for young children (Hohmann, Banet, & Weikart, 1979). Proponents of *direct instruction*, on the other hand, maintain that such structuring of learning by the adult is not only more efficient, but also a more effective way to enhance children's learning, especially that of disadvantaged or delayed children (Gersten, Woodward, & Darch, 1986). Whatever the setting in which young children with disabilities are educated, many professionals in ECSE agree with the position (Wolery & Fleming, 1993) that their learning needs must be addressed through carefully planned, assessment-based, individually tailored, systematically monitored direct instruction, employing an array of "instructional manipulations."

Most young children may thrive under minimal externally imposed structure and adult direction, actively exploring, independently learning, and internalizing experiences in organized structures. However, fundamental concerns in teaching many young children with developmental delays involve difficulties these children often have in *spontaneous engagement with the environment, incidental learning,* and *generalization* (Beckman, Robinson, Jackson, & Rosenberg, 1988; Carta et al., 1991). Intervention, according to Bricker and Cripe (1992), is therefore intended "to improve children's acquisition and use of important motor, social, affective, communication, and intellectual (e.g., problem solving) behaviors that, in turn, are integrated into response repertoires that are generative, functional, and adaptable" (pp. 10–11). Current models and approaches in ECSE share that goal, though it is addressed in different ways and expressed in different terminology. Those programs emphasizing cognitive development (e.g., Haywood, Brooks, & Burns, 1990) generally attempt to address *processes* necessary for intentional behavior, goal-directed action, making choices and decisions, problem solving, and generalization, rather than attainment of successive levels. While they differ in various ways, most such models continue to reflect Piagetian notions, but in combination with ideas drawn from such sources as Vygotsky, Feuerstein, information theory, and the pragmatic dimension of language, which emphasizes its social context and functional use. Some also challenge a convention that has become "traditional" in ECSE: compartmentalization on the basis of developmental domains.

Redefining and Transcending Domains in ECSE

The concept of *linked systems* of assessment and intervention has constituted a major advance in ECSE (Bricker & Cripe, 1992), but the typical organization of developmental assessment on the basis of domains constitutes a major difference between developmental and functional perspectives (Mallory, 1992) and can lead to artificial compartmentalization of curriculum. Goodman and Pollack (1993) found that a "core cognitive curriculum" in ECSE programs they surveyed was defined by common cognitive domain items in widely used developmental inventories. This segmentation of development has been a convenient way to organize information about children, but it implies and may sometimes impose artificial boundaries, as in distinguishing early cognitive, language, and social development. Most professionals, and parents, would agree with Berkeley and Ludlow's (1992) assertion that "when applied to developmental complexity (especially that which takes place in infancy), the very notion of domains as now understood becomes irrelevant and/or simplistic" (p. 14). They suggest that "commercially published curriculum packages for young children with disabilities, . . . based on developmental domains, reflect an American penchant for convenience, rather than a professional respect for theory" (p. 14). Arguing instead for an "integrated view of development" (p. 17) focusing on children's acquisition and application of generalization strategies across contexts, they endorse Lewis and Starr's (1979) *salient response model*, which identifies attributes or processes that develop continuously and are expressed in all spheres of development.

A similarly integrated conception that focuses on *how* young children learn is reflected in the HCEEP curriculum model known as the Early Recognition Intervention Network (ERIN) (Hainsworth & Hainsworth, 1979). In this model, based on information-processing theory, children's learning is seen as proceeding in parallel fashion across all domains. Assessment and intervention are linked, but structured on the basis of successive receptive and expressive processes.

Various "approaches" addressing learning skills across domains have been developed for more or less general application with young children with disabilities, notably *Activity Based Intervention* (ABI) (Bricker & Cripe, 1992) and the individualized assessment and systematic intervention strategies described by Bailey and Wolery (1992) and Wolery and Fleming (1993). Some have been devised for young children with specific disabilities such as autism. The approach employed at the Language and Cognitive Development Center in Boston (Miller & Eller-Miller, 1989), based on the developmental theories of Werner,

Piaget, and Vygotsky and the information-processing theory of von Bertalanffy, is designed to help the child organize behavior and develop more functional and flexible repertoires through increased awareness of their own bodies, other people, and the functional use of objects in the environment. The child's present "rituals," or systems, are expanded, with new behaviors selected on the basis of their relationship to familiar experiences and potential interest. While the activities themselves are congruent with DAP, the intervention strategies may be directive, even intrusive, such as placing the child in challenging, and initially distressing, situations.

Fostering Engagement in ECSE

All the "approaches" noted above share the goal of enhancing the child's ability to become involved with the social environment, the context for learning. Various procedures have been employed to address the fundamental concern for young children with developmental delays and disabilities to be actively involved in learning (Bailey & Wolery, 1992; Carta et al., 1991) by building on and enhancing children's interest in their environment. Considerable research attention has been given to strategies for increasing children's engagement with objects in the environment (e.g., McGee, Daly, Izeman, Mann, & Risley, 1991), but more important than acquisition of isolated skills may be fostering the child's inclination to actively explore, participate, and interact with peers. Thus, Norris (1991) maintains that engagement with a toy should be embedded within a social context, wherein the adult (teacher or parent) supports the child's progress toward joint attention. The goal is not to teach a specific skill but to have the child become interested in the actions of others, intentionally control events, and use objects in functional ways.

Engagement is also the goal of the *Transactional Intervention Project* (TRIP) model (Mahoney & Powell, 1986). This model focuses on the interaction between adult and child as the milieu in which children can become more proficient interactive partners and thus increase engagement with people and objects in their environment. The approach involves assessing the child's current level and style of involvement and building on children's current functioning to enhance interest, curiosity, self-esteem, and ability to make choices. Research with this model (e.g., Mahoney, Finger, & Powell, 1985) has suggested that nondirective interaction strategies are more effective than direct instruction in accomplishing these goals and that child-initiated activity is more likely to occur in natural settings than in artificially imposed contexts.

Natural Environments and ECSE

Recent ecological perspectives in ECSE have suggested a means of reconciling child-initiated activity and adult-planned intervention (Bricker & Cripe, 1992; Warren & Kaiser, 1986). Through ecological assessment, children's actual participation in routines and activities in important environments can be observed and analyzed in order to identify ways to enhance involvement and opportune points in time for such interventions as adapting materials, providing partial assistance, use of peer-mediated methods, and/or targeting key instrumental physical or social skills. Play settings, both planned and impromptu, provide natural environments in which children's skills, across domains, can be assessed and enhanced through appropriate intervention. Play is the "work" of the child in many senses, including the development of representational, motor, communication, and social skills and coping with feelings, fantasies, and fears. Young children obtain information from play actions that is then generalized to new learning situations. Since play is the primary mode of learning in young children, particularly with respect to incidental learning, it is the core of early childhood curriculum. And since play is central to early learning for all young children, as Linder points out in Chapter 4, but both incidental acquisition and generalization of skills through play are areas of difficulty for many young children with disabilities, we have a second, related major challenge for ECSE.

Difficulties experienced by many young children with delays and disabilities in learning through play involve any or all of a variety of play skills. These include maintaining attention, physical manipulation, gaining sensory information from a toy, acquiring knowledge inherent in a toy and generalizing knowledge gained from interacting with a toy, imitating peer or adult models, engaging in mutual or reciprocal play with peers, and making choices within the play environment. Yet, young children with disabilities also learn through play, benefit from the repetitive rehearsal of schemes that characterizes young children's play behavior, and often can be enabled to participate through adaptation of the setting or of specific play materials. Play should not entail onerous, even painful tasks, nor should it be a source of frustration and failure; rather it should be a source of pleasure, of joy, for all young children. The problem is then how to provide the guidance and support some young children may need in order to experience both the enjoyment and the learning benefits of play experienced by their typical peers (Odom & McEvoy, 1990).

Activity Based Intervention (ABI) (Bricker & Cripe, 1992) represents an integration of transactional models of development, especially language development, applied behavior analysis methodology, and developmentally appropriate practice. It aims to capitalize on "child-initiated" as well as "routine and planned . . . activities that children choose or enjoy" (p. 29) in developing an adaptive, *generative* repertoire of functional skills. In ABI, instructional objectives are established, but these may be stated in less specific, more open-ended language than has typically been used in early intervention programs, and planned activities occur in natural rather than contrived environments. Children's progress is carefully monitored, but instruction is responsive to the emerging, and changing, interests of the child. In addition to its other promising features, ABI has the important merit of being adaptable to (1) use by parents as well as professionals; (2) the differential needs of infants, toddlers, and preschoolers; (3) the various settings in which young children learn and are served; (4) group programs that integrate typically developing children with those with disabilities; and (5) the transdisciplinary nature of early intervention and ECSE.

CONCLUSION: SOURCES OF ECSE CURRICULUM

The history of ECSE instructional models, though influenced by various societal events and trends, personal values, professional disciplines, and scholarly conventions, has until recently reflected more of a "vertical extension" of practices with older exceptional learners than application of practices with young children whose development is typical. That is to some degree specifically the case with the content of instruction. The future-oriented, functional-skill orientation of special education implies certain variations of curriculum-based and ecological assessment as guides for curriculum and instruction in ECSE, best expressed by the phrase "criterion of the next environment" (Salisbury & Vincent, 1990). Identification of the skills actually needed by a child to function effectively within anticipated future environments (as well as present ones) has been generally considered more valid than assuming, based on hypothesized developmental hierarchies, that certain accomplishments must always precede others, in a predictable sequence.

Another source of curriculum is federal and state policies and guidelines governing the education of students, including young children, with disabilities. The topic of "DAP-IEP compatibility," discussed in depth by Mahoney and Wheatley in Chapter 6, addresses the *normalization–accountability* problem referenced earlier. Additionally, at least one author (Goodman, 1993) suggests that even the Least Restrictive Environment (LRE) provision can result in practices not appropriate to the characteristics and needs of young children. She observes that the goal of preparing young children for more normalized future environments often creates an "acceleration imperative" (p. 182) incompatible with DAP and, in her view, both stressful and of questionable efficacy. Evidence of ineffectiveness is suggested by indications that some children's highly specific IEP objectives may be repeated from one year to the next, which Goodman and Lloyds (1993) interpret as revealing "the assignment of too difficult tasks taught through too much repetition" (p. 191), though apparently not learned.

But the goal for children with disabilities of "integration of learned responses into generative, functional, and adaptable repertoires" (Bricker & Cripe, 1992, p. 11) seems to imply a less segmented conception of children's development and a focus on learning *processes*, rather than on acquisition of isolated, noncontextual skills. Such a goal also suggests activities that are pleasant and interesting to young children and that occur in the natural course of events or can be embedded within such events. To the extent that inclusion of young children with delays and disabilities in "regular" early childhood programs with typically developing peers becomes more the norm than the exception, such "developmentally appropriate" practices appear likely to define early childhood special education far more than they have in the past. They suggest a more comprehensive developmental model than the maturationist, laissez-faire one attributed to "traditional" developmentalists and a more normalized approach than that identified with "traditional" interventionists.

Finally, the *family-focused* principle that undergirds early intervention services for infants and toddlers, represented by the Individualized Family Services Plan (IFSP), suggests perhaps the most important source of curriculum in ECSE for preschool-age children, as well, and, with respect to social validity, the source most useful in addressing the criterion of *individual appropriateness*. Although the IFSP is the required vehicle for planning of services only until age 3, it may continue to be used, as long as the process and content legally mandated for the IEP are followed. Most importantly, it epitomizes a set of principles for collaboration *of* professionals *with* families in creating futures for young children with special needs.

REFERENCES

Anastasiow, N. J. (1981). Early childhood education for the handicapped in the 1980s: Recommendations. *Exceptional Children, 47*(5), 276–282.

Bailey, D. B., Clifford, R. M., & Harms, T. (1982). Comparison of preschool environments for handicapped and nonhandicapped children. *Topics in Early Childhood Special Education, 7*(1), 73–88.

Bailey, D. B., & Wolery, M. (1992). *Teaching infants and preschoolers with disabilities* (2nd ed.). New York: Merrill.

Beckman, P. J., Robinson, C. C., Jackson, B., & Rosenberg, S. A. (1988). Translating developmental findings into teaching strategies for young handicapped children. *Journal of the Division for Early Childhood, 12*, 45–52.

Berkeley, T. R., & Ludlow, B. L. (1992). Developmental domains: The mother of all interventions; or, the subterranean early development blues. *Topics in Early Childhood Special Education, 11*(4), 13–21.

Billingsley, F. F. (1993). In my dreams: A response to some current trends in education. *Journal of the Association for Persons with Severe Handicaps, 18*(1), 61–63.

Bredekamp, S. (1987). *Developmentally appropriate practice in early child- hood programs serving children from birth through age 8* (expanded ed.). Washington, DC: National Association for the Education of Young Chil- dren.

Bredekamp, S. (1991). Redeveloping early childhood education: A response to Kessler. *Early Childhood Research Quarterly, 6*, 199–209.

Bricker, D. (1993). A rose by any other name, Or is it? *Journal of Early Intervention, 17*(2), 89–96.

Bricker, D., & Cripe, J. W. (1992). *An activity-based approach to early inter- vention*. Baltimore: Paul H. Brookes.

Bricker, W., & Bricker, D. (1974). Mental retardation and complex human behavior. In J. Kaufman & J. Payne (Eds.), *Mental retardation*. Colum- bus, OH: Merrill.

Bricker, W., Macke, P., Levin, J., & Campbell, P. (1982). The modifiability of intelligent behavior. *Journal of Special Education, 15*, 145–163.

Bronfenbrenner, U. (1979). *The ecology of human development*. Cambridge: Harvard University Press.

Burton, C. B., Hains, A. H., Hanline, M. F., McLean, M., & McCormick, K. (1992). Early childhood intervention and education: The urgency of professional unification. *Topics in Early Childhood Special Education, 11*(4), 53–69.

Carta, J. J., Schwartz, I. S., Atwater, J. B., & McConnell, S. R. (1991). Developmentally appropriate practice: Appraising its usefulness for young children with disabilities. *Topics in Early Childhood Special Education, 11*(1), 1–20.

Fagan, T. K., & Delugach, F. J. (1985). Literary origins of the term school psychologist. *School Psychology Review, 10*, 216–220.

Feuerstein, R., Rand, Y., Hoffman, M. B., & Miller, R. (1980). *Instrumental enrichment: An intervention program for cognitive modifiability*. Balti- more: University Park Press.

Fewell, R. R., & Neisworth, J. T. (1991). Foreword. *Topics in early childhood special education, 11*(1), xvi–xviii.

Fraiberg, S. (1977). *Insights from the blind: Comparative studies of blind and sighted infants*. New York: Basic Books.

Furman, R. A., & Katan, A. (1969). *The therapeutic nursery school: A contribution to the study and treatment of emotional disturbances in young children*. New York: International Universities Press.

Gersten, R., Woodward, J., & Darch, C. (1986). Direct instruction: A research-based approach to curriculum design and teaching. *Exceptional Children, 53*(1), 17–31.

Gesell, A. (1923). *The preschool child from the standpoint of public hygiene and education*. Boston: Houghton Mifflin.

Gesell, A. (1924). The care of intellectually inferior children. In M. V. O'Shea (Ed.), *The child: His nature and his needs* (pp. 216–276). New York: The Children's Foundation.

Goodman, J. F. (1993). Curriculum issues in early intervention preschool programs. *Early Education and Development, 4*(3), 182–183.

Goodman, J. F., & Lloyds, W. (1993). Repetition in early intervention programs. *Early Education and Development, 4*(3), 184–192.

Goodman, J. F., & Pollack, E. (1993). An analysis of the core cognitive curriculum in early intervention programs. *Early Education and Development, 4*(3), 193–203.

Hainsworth, P. K., & Hainsworth, M. L. (1979). *Getting started in ERIN*. Dedham, MA: Early Recognition Intervention Network.

Haywood, H. C., Brooks, P., & Burns, S. (1990). *Cognitive curriculum for young children* (Experimental Version). Watertown, MA: Charlesbridge Publishing.

Hohmann, M., Banet, B., & Weikart, D. P. (1979). *Young children in action: A manual for preschool educators*. Ypsilanti, MI: High/Scope Press.

Homme, L. E., DeBaca, P. C., DeVine, J. V., Steinhorst, R., & Rickert, E. J. (1963). Use of the Premack Principle in controlling the behavior of nursery school children. *Journal of the Experimental Analysis of Behavior, 6*, 544.

Hymes, J. (1955). *The child development point of view*. Englewood Cliffs, NJ: Prentice-Hall.

Jipson, J. (1991). Developmentally appropriate practice: Culture, curriculum, connections. *Early Education and Development, 2*(2), 120–136.

Kamii, C., & DeVries, R. (1993). *Physical knowledge in preschool education: Implications of Piaget's theory*. New York: Teachers College Press. Original work published 1978.

Kaufman, B. A. (1980). Early childhood education and special education: A study in conflict. *Volta Review, 80*, 15–24.

Kessler, S. A. (1991). Early childhood education as development: Critique of the metaphor. *Early Education and Development, 2*(2), 137–152.

Kostelnick, M. J. (1992). Myths associated with developmentally appropriate practice. *Young Children, 47*(4), 17–23.

Leigh, J. E., & Riley, N. (1982). Learning disabilities in the early years: Characteristics, assessment, and intervention. *Topics in Learning and Learning Disabilities, 2*(3), 1–15.

Lewis, M., & Starr, M. (1979). Developmental continuity. In J. D. Osofsky (Ed.), *Handbook of infant development* (pp. 635–670). New York: Wiley.

Mahoney, G., Finger, L., & Powell, A. (1985). Relationship of maternal behavioral style to the development of organically impaired mentally retarded infants. *American Journal on Mental Retardation, 90,* 296–302.

Mahoney, G., & Powell, A. (1986). *The Transactional Intervention Program: Teachers' guide.* Farmington, CT: Pediatric Research and Training Center.

Mallory, B. L. (1992). Is it always appropriate to be developmental? Convergent models for early intervention practice. *Topics in Early Childhood Special Education, 11*(4), 1–12.

McDonnell, A., & Hardman, M. (1988). A synthesis of "Best Practice" guidelines for early childhood services. *Journal of the Division for Early Childhood, 12,* 328–341.

McGee, G. G., Daly, T., Izeman, S. G., Mann, L. H., & Risley, T. R. (1991). Use of classroom materials to promote preschool engagement. *Teaching Exceptional Children, 23*(4), 44–47.

Mercer, J. R. (1973). *Labeling the mentally retarded: Clinical and social system perspectives.* Berkeley: University of California Press.

Miller, A., & Eller-Miller, E. (1989). *From ritual to repertoire: A cognitive-developmental systems approach with behavior-disordered children.* New York: Wiley.

Miller, P. S. (1992). Segregated programs of teacher education in early childhood: Immoral and inefficient practice. *Topics in Early Childhood Special Education, 11*(4), 39–52.

Moore, P., & Kester, D. G. (1953). Historical notes on speech correction in the pre-association era. *Journal of Speech and Hearing Disorders, 10,* 48–53.

Norris, J. A. (1991). Providing developmentally appropriate intervention to infants and young children with handicaps. *Topics in Early Childhood Special Education, 11*(1), 21–35.

Odom, S. L., & McEvoy, M. A. (1990). Mainstreaming at the preschool level: Potential barriers and tasks for the field. *Topics in Early Childhood Special Education, 10*(2), 48–61.

Padden, C., & Humphries, T. (1988). *Deaf in America: Voices from a culture.* Cambridge: Harvard University Press.

Peterson, N. L. (1987). *Early intervention for handicapped and at-risk children: An introduction to early childhood special education.* Denver: Love.

Salisbury, C. L., & Vincent, L. J. (1990). Criterion of the next environment and best practice: Mainstreaming and integration 10 years later. *Topics in Early Childhood Special Education, 10*(2), 78–89.

Sameroff, A. J., & Fiese, B. H. (1990). Transactional regulation and early intervention. In S. J. Meisels & J. P. Shonkoff (Eds.), *Handbook of early childhood intervention* (pp. 119–149). New York: Cambridge University Press.

Sarason, S. B., & Doris, J. (1969). *Psychological problems in mental deficiency* (4th ed.). New York: Harper & Row.

Shapiro, E., & Biber, B. (1972). The education of young children: A development interaction approach. *Teachers College Record, 70*(1), 55–79.

Snell, M., & Brown, F. (1993). Instructional planning and implementation. In M. Snell (Ed.), *Instruction of students with severe disabilities* (4th ed., pp. 99–151). New York: Macmillan.

Spodek, B. (1991). Early childhood curriculum and cultural definitions of knowledge. In B. Spodek & O. N. Saracho (Eds.), *Yearbook in Early Childhood Education, Vol. 2: Issues in Early Childhood Curriculum* (pp. 1–20). New York: Teachers College Press.

Strain, P. S., McConnell, S. R., Carta, J. J., Fowler, S. A., Neisworth, J. T., & Wolery, M. (1992). Behaviorism in early intervention. *Topics in Early Childhood Special Education, 12*(1), 121–141.

Suarez, T. M., Hurth, J. L., & Prestridge, S. (1988). Innovation in services for young children with handicaps and their families: An analysis of the Handicapped Children's Early Education Program projects funded from 1982 to 1986. *Journal of the Division of Early Childhood, 12*(3), 224–237.

Swadener, B. B., & Kessler, S. (1991). Introduction to the special issue. *Early Education and Development, 2*(2), 85–94.

Talbot, M. E. (1964). *Edouard Seguin: A study of an instructional approach to the treatment of mentally defective children.* New York: Teachers College Press.

Walsh, D. J. (1991). Extending the discourse on developmental appropriateness: A developmental perspective. *Early Education and Development, 2*(2),109–119.

Warren, S., & Kaiser, A. (1986). Incidental language teaching: A critical review. *Journal of Speech and Hearing Disorders, 51,* 291–299.

Weikart, D., Rogers, L., Adcock, C., & McClelland, D. (1970). *The cognitively oriented curriculum: A framework for preschool teachers.* Washington, DC: National Association for the Education of Young Children.

Widerstrom, A. H. (1986). Education of young handicapped children: What can early childhood contribute. *Childhood Education, 60*(2), 78–83.

Wolery, M., Doyle, P. M., Gast, D. L., Ault, M. J., & Simpson, S. L. (1993). Comparison of progressive time delay and transition-based teaching with preschoolers who have developmental delays. *Journal of Early Intervention, 17*(2), 160–176.

Wolery, M., & Fleming, L. A. (1993). Implementing individualized curricula in integrated settings. In C. A. Peck, S. L. Odom, & D. D. Bricker (Eds.), *Integrating young children with disabilities into community programs: Ecological perspectives on research and implementation* (pp. 109–132). Baltimore: Paul H. Brookes.

Wolery, M., Strain, P. S., & Bailey, D. B. (1993). In S. Bredekamp & T. Rosegrant (Eds.), *Reaching potentials: Appropriate curriculum and assessment for young children, Vol. 1* (pp. 92–111). Washington, DC: National Association for the Education of Young Children.

Wood, M. W. (1975). *Developmental therapy: A textbook for teachers as therapists for emotionally disturbed young children.* Baltimore: University Park Press.

Ysseldyke, J. E., & Algozzine, B. (1982). *Critical issues in special and remedial education.* Boston: Houghton Mifflin.

CHAPTER 6

Reconceptualizing the Individual Education Program: A Constructivist Approach to Educational Practice for Young Children with Disabilities

Gerald Mahoney and Amy Powell Wheatley

A key practical issue associated with integrating young children with disabilities into community preschool programs with typical peers is the apparent incompatibility of the Individual Education Program (IEP) mandated for students eligible for special education with the *constructivist* model undergirding developmentally appropriate practice (DAP; Bredekamp, 1987). This problem of "DAP–IEP compatibility" is, we believe, a potential barrier to effective inclusion of young children with disabilities in regular programs, since inclusion depends on the extent to which children's individualized programs can be integrated within the regular curriculum. Discrepancies between the educational models used for children with disabilities and those whose functioning is typical increase the demands placed on the teacher and lead to the social isolation of children with disabilities during major portions of the day (Mahoney, Robinson, & Powell, 1992; Odom & McEvoy, 1990).

While the focus of this chapter is the IEP, the underlying issue is what constitutes "best" practice for young children with disabilities. The IEP was originally designed to assure that children with disabilities receive educational experiences that are appropriately tailored to their individual educational needs. Mandated for school-age children during the 1970s, IEPs developed by state and local school districts were designed to reflect state-of-the-art practice in special education, which, at that time, was practice derived from models of behavioral psychology. The structure or form of the IEP has undergone little change since it was introduced. This reflects the continued belief, prevalent among special educators, including those involved in early childhood special education (ECSE), that behavioral strategies are still a key component of best practice. Although for the past 20 years the IEP has been instrumental in enhancing the education of children with disabilities, its current form discourages non-behaviorally oriented models such as constructivism, which hold great potential for children, especially young children with disabilities.

This chapter is divided into four sections. We first discuss the rationale for using a behavioral model as best practice for preschool-age children with disabilities. We then describe research that supports the use of an alternative constructivist model. Next, we describe how the structure of the traditional IEP discourages the use of models other than those that are derived from behavioral psychology. Finally, we offer guidelines for developing IEPs that support the use of practices compatible with the constructivist model.

EARLY CHILDHOOD SPECIAL EDUCATION "BEST" PRACTICE

During the past 10 years there has been extensive discussion of best practices in ECSE. Generally, these reflect the opinions of highly regarded professionals about the strategies and services they believe to be the most effective for young children with disabilities. This concept evolved as a mechanism for the professional community to provide leadership and direction to practitioners in the absence of clear research findings regarding the efficacy of special education practice. While, as Wolery, Strain, and Bailey (1992) note, best practice is based on research, discussion, experience, and beliefs, the relative contribution of each of these is unclear. Although research studies are often cited to support most of the endorsed practices, few of these studies are of the scope and quality needed to establish the efficacy of the practice or to rule out alternative approaches.

Since the late 1960s, special education instructional practices have been dominated by behavioral concepts, particularly as derived from operant learning theory. At least four factors contributed to behaviorism's taking root in special education. First, the period of rapid growth in special education corresponded to the emergence of behavioral psychology as the "cutting edge" in theory and research concerning child development and educational psychology. Behavioral methodologies were considered to hold great promise in all areas of education, as well as special education. Second, behavioral techniques, in marked contrast with the perceptual-motor, psychodynamic, and other intrinsic process–oriented approaches commonly used in instruction and treatment, were demonstrated to have relatively rapid and often dramatic impact on the learning of targeted objectives by persons with disabilities. Reviews of research published in the early 1970s pointed out the lack of evidence to support the belief that procedures designed to remediate deficient or delayed mental processes actually enhanced children's competence and functioning. Thus, behaviorism provided a viable alternative to ineffective practices that were then in use. Third, the emphasis of behaviorism on observation and measurement provided a framework that required teachers to specify and operationalize the objectives identified for each child. This was seen as an antidote to some of the laissez-faire attitudes that had permeated special education. Fourth, behaviorism was a highly positive and activist-oriented educational model, grounded in the belief that all persons, including persons with severe disabilities, could learn and change.

Consistent with this general orientation of special education, many of the instructional procedures designated as best practice in ECSE are also closely associated with the principles and methodology of applied behavioral analysis. In particular, five elements associated with behaviorism are consistently included in best-practice descriptions:

1. Educational goals and objectives that are functional and contribute to children's social adaptation (Bailey & McWilliam, 1990);
2. Instructional activities that are directly related to educational objectives (Carta, Schwartz, Atwater, McConnell, 1991; Wolery et al., 1992);
3. Strategies that guide or direct children to engage in instructional activities (Carta et al., 1991; McConnell & Hardman, 1988);
4. Reinforcement procedures that encourage children to perform predetermined behaviors and/or respond in the desired manner to instructional activities (McConnell & Hardman, 1988);
5. Systematic observational procedures that can be used on a regular basis to monitor children's performance in relationship to their educational objectives (Strain, McConnell, Carta, Fowler, Neisworth, & Wolery, 1992).

These elements are discussed by Odom and McEvoy (1990), who observe that ECSE programs, like special education in general, have tended to have a didactic character, incorporating psychological learning theories with the concept of mastery learning, drawn from educational psychology, and the belief, supported by the effective schools literature, that student progress is directly related to time spent in direct instruction:

> The implicit assumption within these programs is that the disability of the child prevents him or her from taking advantage of the typical environmental experiences that promote normal child development. . . . ECSE programs have been more teacher directed, have included the development of specific and more individualized goals and objectives for the child, and have designed learning activities to meet those specific objectives. (pp. 51–52)

Support for this model of best practice has been based on two factors. The first is evidence from single-subject research studies that points to the effectiveness of behavioral procedures; the second involves commonly accepted beliefs about the characteristics of children with disabilities. As we will discuss, there are significant flaws with both lines of support. While studies have demonstrated the power of behavioral techniques in producing predetermined changes in children's behavior, the question remains as to whether children are better off as a result. Moreover, there are substantial inconsistencies between research findings regarding the characteristics of children with disabilities and some of the presumed characteristics that behavioral techniques are designed to address.

Effectiveness of Behavioral Instructional Procedures

Behavioral methods assume that children's development and adaptive functioning can be enhanced through instruction in skills identified with desired levels of developmental and adaptive functioning (Strain et al., 1992). This assumption is partially supported by a substantial body of research on behavioral instructional practices with preschool-age children. Many studies have reported causal relationships between direct instructional procedures such as modeling, shaping, prompting, and reinforcement and the acquisition of key developmental and adaptive functioning milestones (cf. Snell, 1993). These studies have demonstrated that preschool-age children with a wide range of disabilities can be taught a variety of cognitive, language, social, motor, and adaptive skills through the combined use of direct instruction and extrinsic incentives, such as praise and tangible reinforcers. Indisputably, these procedures can be, and often are, effective in helping children attain objectives. However, the effectiveness of this mode of instruction in enhancing long-term competence or adaptive functioning is far less clear. Over the past 20 years, studies of the efficacy of behavioral interventions in promoting children's early developmental functioning have indicated that almost all children attain significant progress over the course of intervention as evidenced by standardized or criterion-referenced tests. However, evidence that such procedures accelerate development beyond expected rates of maturation is neither consistent nor convincing (e.g., Casto & Mastropieri, 1986; Dunst, 1986; Farran, 1990; Guralnick & Bennett, 1987).

The methodological flaws of many of these studies prevent definitive conclusions regarding the value of behavioral procedures. Reviewers have observed that treatment effects may have been underestimated due to the use of inappropriate and insensitive evaluation instruments. Yet in the absence of evidence to the contrary, it is possible that findings from these studies do, in fact, suggest that the behavioral interventions being implemented are not as effective at promoting development as hoped.

Characteristics of Children with Disabilities

The behavioral model of best practice is also based on the belief that children with disabilities are not likely to engage in the kinds of activities needed to promote learning and development unless they are provided with directed instruction (Carta et al., 1991; Wolery et al., 1992). Assumptions that have been made about the spontaneous behavior of children with disabilities are directly linked to views about what is needed to promote learning and development. If learning and development occur as the result of children's spontaneous and repeated performance of the behaviors that reflect higher levels of functioning, then directed instruction is necessary because children are not likely to produce behaviors beyond their present level. If, on the other hand, learning and development occur as the result of children's spontaneous and repeated performance of behavior at their present level, then directed instruction is not necessary, since the kinds of behaviors that children normally produce while playing or socializing are the basis for higher levels of functioning.

Since 1980, more than 30 studies have examined the quality of play of preschool-age children with various disabilities. These studies have had a variety of designs and subject samples but are relatively homoge-neous in the conclusions they have drawn. As Linder discusses in Chap-ter 4, when the play of children with disabilities has been compared with that of typically developing, same-age peers, findings indicate that children with disabilities have less frequent play (Jennings, Connors, & Stegman, 1988; Li, 1985; Turner & Small, 1985), less varied play (Beeghly, Weiss-Perry, & Cicchetti, 1990; Parsons, 1986), and lower developmental levels of play (Brophy & Stone-Zukowski, 1984; Jen-nings, Connors, & Stegman, 1988; Li, 1985). However, when com-pared with typically developing children at the same developmental age level, few if any of these differences are observed (Brooks-Gunn & Lewis, 1982; Gowen, Goldman, Johnson-Martin, & Hussey, 1989). Such comparisons indicate that children with disabilities demonstrate comparable levels and intensity of play and progress through the same play stages as do typically developing children (Beeghly et al., 1990; Brooks-Gunn & Lewis, 1982).

Studies of the relationship between play and other developmental skills indicate that the quality of play displayed by children with disa-bilities is correlated with their language functioning (Beeghly et al., 1990), interpersonal skills (Hill & McCune-Nicholich, 1981; Motti, Cic-chetti, & Stroufe, 1983), and cognitive development (Hill & McCune-Nicholich, 1981; Power & Radcliff, 1989). These findings suggest that, as with typically developing children, play is a vehicle through which children acquire the competencies and skills that lead to higher levels of developmental functioning. However, the fact that children with disabilities remain at specific play levels for extended periods suggests that they need more time to learn from these experiences than do typi-cally developing children.

In summary, while research evidence is often cited as the basis for current notions of best practice in ECSE, a careful analysis of this research indicates that behaviorism's value has yet to be fully estab-lished. It appears that much of the learning attained by children with disabilities through the use of behavioral procedures does not generalize to spontaneous behavior (Kaiser, Yoder, & Keets, 1992). In addition, most descriptive research conducted with children with disabilities indi-cates that these children display types of play behavior similar to those of typical children who are at the same developmental age level. Thus, there is little research support for the belief that children with disabili-ties need directed instruction to guide them to participate in develop-mentally stimulating activities. On the contrary, the same types of con-structive activities that are associated with the functioning of typically developing children are also related to the emergence of early developmental skills in children with disabilities (Weisz & Zigler, 1979). While behaviorism has considerable promise as an educational strategy for children with disabilities, claims regarding best-practice status for it appear to be more a reflection of current practice in ECSE than of evidence.

CONSTRUCTIVIST PROCESSES AND CHILDREN WITH DISABILITIES

While constructivism has yet to be evaluated as an educational strategy for children with disabilities (Carta et al., 1991), there is at least as much empirical justification for using this approach as there is for using behaviorism. There is an emerging body of research examining the relationship of adult-child interaction to the functioning of children with disabilities that is generally supportive of the constructivist model of education, particularly as described in DAP (Bredekamp, 1987). Since most of this evidence has been based on descriptive rather than experimental research designs, results from these studies can provide only circumstantial support. Nonetheless, the general pattern of findings consistently indicates that styles of parental interaction that support and encourage children's play, communication, and other forms of constructive behavior affect children with disabilities much in the same manner as constructivist instructional procedures affect typical children.

Three questions addressed in parent-child interaction research have direct implications for the use of a constructivist model of education with children with disabilities:

1. How do parents impact the development of children with disabilities?
2. How is active participation of children with disabilities influenced by adult interactive style?
3. How does promoting a responsive style of interaction influence the development of children with disabilities?

Parental Influences on Development

At least four studies have examined interactive influences on the development of children with disabilities. Brooks-Gunn and Lewis (1984) examined interactions among a sample of 111 dyads with children 3–36 months, including children with Down syndrome, cerebral palsy, and developmental delays. Mother-child play was rated using a discrete-time sampling procedure. Results indicated that variability in children's mental age was significantly related to the degree to which mothers responded to their children's behavior. Children were likely to have higher developmental scores the more frequently their mothers vocalized, looked, or smiled in a meaningful manner.

Mahoney, Finger, and Powell (1985) examined patterns of mother-child play with dyads that included children with mental retardation who were between 12 and 36 months of age. Mothers' behavioral style was assessed across a number of global characteristics including responsiveness, enjoyment, sensitivity, stimulation, directiveness, and teaching. Children with the highest levels of developmental functioning had mothers who were rated as being highly responsive and child-oriented. These mothers enjoyed playing with their children and were sensitive to their children's feelings and interests. They responded to and followed activities their children initiated, and they were effective at gaining their children's cooperation. Lowest levels of functioning were associated with maternal interactional styles that were directive and teaching-oriented. These mothers structured their play around activities that would promote specific developmental skills and behaviors and frequently attempted to engage their children in activities that they had chosen.

Bradley (1989) used an adapted version of the HOME Inventory Scale (Caldwell & Bradley, 1984) to investigate parent-child interaction. The HOME was administered to 261 caregivers during two separate home visits. All parents had children between 6 months and 12 years of age with a diagnosed disability. Parental responsiveness was assessed by rating the degree that caregivers responded to or facilitated their children's interaction during the visit. Correlations between parental responsiveness and developmental quotient scores were, for preschool-age children, in the low to moderate range. However, for school-age children, correlations between parental responsiveness and intelligence quotients were much stronger.

Mahoney (1989a, 1989b) investigated the relationship of maternal communication style to children's rate of communication development. The sample included the same 60 dyads described in Mahoney et al. (1985). Results indicated that mothers who communicated by responding to their children's nonverbal behavior as if it were a meaningful part of a conversation had children who both communicated frequently with their mothers and had relatively high expressive language age scores. Mothers who modeled and encouraged children to use appropriate words or phrases tended to be less responsive to their children's nonverbal communication. Their children communicated less frequently and had lower expressive language age scores than children of more responsive mothers.

These descriptive studies provide evidence that children with disabilities attain higher levels of developmental functioning when their parents use a style of interaction that (1) accepts and values the behaviors that children are able to do, (2) is highly responsive to their interests, and (3) provides their children ample opportunity to exercise control over the activities in which they are involved. None of these studies reported that children with disabilities had high levels of development when their parents' interactive style reflected the directive and instructional characteristics associated with the ECSE best-practice model. On the contrary, the kinds of child-oriented relationships that constructivist theories presume motivate children to engage in developmental activities were consistently associated with higher levels of developmental growth.

Effects of Style on Children's Engagement

Several studies have examined the quality of children's engagement in relationship to adult style of interaction. Findings from these studies indicate that children with disabilities are more active when interacting with adults who are responsive and child-oriented rather than directive and performance-oriented. This relationship has been observed in investigations of both parent-child and teacher-child interaction. Dedrick, Mahoney, and Dedrick (in preparation) examined the effects of maternal interactive style on the play and social interactions of 32 children with disabilities who ranged from 9 to 31 months of age. Two matched groups of mother-child dyads were established on the basis of their mothers' level of directiveness (directive/nondirective) while playing with their children. Children's engagement was assessed while they played alone and with their mothers. The two groups of children showed no differences in their developmental level of play (maturity) or level of engagement while playing alone. However, while playing with their mothers, children of directive mothers were 25 percent less actively engaged in play and displayed higher levels of passivity, crying, and fussing than children of responsive parents.

Wolock (1990) examined the effects of teachers' style of interaction on the interactive engagement of preschool-age children with disabilities. Forty-nine children enrolled in special education classes were observed in three situations: playing alone, playing with their teacher, and receiving individualized instruction from their teacher. Children's level of engagement with their teachers was unrelated to the children's developmental status or level of engagement while playing alone. However, children's participation in both the play and instruction situations was highly associated with their teachers' style of interaction. Children were more likely to initiate play and communication when their teachers used a responsive, child-oriented style rather than a directive, instructionally oriented style.

Bressanutti, Mahoney, and Sachs (1992) examined the quality of children's compliance to their mothers' behavior requests. Subjects were 36 mother-child dyads. One group included children with Down syndrome, the other typically developing children. Children in the two groups were matched on developmental age (MDA = 17.5 months). Maternal requests were rated according to their contingent relationship to children's current interests and the relative difficulty of the behavior being requested. In both groups, the contingency and difficulty of mothers' behavior requests were highly associated with the quality of children's compliance. Children were more likely to comply with requests that were contingently related to their current interests and at a relatively low level of difficulty.

The constructivist model places great importance on children's active engagement and participation. It is believed that child-centered (rather than adult-directed) instructional strategies encourage children's active participation. Investigations of interactive influences on children's engagement support this belief. Children with disabilities are more actively engaged when involved in interactions that are child-centered rather than adult-directed, that are responsive to their interests, and that are supportive of the behaviors they are able to produce. Adult-directed interactions do not appear to encourage children to either perform developmentally advanced behaviors or to sustain higher levels of engagement.

Effects of Parental Style in Early Intervention

A number of intervention studies, three of which are pertinent to this discussion, have attempted to promote children's developmental functioning by encouraging parents to adopt the responsive child-oriented characteristics of interaction described above. Mahoney and Powell (1988) reported the results from an intervention program that attempted to promote high levels of parental responsiveness and acceptance and low levels of parental directiveness. Parents were encouraged to use the interactive strategies of turn-taking and interactive match as means of monitoring their daily interactions with their children. They were asked to support and encourage their children's active engagement in routine interactions and were discouraged from teaching specific developmental skills. This program was assessed with a sample of 41 children with disabilities ranging from 2 to 32 months of age. Children who made the greatest developmental gains after one year of intervention had parents who were the most child-oriented and responsive. Their developmental gains were 48 percent greater than the gains made by children of more directive parents.

The ecological (ECO) communication intervention program (Macdonald, 1989) focuses on parent-child communication. Parents are coached to use interactive strategies to help them become more sensitive and responsive to their children's communicative behavior, to be better matched to the children's current level of functioning, and to sustain longer episodes of reciprocal interaction with their children. This program was evaluated with a sample of 25 parent-child dyads in which each of the children had at least a one-year delay in language functioning and ranged in age from 23 to 64 months at the time of the first observation. Mother-child dyads received weekly instruction in the ECO model at a speech clinic over a six-month time period. Ratings of videotapes of parent-child communication indicated little or no improvement in children's language and communicative functioning or in the adults' interactive style during a one-month baseline period. However, during the course of intervention, adults became more communicatively responsive in interacting with their children, and children showed marked improvement in their language and communicative functioning. One-month follow-up assessment indicated continued progression in parent–child interaction and children's communicative functioning.

Greenberg, Calderon, and Kusche (1984) reported a study that involved parents of infants with severe or profound deafness. Twelve families received systematic weekly intervention in which they were trained to use a total communication approach emphasizing responsivity to the child's communication. The 12 comparison families did not receive systematic intervention because of their inability to attend this program. At the end of this project, the communication skills of parents in the experimental group were characterized as more positive and less directive and controlling than comparison parents. They appeared to be more in tune with and responsive to their children. Compared with the comparison children, children in the experimental group were more advanced in receptive and expressive communication skills and in the expression of time concepts. The authors concluded that the experimental families demonstrated a more "natural and rich communication" style.

Results from these intervention programs provide additional support for strategies associated with constructivist educational practices. Evaluations of these projects indicate that children with disabilities achieve desirable developmental outcomes when their primary caregivers adopt a responsive, child-oriented style of interaction. These results suggest that strategies associated with constructivist educational practices effectively promote the cognitive, language, and social development of children with disabilities. They also provide further indication that the constructivist educational philosophy and procedures associated with the DAP model may be very appropriate for addressing the developmental and educational needs of preschool children with disabilities.

DISCREPANCIES BETWEEN IEPs AND CONSTRUCTIVIST PROCEDURES

IEPs are required for all children who receive special education services to ensure placements that are appropriately responsive to developmental and educational needs associated with each child's disability; assure that children's educational and remedial programs address their specific educational and developmental needs; monitor and evaluate children's developmental, educational, and socio-adaptive progress; and involve parents as key decision makers in the educational process. Each student's IEP must include

1. A statement of the student's present level of educational performance
2. Annual goals, including short-term instructional objectives
3. A statement of the specific special education and related services to be provided, and the extent to which the student will be able to participate in regular education
4. Projected dates for initiating services and the anticipated duration of services
5. Appropriate objective criteria and evaluation procedures and schedules for determining, on at least an annual basis, whether the objectives are being achieved

These guidelines are broad enough to accommodate a range of educational approaches. Nonetheless, as mentioned at the beginning of this chapter, most of the IEP protocols developed by state and local school districts were designed on the assumption that practices derived from a behavioral model were the most effective for children receiving special education. Thus, most IEP forms have been developed so that children's instructional plans are outlined in a manner that reflects behavioral instructional strategies. IEPs require long-term goals and short-term objectives for each educational and developmental need identified by the diagnostic team. Short-term objectives are generally sets of specific subskills, which are logically linked to children's performance of the overall instructional goal and can be observed and measured objectively. Required outcome criteria often focus on the performance of subskills to a certain level (e.g., 8 out of 10 trials, 80 percent accuracy) under highly specified conditions (e.g., either in the instructional setting or under conditions that are very similar to the instructional setting) (Bricker, 1989). Although not designed to be lesson plans, IEPs generally include statements indicating that children will receive directed instruction in activities that target each of the goals and objectives on the IEP.

Surprisingly little research has been conducted on the IEP. There is some evidence, however, that a significant number of special education personnel do not use the IEP to guide daily instructional activities (Mahoney & O'Sullivan, 1989; Margolis & Truesdale, 1987). Nevertheless, three aspects of the legislation related to IEPs underscore the important role the document is intended to have for those who educate children with disabilities. First, schools must assure that all IEPs are implemented as approved by parents and the IEP team. Second, state and federal funding for special education services requires monitoring of local school districts to assure that IEPs are developed and implemented as required by law. Third, service providers are required to keep the IEP on file where they work with the child and must be able to demonstrate how a child's educational program is responsive to the goals and objectives identified on the IEP.

To the extent that service providers feel compelled to use the IEP as a framework for children's educational services, there are a number of features of the IEP that discourage the use of constructivist educational procedures. Constructivist and behavioral educational practices are based on assumptions about learning and development that in many cases are diametrically opposed. Consequently, descriptions of children's educational programs from a behavioral framework often imply the use of instructional procedures and activities that are in direct conflict with constructivist practices, as suggested in the following:

General vs. Specific Experiences

While constructivism and behaviorism both provide a framework for maximizing children's developmental and functional competence, these two practices have conflicting conceptualizations about how higher levels of competence are achieved (Mahoney et al., 1992). Constructivism conceptualizes competence as the result of children's evolving understanding of their world. In the process of engaging in a variety of developmentally appropriate activities and experiences, children discover or begin to recognize new relationships or meanings. These "child-initiated" discoveries and children's attempts to "make sense of them" through the process of accommodation and assimilation (Piaget, 1963) are considered crucial for children's acquisition of new skills and behaviors that reflect higher levels of competence. Behaviorism, on the other hand, views competence as resulting from the acquisition of subskills or component behaviors. Behavioral IEPs thus foster competence by encouraging children to acquire a sequence of predetermined skills.

To illustrate the difference between the two approaches, consider communicative competence. Constructivism would view children's acquisition of language as the result of their use of communication in a number of forms (e.g., gestures, sounds) and in a wide variety of situations. Thus, constructivist educational practices would focus on enhancing children's opportunities to engage in any kind of communication that is at the child's current level of functioning. Behaviorism, on the other hand, would view children's acquisition of language as the result of their ability to use words. As a result, behaviorally oriented IEPs would prescribe instructional activities that require children to make specific sounds or words that characterize higher levels of communicative competence rather than encourage more general communication efforts (Lerner, Mardell-Czudnowski, & Goldenberg, 1981).

Integrated vs. Isolated Experiences

Constructivism is based on the belief that each of the activities that take place in an educational setting can, and does, have a multitude of developmental consequences. The impact that a particular activity has on a child's development is determined less by the nature of the activity than by the manner in which children engage in the activity. For example, a sand-table activity has the potential to promote children's creativity, problem solving, fine motor skills, and communication and social skills. Behaviorism, in contrast, assumes that specific instructional activities are necessary for the development of specific skills. Thus, for example, behaviorally oriented IEPs would prescribe specific fine motor activities to develop fine motor skills and "language arts" activities to develop communication skills (Bagnato, Neisworth, & Munson, 1989). Although there is no inherent contradiction between constructivism and

descriptions of children's development from the perspective of developmental domains (e.g., cognitive, language, social, motor), constructivism tends to view early child development as a holistic, integrated process in which all dimensions of children's development benefit to
varying degrees from every activity in which they participate (Norris,
1991). IEPs that prescribe specific instructional activities for each developmental domain militate against this holistic view of development.

Child-Initiated vs. Teacher-Directed

Constructivism is a child-directed model of education and development that assumes that children will voluntarily choose and initiate
activities that promote the acquisition of new knowledge and behavior,
provided there is sufficient opportunity. In contrast, behaviorism is
an adult-directed model of learning and development. Behaviorally
oriented objectives are usually formulated on the assumption that adult
direction is necessary for children to perform the tasks most likely to
promote higher levels of competence. Generally, behaviorally oriented
IEPs convey the notion that personnel will guide and direct children
to engage in learning activities to implement the child's educational
program. This conflicts with constructivist biases toward encouraging
children to make choices and initiate activities.

Strength vs. Deficit Orientation

Constructivist-oriented curricula emphasize children's strengths,
creating a classroom environment replete with opportunities to become
involved in activities and interactions that are commensurate to children's current level of functioning. Behaviorism, in contrast, has a
strong deficit orientation. It assumes that development occurs by children's learning to perform behaviors that they currently are unable to
do (i.e., the subskill required to reach a desired behavior). As a result,
behaviorally oriented IEPs emphasize educational activities that direct
or guide children to perform behaviors or skills related to their deficits
as opposed to activities that encourage behaviors currently within children's behavioral repertoire.

TOWARD AN IEP THAT SUPPORTS
A CONSTRUCTIVIST APPROACH

What would an IEP that is consistent with the principles of constructivism look like? While it is impossible to prescribe a single form or

specific content for such an IEP, the following guidelines for identifying, accomplishing, and evaluating IEP goals and objectives are consistent with the principles of a constructivist model and offer an alternative to the traditional behavioral framework for developing and implementing the IEP. Table 6.1 highlights some key differences between an IEP based on a constructivist model and one based on a

Table 6.1. Contrasting Approaches to Developing an Individual Education Program (IEP)

BEHAVIORAL MODEL	CONSTRUCTIVIST MODEL
IDENTIFYING GOALS AND OBJECTIVES	
Specific skills	Active engagement
Isolated behaviors	Broad competencies
Above present level of functioning	Matched to present level of functioning
Chronological Age appropriate	Developmental age appropriate
ACCOMPLISHING GOALS AND OBJECTIVES	
Direct instruction	Play
Instructional activities	Daily routines & activities
Adult initiated/controlled	Child initiated/controlled
Performance oriented	Process oriented
Extrinsic rewards	Intrinsic motivation
EVALUATING GOALS AND OBJECTIVES	
Assessment identifies deficits	Assessment identified strengths
Assessment identifies objectives	Assessment used to monitor
Test/Trial	Observation
Behavior elicited and/or directed by an adult	Behavior demonstrated spontaneously by child
Specific, isolated interactions and activities	General integrated interactions and activities

behavioral model. Many of the principles and practices derived from behaviorism that have guided the development of traditional IEPs are outlined and contrasted with an alterative approach, based on the principles of constructivism and practices associated with this model. The following guidelines provide a framework for developing an IEP that supports a constructivist approach to educating young children with disabilities.

Identifying Goals and Objectives

- Since children's active engagement in interactions with people, materials, and ideas is the most critical component of early learning in all domains, emphasize active engagement by identifying goals and objectives that focus on the nature and quality of children's engagement. Use words such as *initiation, persistence, practice, manipulation, exploration, experimentation, attention, problem solving, expansion,* and *participation*.
- Focus on broad competencies, rather than specific skills and isolated behaviors. Children's competence and higher levels of functioning are viewed as the result of their evolving understanding of the world through use of existing schemata, or general patterns of behavior, in a wide variety of interactions and activities. Specific higher-level skills and behaviors to be repeatedly performed are not identified as objectives on the IEP, because it is assumed that the performance of these skills and behaviors does not necessarily lead to overall higher levels of functioning. If specific skills and behaviors are identified on the IEP, they are identified not as objectives in themselves, but as examples of the kinds of behavior one might look for as the child's competence in a particular domain increases.
- Project long-term goals on the basis of a child's personal developmental history. A statement of annual goals identifies broad competencies within each domain. The level of functioning that children would be expected to achieve in any domain during the course of a year is consistent with the child's current rate of development. Realistic predictions can be made based on the rate of gain that the child has made up to that point. Thus, a 48-month-old child whose cognitive functioning is estimated to be at the 24-month level might be expected to make a gain of six months during one year. The predicted rate is based on the child's current rate of gain, which is 24/48 or .5 years for each year of life.
- Match short-term objectives to both present and expected levels of development. The IEP emphasizes the importance of a child's current

behavior as the foundation on which new behaviors develop. There-fore, short-term objectives focus on the child's increasing and ex-panded use of current knowledge, behaviors, and skills, reflecting the belief that children learn by doing more of what they already can do. Short-term objectives also focus on the emergence of new knowledge, behaviors, and skills, as consistent with expected levels of development.

Accomplishing Goals and Objectives

- Integrate objectives within a wide variety of play routines and activi-ties. The constructivist model assumes that every interaction and activity has the potential to provide opportunities for learning and development in a variety of domains. For example, strategies for accomplishing a fine motor objective that emphasizes the child's in-creasingly coordinated eye-hand movements might include providing opportunities for the child to initiate these movements in play at the sand table, in the block area, on the playground, and at snack time.
- Emphasize the importance of child-initiated activities. Constructiv-ism is a child-directed model. It assumes that children will volun-tarily choose and initiate activities that will lead to the acquisition of new understandings and behaviors, provided there are sufficient opportunities for interaction with people and the environment.
- Assume a process rather than performance orientation. Constructiv-ism assumes that the impact an activity or interaction has on a child's development is determined mainly by the degree and manner in which the child engages in that interaction or activity. IEP objectives emphasize the quality of children's engagement with people and ma-terials (e.g., as indicated by words like *practices, initiates, manipu-lates, experiments, participates*) rather than performance of a task or completion of a product, as indicated by words like *completes, identifies, responds correctly, uses x times daily, or demonstrates to 80 percent criterion.*
- Emphasize intrinsically motivated rather than extrinsically motivated behavior. Constructivism stresses the importance of active engage-ment for learning and development. Models of intrinsic motivation suggest that children are most likely to be actively engaged in (and therefore be most likely to learn from) interactions and activities that are enjoyable, support feelings of control, match their interests, and match their developmental level of functioning (Mahoney, 1988). These concepts imply that adults can enhance and capitalize on chil-dren's intrinsic motivation by creating educational environments that

are personally enjoyable and satisfying to children, that allow children to experience a high degree of success, and that are highly
sensitive and responsive to children's interests. Curricula based on
developmentally appropriate practices emphasize these concepts by
creating environments that offer a variety of materials and activities
that match children's developmental level and interests. Children are
encouraged to become involved in activities of their choice. Adults
strive to make preschool an enjoyable, exciting, and personally satisfying experience for each child. To support the constructivist model,
IEPs must be designed to encourage instructional practices that are
consistent with these concepts of intrinsic motivation.

- Describe what adults will do to support the child's active engagement
  in interactions and activities. Adults can effectively promote the ac-
  complishment of developmental objectives by supporting children's
  active engagement in interactions with people, materials, and ideas.
  Adult support strategies describe ways the adult will create an environment that facilitates active engagement, provide experiences that
  encourage active engagement, and interact with children in ways
  that develop and maintain their active engagement.

Evaluating Goals and Objectives

- Identify present level of functioning and developmental strengths
  (current behaviors and interests) as the foundation for higher levels
  of functioning. The statement regarding the child's present level of
  functioning required in the IEP focuses on the nature of the child's
  engagement in interactions with people and materials. It describes
  the child's current behavior in terms of strength—present abilities
  and interests—and emphasizes that these abilities and interests provide a critical "precursor" to the next stage of development.
- Assess to monitor development, rather than to identify objectives.
  Assessments of children provide information regarding current levels
  of functioning, which allows adults to monitor progress and changes
  in children's development over time. Assessment instruments (e.g.,
  criterion-referenced tests) have been used extensively in behavioral
  approaches as the basis for identifying IEP objectives. This approach
  assumes that the specific skills and behaviors that comprise items on
  an assessment (e.g., names 3 out of 5 colors, completes a 7-piece
  puzzle, walks up stairs alternating feet without adult assistance) are
  the skills and behaviors the child must acquire to reach higher levels
  of functioning. Using this approach, for example, a service provider
  administering a test to a child notes the items that the child did not

"pass" or demonstrate in a specific domain, identifies these items (e.g., names 3 out of 5 shapes presented, completes a 7-piece puzzle, walks up stairs alternating feet without adult assistance) as short-term objectives in the cognition, fine motor, and social domains, and transfers them directly to the child's IEP. In a constructivist approach, the service provider uses information from assessment instruments to estimate the child's developmental level of functioning and to monitor changes and progress in the child's level of functioning over time. Individual assessment items are viewed only as examples of the kinds of behavior children demonstrate at a particular level of functioning, not as objectives in and of themselves.

- Use regular observation of children's engagement and behavior as the primary method for evaluating IEP goals and objectives. Regular observation is the most valid method for documenting and evaluating IEP goals and objectives that emphasize children's engagement and spontaneous behavior. Criteria for evaluating goals and objectives emphasize the wide variety of interactions and activities in which children's engagement, current and emerging behavior can be observed and documented on a regular basis.
- Focus on those behaviors that the *child* initiates. IEP objectives that are consistent with a constructivist model of development emphasize the importance of child-initiated behavior. Therefore, IEP objectives are evaluated in the context of those interactions and activities in which spontaneous child-initiated behavior can be observed, rather than in test or "trial" situations in which children's behavior is elicited or directed by an adult.
- Focus on children's engagement and behavior in a wide variety of interactions and activities. In the constructivist model of development, competence and higher levels of functioning are viewed as the result of children's use of existing schemata, or general patterns of behavior, across a wide variety of interactions and activities. Therefore, individual IEP objectives are evaluated in the context of many kinds of interactions and activities.

CONCLUSION

Although the education of children with disabilities has clearly been enhanced through the IEP, the current form and use of IEPs interfere with the implementation of innovative curriculum approaches such as those based on constructivist theory. The restrictions on the use of these innovative practices stem from the long-standing belief that behaviorism is a critical component of best practice in special education, as well as from the efforts of state and local agencies to assure that children receive state-of-the-art services. We believe that the disappointing results of behavioral instructional practices, and research evidence supporting innovative practices such as constructivism, necessitate a reconceptualization of the IEP process.

We have proposed a series of guidelines that can be used to modify IEP forms. These guidelines reflect three essential elements of the constructivist model. They encourage the use of educational practices that are derived from constructivist theories of child development; they promote the development of individually appropriate developmental goals and objectives that view children's current developmental behaviors as the foundation for higher-level accomplishments; and they foster instructional methods that are designed to promote and use children's intrinsic motivation. Modification of IEP forms consistent with these guidelines will be instrumental in fostering the implementation of innovative practices such as constructivist models of instruction. Such modifications will foster the inclusion of children with disabilities in regular education settings by integrating the instructional goals and objectives for the children into the regular curriculum.

REFERENCES

Bagnato, S., Neisworth, J., & Munson, S. M. (1989). *Linking developmental assessment and early intervention: Curriculum-based prescriptions (2nd ed.).* Rockville, MD: Aspen.

Bailey, D., & McWilliam, R. (1990). Normalizing early intervention. *Topics in Early Childhood Special Education, 10*(2), 33–47.

Beeghly, M., Weiss-Perry, B., & Cicchetti, D. (1990). Beyond sensorimotor functioning: Early communicative and play development of children with Down syndrome. In D. Cicchetti & M. Beeghly (Eds.), *Children with Down syndrome: A developmental perspective* (pp. 329–368). New York: Cambridge University Press.

Bradley, R. (1989). HOME measurement of maternal responsiveness. In M. H. Bornstein (Ed.), *Maternal responsiveness: Characteristics and consequences. New Directions for Child Development, 43,* 63–74.

Bredekamp, S. (1987). *Developmentally appropriate practices in early childhood programs serving children from birth through age 8* (expanded ed.). Washington, DC: National Association for the Education of Young Children.

Bressanutti, E., Mahoney, G., & Sachs, J. (1992). Predictors of young children's compliance to maternal requests. *International Journal of Cognitive Education and Mediated Learning, 2,* 198–209.

Bricker, D. D. (1989). *Early intervention for at-risk and handicapped infants, toddlers, and preschool children*. Palo Alto, CA: Vort.

Brooks-Gunn, J., & Lewis, M. (1982). Development of play behavior in handicapped and normal infants. *Topics in Early Childhood Special Education*, 2(3), 14–27.

Brooks-Gunn, J., & Lewis, M. (1984). Maternal responsivity in interactions with handicapped infants. *Child Development, 55*, 782–793.

Brophy, K., & Stone-Zukowski, D. (1984). Social needs of special needs and nonspecial needs toddlers. *Early Child Development and Care, 13*, 137–154.

Caldwell, B., & Bradley, R. (1984). *Home observation of measurement of the environment*. Little Rock: University of Arkansas Press.

Carta, J., Schwartz, I., Atwater, J., & McConnell, S. (1991). Developmentally appropriate practice: Appraising its usefulness for young children with disabilities. *Topics in Early Childhood Special Education, 11*(1), 1–20.

Casto, G., & Mastropieri, M. (1986). The efficacy of early intervention programs: A meta-analysis. *Exceptional Children, 52*, 417–424.

Dedrick, C., Mahoney, G., & Dedrick, R. *Effects of maternal directiveness on the play and social interactions of young developmentally delayed children*. Manuscript submitted for publication.

Dunst, C. J. (1986). Overview of the efficacy of early intervention programs. In L. Bickman & D. L. Weatherfield (Eds.), *Evaluating early intervention programs for severely handicapped children and their families*. Austin, TX: PRO-ED.

Farran, D. C. (1990). Effects of intervention with disadvantaged and disabled children: A decade review. In S. J. Meisels & J. P. Shonkoff (Eds.), *Handbook on early intervention* (pp. 501–539). Cambridge: Cambridge University Press.

Gowen, J., Goldman, B., Johnson-Martin, N., & Hussey, B. (1989). Object play and exploration of handicapped and nonhandicapped infants. *Journal of Applied Developmental Psychology, 10*, 53–72.

Greenberg, M., Calderon, R., & Kusche, C. (1984). Early intervention using simultaneous communication with deaf infants. *Child Development, 55*, 607–616.

Guralnick, M. J., & Bennett, F. C. (Eds.). (1987). *The effectiveness of early intervention for at-risk and handicapped children*. New York: Academic Press.

Hill, P., & McCune-Nicholich, L. (1981). Pretend play and patterns of cognition in Down syndrome children. *Child Development, 52*, 611–617.

Jennings, K., Connors, R., & Stegman, C. (1988). Does a physical handicap alter the development of mastery motivation during the preschool years? *American Academy of Child and Adolescent Psychiatry, 27*(3), 312–317.

Kaiser, A., Yoder, P., & Keets, A. (1992). Evaluating milieu teaching. In S. F. Warren & J. Reichle (Eds.), *Causes and effects in communication and language intervention* (pp. 9–47). Baltimore: Paul H. Brookes.

Lerner, J., Mardell-Czudnowski, C., & Goldenberg, D. (1981). *Special education for the early childhood years*. Englewood Cliffs, NJ: Prentice Hall.

Li, A. (1985). Toward more elaborate pretend play. *Mental Retardation, 23*(3), 131–136.

Macdonald, J. D. (1989). *Becoming partners with children: From play to conversation.* San Antonio, TX: Special Press.

Mahoney, G. J. (1988). Enhancing children's developmental motivation. In K. Marfo (Ed.), *Parent-child interactions and developmental disabilities* (pp. 203–259). Westport, CT: Praeger.

Mahoney, G. J. (1989a). Maternal communication style with mentally retarded children. *American Journal of Mental Retardation, 93,* 352–359.

Mahoney, G. J. (1989b). Communication patterns between mothers and developmentally delayed infants. *First Language, 8,* 157–172.

Mahoney, G. J., Finger, I., & Powell, A. (1985). The relationship between maternal behavioral style to the developmental status of mentally retarded infants. *American Journal of Mental Deficiency, 90,* 296–302.

Mahoney, G. J., & O'Sullivan, P. (1989). A national study of the practices of early intervention service providers. *Pediatric Research and Training Center Monograph, 10.* Farmington: University of Connecticut.

Mahoney, G. J., & Powell, A. (1988). Modifying parent-child interaction: Enhancing the development of handicapped children. *Journal of Special Education, 22,* 82–96.

Mahoney, G. J., Robinson, C., & Powell, A. (1992). Focusing on parent-child interaction: The bridge to developmentally appropriate practices. *Topics in Early Childhood Special Education, 12*(1), 105–120.

Margolis, H., & Truesdale, L. A. (1987). Do special educators use IEPs to guide instruction? *The Urban Review, 19,* 151–159.

McConnell, A., & Hardman, M. (1988). A synthesis of 'best practice' guidelines for early intervention services. *Journal of Early Intervention, 12,* 328–341.

Motti, F., Cicchetti, D., & Stroufe, L. (1983). From infant affect expression to symbolic play: The coherence of development in Down syndrome children. *Child Development, 54,* 1168–1175.

Norris, J. A. (1991). Providing developmentally appropriate intervention to infants and young children with handicaps. *Topics in Early Childhood Special Education, 11*(1), 21–35.

Odom, S., & McEvoy, M. A. (1990). Mainstreaming at the preschool level: Potential barriers and tasks for the field. *Topics in Early Childhood Special Education, 10*(2), 48–61.

Parsons, S. (1986). Function of play in low vision children (part 2): Emerging patterns of behavior. *Journal of Visual Impairment and Blindness, 80*(6), 777–784.

Piaget, J. (1963). *The origins of intelligence in children.* New York: Norton.

Power, T., & Radcliff, J. (1989). The relationship of play behavior to cognitive ability in developmentally disabled preschoolers. *Journal of Autism and Developmental Disorders, 19*(1), 97–107.

Snell, M. (Ed.). (1993). *Instruction of students with severe disabilities.* New York: Merrill.

Strain, P. S., McConnell, S. R., Carta, J. J., Fowler, S. A., Neisworth, J. T., & Wolery, M. (1992). Behaviorism in early intervention. *Topics in Early Childhood Special Education, 12*(1), 121–141.

Turner, I., & Small, J. (1985). Similarities and differences in behavior between mentally handicapped and normal preschool children during play. *Child: Care, Health and Development, 11*, 391–401.

Weisz, J., & Zigler, E. (1979). Cognitive development in retarded and nonretarded persons: Piagetian tests of the similar sequence hypothesis. *Psychological Bulletin, 86*, 831–851.

Wolery, M., Strain, P., & Bailey, D. (1992). Reaching potentials of children with special needs. In S. Bredekamp & T. Rosegrant (Eds.), *Reaching potentials: Appropriate curriculum and assessment for young children* (pp. 92–111). Washington, DC: National Association for the Education of Young Children.

Wolock, E. (1990). *The relationship of teacher interactive style to the engagement of developmentally delayed preschoolers.* Unpublished doctoral dissertation, University of Michigan, Ann Arbor.

CHAPTER 7

Transitions to and from Preschool in Early Childhood Special Education

Susan A. Fowler and
Michaelene M. Ostrosky

Each year thousands of young children with developmental delays turn 3 and with their families make the transition from early intervention programs to preschool services. Two years later, these same children will make the transition from preschool to kindergarten. A limited number of choices or an overwhelming number of options may be available to their families at each transition point. Whether the choices appear simple or complex, they include a number of significant changes that these families and their children will experience.

First, transitions reflect change in *who* receives services, *what* services are received, *where* services are received, *how* they are delivered, and *by whom* they are delivered. Changes in services may coincide with changes in eligibility requirements, thus affecting *who* receives services (Harbin, Gallagher, & Terry, 1991). The auspices, structure, and philosophy of services may be different, thus affecting how and where services are delivered (Caldwell, 1991). Likewise, the content of services may change, moving from family-directed approaches, which include support and training for the family, to more child-directed approaches, which focus on the child as the primary recipient of services (Hains, Rosenkoetter, & Fowler, 1991; Lazzari & Kilgo, 1989). Finally, who delivers the services may vary. Such shifts may be across disciplines (e.g., speech therapist, infant specialist) or across certifications (early childhood, elementary education, special education), often accompanied by shifts in pedagogy and philosophy (Peterson, 1986; Spodek, 1991).

Second, transitions between programs reflect change often based on administrative convenience, rather than child or family readiness. Children with developmental delays or disabilities move from early intervention services on or near their third birthday because the funding for such services is restricted by age. Likewise, children typically enter kindergarten in the fall following their fifth birthday. Again, funding for preschool special education services is restricted to ages 3 through 5. The pressure of new and younger children identified as in need of services also serves as a force to move older children to their next age-based placement (Thurlow, Ysseldyke, & Weiss, 1988). The potential number of changes creates the opportunity for uncertainty, confusion, and anxiety for the family and the child. At the same time, the changes and resulting diversity of options available can allow for considerable choice and flexibility in how the child's next program is designed. Planning for change, while maintaining continuity and quality of services, becomes the critical element of transition preparation.

This chapter will address the major concerns surrounding these two transition points in the lives and services for young children and their families. It will describe the impetus for transition planning within the field of early intervention and the issues it raises for families, service providers, program administrators, and policymakers. Barriers to transition will be described as well as strategies for obviating such barriers.

THE CURRENT IMPETUS

The passage of P.L. 99-457 in 1986 created two programs for young children: the Early Intervention Program for Infants and Toddlers with Disabilities and Their Families (Part H), which serves children from birth to age 3; and the Preschool Incentives Grant Program (Section 619, Part B), which serves children 3 through 5. States were provided five years in which to implement special education preschool services for all eligible children. Although many communities had provided preschool services for children with disabilities, the provision of such services was not required prior to this legislation. In fact, only 22 states had legislation guaranteeing preschool services for children with disabilities (Thiele & Hamilton, 1991; Trohanis, 1989). By the October 1991 deadline, all states had passed legislation mandating these services. As a result, the number of children in preschool increased from an estimated 265,814 in 1986 to more than 399,000 in 1991 (Office of Special Education Programs [OSEP], 1992). Many new programs were developed at the community level, and schools began experimenting with a variety of ways in which to deliver services, both through new programs and through existing community preschool and child care programs (NEC*TAS, 1992).

During this same time, states began planning and implementing early intervention services for infants and toddlers. As with preschool special education services, many communities were already providing early intervention services, but such services were legislated in only five states and the range and extent of services varied considerably (Thiele & Hamilton, 1991). By 1991, an estimated 200,000 children were receiving some early intervention services (OSEP, 1992). At this time, states are continuing to refine and implement services; states are expected to have a mandate in place for such services by 1993 if they are to continue to receive federal funds. As of 1992, only six states had mandated services for infants and toddlers.

The intention of the two federal programs is to provide uninterrupted services to children with developmental delays or disabilities and their families from birth, or the point at which their delay or disability is identified, through age 5, at which time the child enters the existing system of services provided through the public schools. Critical juncture points occur as children move from early intervention to preschool and from preschool to kindergarten. The degree to which transitions at these junctures are smooth or disrupted depends on a number of variables. These can best be summarized by discussing who administers the programs, who is eligible to receive services, what services are received, where services are received, how services are delivered and by whom.

FACTORS INFLUENCING TRANSITION

Who Administers the Programs

At the federal level, the Early Intervention Program and the Preschool Incentives Grant Program are administered through the Office of Special Education Programs (OSEP) in the U. S. Department of Education. At the state level, however, these programs may reside in different agencies: The Preschool Incentives Grant Program is located in the state department of education, but the Early Intervention Program may reside in another department (e.g., health or social services) based on the governor's designation of which agency is most appropriate to manage the program. The differences in program jurisdiction may translate to differences in program philosophies and regulations, which can impact local service delivery and potentially impede coordination between programs and movement of children and families from one program to another.

At the local level, early intervention services may be delivered by a range of different private or public agencies, and may be based within a health, social service, or education framework. In most instances, preschool services at the community level are administered or delivered through the local public schools, although in some communities public schools may choose to contract with another agency for the delivery of services.

The flexibility in program jurisdiction allows communities to implement services based on their resources, geographic needs, past history of service delivery, and vision of best practice. It allows for a range and diversity of services, which can be comforting to families and agencies desiring a range of choices for a child's next placement. Yet such a range can be challenging to coordinate. The variety of possible jurisdictions and the involvement of different agencies in service delivery necessitate interagency coordination at the community and state level (Fowler, Hains, & Rosenkoetter, 1990; Peterson, 1991).

Who Receives Services

Children who are eligible for services in one program may or may not be eligible for services in the next program. The extent to which the family is viewed as a recipient of services may shift as well. Child eligibility will change if a child's development progresses to the extent that the child no longer needs (or qualifies for) special services. For some 3-year-olds, early intervention is sufficient for facilitating the young child's development to expected age norms. These children thus face a transition from special services to other community services (e.g., preschool or child care) or to no further services. Likewise, for some 5-year-olds, the preschool experience may result in development to within normal ranges and in kindergarten they no longer need support services, other than the monitoring of their continued development.

In contrast, some children may demonstrate the same needs and delays, but no longer qualify for special services. This happens when the criterion for the next program is more restrictive, thus reducing the number of children who are eligible. This is most likely to happen in states in which the eligibility definition for developmental delay for early intervention is different from the definition used for preschool services. This most often occurs when the state's Early Intervention

Program includes the category of children identified as at-risk for developmental delay; this category is not included for preschool services (Fowler et al., 1990).

In most states, the developmental-delay category used for preschoolers is not allowable once the child turns 6 or enters kindergarten. It is important for parents to understand that the term *developmental delay* is a temporary label that may either no longer apply or may be replaced by a more specific disability label (e.g., learning disability, speech and language impaired) at age 6, in order for their child to continue to be eligible for special and related services (McLean, Smith, McCormick, Schakel, & McEvoy, 1991). The extent to which the introduction of a categorical label may depress the number of children who receive services is not known yet. So far studies have shown only that many recent graduates of early childhood special education programs enter regular kindergarten programs without the need for special services (Edgar, Heggelund, & Fischer, 1988; Edgar, McNulty, Gaetz, & Maddox, 1984; Hume & Dannenbring, 1989). However, it is unclear if this reduction in numbers is due to the effectiveness of preschool programs or to changes in eligibility criterion. The transition to kindergarten for those children who enter with a categorical label may be difficult for families who hoped that their child's development would "catch up" by school age. Accepting the label and its implications may cause additional stress for families (Fowler & Titus, in press).

Families also may be recipients of services in one program and find their roles significantly changed in the next program. The philosophy associated with the Early Intervention Program is one in which services are to be delivered within the context of the family (McGonigel, Kaufmann, & Johnson, 1991). Thus, families are encouraged to identify resources and concerns that can be considered in the design of the Individualized Family Services Plan (IFSP), which specifies activities and outcomes for individual families and their child. It is not uncommon for families to develop close relationships with their service coordinator or a child's service provider over the course of the one to three years in which their child is enrolled in the Early Intervention Program. Breaking these ties and adapting to a change in program philosophy in the next program (Hains et al., 1991; Hanline, 1988; Hanline & Knowlton, 1988) can be difficult for parents, children, and staff.

The philosophy and services provided in the preschool program and later in kindergarten may also be quite supportive of families and provide high levels of contact and support. But many families experience a reduction in contact with service providers as their child advances to the next program. The reduction may coincide with a change in service delivery (from home-based to center-based) or change in transportation method (from parent-provided to school van or bus). It may also coincide with a change in philosophy. The staff may hold different views regarding parents' roles, ranging from parents as detached from the child's program, to parents as learners, to parents as resources or partners (Powell, 1991). Some families are ready for reduced contact, regardless of the reason for it, and others are not (Johnson, Chandler, Kerns, & Fowler, 1986). The change in family roles, support, and contact is one that may require preparation and planning so that it is not an added stress or source of conflict for families or staff.

What, Where, and How Services Are Delivered

The types of services and their location and form may change when children move from early intervention to preschool and from preschool to kindergarten. Some of these changes are superficial and some may be substantive. Ideally, a change in type of services, frequency of services, and method of delivery should be in response to the identified needs of the child. A plan is developed for each child annually by a team of specialists, which specifies the child's strengths and needs and identifies goals and objectives for meeting the child's developmental needs. The plan is intended to supersede and, in fact, drive the program placement decisions. It identifies what, where, and how often services are delivered, as well as by whom. The Individualized Family Services Plan (cf. McGonigel et al., 1991), used during early intervention, is replaced in most states and communities as children move to preschool and later to kindergarten by the Individual Education Program (IEP) (cf. Strickland & Turnbull, 1990). There is, however, a growing movement to extend the IFSP through the preschool years in order to maintain a focus on family services and to increase philosophical and programmatic continuity between early intervention and preschool programs.

When a new plan is developed, concomitant with the change in services, staff from both the sending and receiving programs should be involved, along with the parents, in order to ensure continuity in the types of services the child receives, as well as in the quality and frequency of services. Parent participation is a guaranteed right and parents have the opportunity to discuss, recommend, and ultimately approve the plan. However, the extent to which parents are active in the development varies (Brinkerhoff & Vincent, 1986; Summers et al., 1990).

The location in which services are delivered also may change. Two principles have been developed to guide families and programs in determining the location of service delivery. The principle used in early intervention is referred to as the child's "natural environment"; in preschool and school programs, it is referred to as the "Least Restrictive Environment" (LRE). The natural environment is defined as "settings that are natural or normal for the child's age peers who have no disability" (Federal Register, 1992, p. 18986). The emphasis is on bringing services to the child and family in the home or community setting.

The principle of Least Restrictive Environment states that "handicapped children must be educated to the maximum extent appropriate with other nonhandicapped children" (OSEP, 1988). The Code of Federal Regulations (300.052) provide three options for providing LRE through preschool programs:

1) linking, even part time, the program for preschool handicapped children, to other preschool programs operated by public agencies (such as Head Start);
2) placing handicapped children in private school programs for non-handicapped preschool children or private preschool programs that integrate handicapped and nonhandicapped children; and
3) locating classes for handicapped preschool children in regular elementary schools. (Federal Register, Jan. 13, 1989)

The transition from early intervention services to preschool services may include a shift in agencies, service delivery modes, service providers, and service plans. The greater the number of changes, the greater the number of potential challenges to coordinating the transition and ensuring continuity of services. For example, some children will move from home-based early intervention visits, which occur weekly, to attendance at a center-based preschool, five half-days a week. The shift in programs may include a change in agencies (perhaps from health to public schools), a change in service providers, a change in location (perhaps from home to a neighborhood school) and concomitantly the addition of transportation (a public van or school bus) and the development of a new plan. Another child, whose early intervention services are provided through consultative visits to the child-care center, may continue to receive similar consultative and support services through the preschool program and experience little or no visible change in the type or content of services, location, or provider.

The transition from preschool to kindergarten likewise can vary along a number of dimensions. Typically these include size of program, consistency of peers across programs, and goals of program. The differences also may include pedagogical styles (role of teacher, type of instruction).

Who Delivers the Services

Differences are likely to occur in who delivers services as children make the transition across programs. These shifts often are related to shifts in program philosophy and staff certification. Programs may deliver special education and related services via a specialist (e.g., speech therapist) who works directly with the child within the program or via a consultation model, in which the specialist consults with the staff and provides assistance and support to the staff in delivering the services.

Certification or licensing of staff also is likely to change across programs. Most states have not yet developed clear licensing or certification standards for early intervention providers, although a multidisciplinary approach to the delivery of services is recommended (cf. McCollum & Bailey, 1991). Preschool programs may be staffed by teachers with early childhood, special education, or a combined early childhood/special education certification (Hurley, 1991). Due to the critical shortage of certified teachers at this age range, many staff may hold provisional certification (OSEP, 1992). Kindergarten programs may be staffed by teachers with early childhood or elementary teaching degrees. Differences in certification usually correspond with differences in training, philosophy, and even pedagogical styles (Spodek, 1991). Coordination and communication across sending and receiving staffs are important to ensure that these differences are not barriers that prevent staff from meeting the child's special needs.

Given the potential differences in service delivery within and across early intervention, preschool, and kindergarten programs, a systems approach to planning is needed to coordinate the transition of children through the service systems. Strategies for coordination at the community and agency level, at the staff and program level, and by the family to facilitate the transition process are described in the following section.

TRANSITION PLANNING AT THE COMMUNITY LEVEL

Developing Local Interagency Agreements and Time Lines

A common framework is needed in most communities to ensure that programs and families have a mechanism for planning and communicating about program changes that must occur. The framework may take the form of a written interagency agreement or a memorandum of understanding between the sending and receiving programs and agencies. The purpose of such written documents is to clarify the steps, time lines, and agency roles associated with the passage of the child and family from one provider to another. Typically such agreements specify responsibility for

1. Obtaining family consent for release of information
2. Conducting additional evaluations
3. Determining eligibility
4. Developing the IEP or IFSP
5. Transmitting records
6. Identifying program options and planning visits
7. Setting dates for beginning new services and ending current services (Fowler, Schwartz, & Atwater, 1991)

Such agreements may be developed by early intervention programs and local public schools that provide preschool services (Fowler et al., 1990); they may also be developed between Head Start agencies or community preschools and public schools for the transition to kindergarten (U.S. Dept. of Health and Human Services, 1988).

Two factors often impede the development of such agreements: time and finances. Planning and release time for staff to meet with families and to attend child staffings and to visit those programs to which they send children or from which they receive children is often cited as inadequate or nonexistent. Financial barriers often include lack of funding for substitutes so that staff have release time for program visits and staffings associated with transition; lack of in-service for staff on the issues related to transition (e.g., teaming, joint meetings, and discussions between sending and receiving programs, family support); and assuming fiscal responsibility for child evaluations. Agreements are useful in identifying these potential impediments and clarifying roles and responsibilities. Such agreements likewise are needed at the state level to ensure that state regulations and policies support such local coordination and planning (McNulty, 1989; Peterson, 1991). As of 1992, 84 percent of the states had written interagency agreements between Head Start and the state education agency for coordinating preschool services and activities, such as transition planning (NEC*TAS, 1992).

Many programs are developing time lines that guide sending and receiving staff and families through the planning process of choosing the next services and transitioning the child. Such time lines typically delineate the specific actions associated with transition planning (e.g., meetings, evaluations), a calendar date for their completion, and the individuals involved or responsible for specific activities. Usually these individuals include the families and representatives of sending and receiving staff (Conn-Powers, Ross-Allen, & Holburn, 1990; Fowler et al., 1991; Thurlow, Lehr, & Ysseldyke, 1987). Figure 7.1 presents a sample transition plan for a child moving from preschool to kindergarten.

Assessing Outcomes

Evaluation of transitions should reflect multiple perspectives: family, child, and sending and receiving agencies. The majority of evalua-

Figure 7.1. Simple Transition Plan for Child Leaving Preschool and Entering Kindergarten

Child: Robbie Burke, aged 4 years, 7 months

By Oct. 15:   Preschool staff invite family to planning meeting to discuss transition process at fall conference.

By Jan. 15   Preschool staff and family develop a transition plan and timeline at midyear conference.

By Jan. 15   Family reviews Robbie's records and, if needed, provides consent for release of information to the next school program during midyear conference.

By Feb. 15   Preschool and appropriate staff from elementary school identify necessary evaluations to determine eligibility for continued special education and related services and conduct evaluations.

By March 15   Staff from the preschool and elementary school meet with family to discuss and identify program options at spring conference.

By May 1   Family and staff visit several placement options.

By May 15   Family and staffs from preschool and elementary school programs meet to determine placement.

By June 1   Family and Robbie visit the new program and meet with the teacher and related service staff. Talk about communication schedules in the fall.

By June 1   Preschool program transfers records to new program and preschool coordinator meets with Robbie's new teacher to exchange information.

Sept. 5   Robbie starts kindergarten; parents receive daily notes for first week of school re: adjustment.

By Sept. 20   Family meets with staff to assess Robbie's adjustment and establish more relaxed schedule of communication, if all is progressing well.

tions reported in the literature reflect satisfaction surveys of professionals and parents. While these are important as a measure of social validity, they should not be the only measures (cf. Schwartz & Baer, 1991). The process of planning should be evaluated to determine the extent to which the planning process facilitated the transition and the match between planned outcomes and actual outcomes was achieved. Informative evaluation cannot be as simple as asking whether the new placement worked or whether the child was ready. Rather, it should ask what worked and how it worked. That is, what accommodations were made by the child, the sending and receiving staffs, and the family during the transition and within the new program? Were these accommodations acceptable and sustainable? To be comprehensive, evaluations should be conducted at a systems level to reflect the roles and responsibilities of all participants. Annual evaluations then can serve as the safety check on how successfully programs are meeting their transition goals and child and family needs and accommodating to one another's differences in program philosophy, structure, and auspices. Additionally, changes can be made based on evaluations to assist with future transitions.

TRANSITION PLANNING AT THE PROGRAM LEVEL

The transition of a young child from one program to another is a process, not a single event (Stephens, 1991). It involves planning, preparation, and perhaps training before the change in programs and it requires support, accommodations, and perhaps training after the change in programs. Planning for transition should include identifying the social, behavioral, and cognitive demands in the next program (Epps, 1992), as well as understanding some of the ways in which that setting differs from the child's current service setting. The child's feelings (sense of competence, self-esteem) and disposition (persistence at task, curiosity, characteristic way of responding) may also influence the child's ability to accommodate to program changes (Katz, 1991). Identification of future expectations and comparisons of these with current expectations can allow families and professionals to determine how well matched the two programs are and what preparations and accommodations may be needed to bridge disparities between programs. Determining the child's vulnerability to stress and ability to manage change may also assist in determining what and how much preparation and support the child, family, and new program may need initially (Kagan, 1991). The competency and skill expectations in the next program should not be regarded as readiness criteria, which the child must master before transition or face exclusion from a placement in the next age-appropriate setting. Rather, they represent preparatory goals, which can be identified in the child's individualized education or family service plan, as competencies and skills that will help the child experience success in the next placement; likewise, they can be identified as expectations that require adjustment in the next program in order for the child to experience success.

Preparation and support for transition should be distributed across sending and receiving programs, the child, and the family so that no one bears all the stress of change. To ensure that planning, training, and subsequent accommodations are shared, professionals and parents should consider the following questions (Caldwell, 1991; Kagan, 1991):

- What will be different for the child and family?
- What skills, knowledge, dispositions, and feelings does the child already have that will be useful in the new program?
- What do the child and family need to learn before a transition occurs?
- How can the sending program best prepare the child and family?
- How can the receiving program modify its demands to meet the family and child's special needs and build on their strengths?

Identifying Differences and Similarities Between Programs

Diverse programs exist at the early childhood level, ranging from private nonprofit, private for-profit, church-sponsored, to various publicly funded ones. The programs rarely exist as a system and rarely adhere to a unifying philosophy. To coordinate transitions across diverse programs, communication between programs is critical. Observations of sending and receiving programs and use of structured interviews and checklists with program staff are ways to identify similarities and differences that may impact a child and family's transition (cf. Fowler et al., 1991, for a review). The following characteristics are useful to consider: program goals; classroom environment and organization; teachers' style, philosophy, attitudes, and expectations; and family involvement.

Ecological differences may exist across programs. For example, the number of staff available, the physical arrangement of classrooms, and the daily schedule may vary. Some of these changes are predictable; some are not. Changes in adult-child ratio are usually predictable: The number of children enrolled in programs tends to increase as children grow older. Guidelines established by the National Association for the Education of Young Children (1984) for its program accreditation standards limit adult-child ratios for 2-year-olds to 1 : 6 and for 3- and 4-year-olds to 1 : 10. For special education programs the ratio tends to be even higher (e.g., 2 : 10 or 3 : 10). Although a ratio of 1 : 10 is recommended for 5-year-olds, kindergartens nationally average a 1 : 23 teacher-child ratio (Boyer, 1991). Such large classes affect the choice and schedule of activities and physical arrangement of programs, as well as expectations and roles of teachers and students. In large classes with few adults to supervise, children are more likely to be scheduled to move as a group, rather than individually; they may have restricted opportunities to exercise choice of activities; and they are expected to show greater compliance (or independence). The demands for social competency and language also can be very different (Ladd, 1990; Rice, Wilcox, & Hadley, 1991) as teacher-child ratios change. Activities are likely to be longer (Sainato & Lyon, 1989) with more time spent in class business (e.g., job assignments, attendance checks) and transition between activities (Carta, Atwater, Schwartz, & Miller, 1990).

Larger classes often necessitate a teaching style that relies on group versus individualized instruction, and is predominantly teacher-directed. Typical professional roles within early childhood classrooms include following the lead of children, encouraging children to initiate interactions and involvement in activities, and adult participation with children in activities. Observations in kindergartens and primary classes, on the other hand, often show professionals assuming roles such as directing children's behavior, encouraging compliance, talking to children, and initiating and organizing activities for children (cf. Carden-Smith & Fowler, 1983; Carta et al., 1990).

Expectations likewise tend to differ. Hains, Fowler, Schwartz, Kottwitz, and Rosenkoetter (1989) investigated the kindergarten entry expectations of 21 preschool and 28 kindergarten teachers in a midwestern community. The kindergarten teachers emphasized classroom skills that were conduct-related and that promoted independence such as following directions, following classroom routines, and participating in group activities. In contrast, the preschool teachers emphasized social interaction and communication skills. The survey used in this study could provide a framework for preschool and kindergarten teachers to discuss and perhaps even adjust their expectations and goals for young children and increase their awareness of programs and expectations within their communities.

Figure 7.2 contains a list of several questions that can be used to identify differences between early childhood programs that could affect

Figure 7.2. A Sample of Factors to Consider When Transitioning into and out of Early Childhood Programs

Classroom composition.

Who makes up the child's peer group? Are any peers familiar?

Are peers of the same age or mixed ages?

Are there other peers with developmental delays or disabilities?

What is the teacher-child ratio?

Are staff assigned to assist children with developmental delays?

How many teachers, aides and volunteers are typically in the room at a given time?

How many adults do children interact with each day?

Schedule and environment.

What does the physical arrangement of the classroom look like?

Are activity areas clearly demarcated?

Where is the bathroom located?

Are support services, such as speech therapy, provided in or outside of the classroom?

How many hours of programming do children receive?

What is the daily schedule?

What are the classroom rules?

What behavior management procedures are used?

Relations between home and program.

Who is the first point of contact for the family?

How do staff communicate with family (e.g., visits, notes, phone calls)?

How often does communication occur typically?

Are family welcome to spend time in the program, assisting or visiting?

What family support activities are provided? When and how often?

Program quality and staff experience and development.

Is the program accredited or licensed?

What is the professional preparation level of staff?

What support and related services staff are associated with the program?

What experience does the staff have with children with disabilities or delays?

What in- service preparation will staff receive during the year?

What are staff expectations for successful child entry and exit from the program?

How comfortable and likely are staff to consult with sending and receiving programs about expectations

and preparations for entering and exiting children?

155

transition. It is unlikely that there will be a universal checklist of transition skills because the requirements of individual classrooms vary too much and the needs of individual children and their families must be considered.

Preparing for the New Program

Elements in the role of the sending program (e.g., preschool) are identifying skills the child is expected to display in the next environment (e.g., kindergarten), focusing on the development of those skills that will be necessary for the child to experience success, and demonstrating that the child does in fact possess those necessary skills before the transition (e.g., Rule, Fiechtl, & Innocenti, 1990; Salisbury & Vincent, 1990; Vincent, Salisbury, Walter, Brown, Gruenewald, & Powers, 1980). But these comprise only one role, as the sending program should not be reformatted to become exactly like the receiving program. That is, the goal of transition planning and preparation should be to integrate transition goals with other developmentally appropriate curriculum goals and activities, routine to the current program. As Chandler (1992) notes, "Transition preparation may be more likely to succeed if preparation activities become an integral part of the core curriculum and are accomplished in the context of typical school activities and routines" (p. 262).

Another way to conceptualize preparation for the next program is to consider the level of support that children need to demonstrate knowledge and skills. Instruction and support can be viewed along a continuum from acquiring new knowledge and skills to expanding the child's use and independent application of current knowledge and skills. Katz (1991) refers to this instruction as "having vertical and horizontal relevance" (p. 63). Instruction should progress horizontally to ensure that children can demonstrate new knowledge and perform new skills in a variety of day-to-day activities, in a variety of settings (classroom, playground, home), with a variety of people (teachers, classmates, family, friends). This suggests that families and professionals should structure activities not only for training in new skills and knowledge (e.g., vertical teaching) but also for practicing recently acquired skills and knowledge to the point at which the child gains confidence and affirmation for mastery and ability to apply these skills and knowledge to a wide variety of situations (horizontal teaching). The amount of support and feedback needed to move children horizontally through maintenance or generalization of skills may vary across time. For instance, teachers may need to provide structure, guidance, and frequent feedback as a child acquires a new skill. Once the skill is acquired, teachers can reduce support while the child practices the skill to the point of mastery. Mastered skills typically need little or no support, but may require temporary teacher facilitation to generalize to a new context. The inclusion of horizontal training and support for skills is critical if children are not only to have certain skills, but to use them consistently in the next environment. There is a danger in focusing attention only on what children "need to know" and ignoring the need for preparation and training to "use what they know" across a wide variety of situations.

Making Accommodations Within the Receiving Program

The ability of the receiving program to adapt to the child's special needs also is a critical ingredient to the success of a child's transition. The staff may need to adapt their expectations regarding the child's entry skills and knowledge and provide support to the child for learning and maintaining new competencies. Other adults may be needed to provide initial structure, support, or consultation. Schedules and room arrangements may have to be altered to optimize the child's ability to participate. Many of these accommodations should be identified prior to placement so that the support necessary to ensure that the child's educational and social needs are met can be provided. Coordination between the sending and receiving agencies and participation by both programs in the development of the child's individualized education or family service plan can facilitate the receiving program's ability to respond to the child's unique needs.

A caution regarding continuity between programs was raised by Caldwell (1991) in her discussion of a national study of early childhood programs in public schools, conducted by Mitchell, Seligson, and Marx (1989). Mitchell et al. found that some teachers and administrators attempted to improve transitions between early childhood and kindergarten programs by extending elementary school practices to the preschool programs. Although there was greater continuity in the goals, philosophies, and curriculum, these were not appropriate to the developmental level of most children. These researchers also found poor continuity between programs when the preschool programs were developmentally appropriate and the kindergartens resembled first grades. As Caldwell, in her review of their research, noted: "This pattern should be viewed with alarm. Both prekindergarten and kindergarten should focus on an upward extension of earlier development rather than a downward extension of schooling" (p. 83). This is a case in which radical accommodations were needed in the receiving programs, not in the sending programs.

TRANSITION PLANNING AT THE FAMILY LEVEL

The role of families as the primary caregivers to the child has often been disregarded in the context of transition planning. Yet, "parents are the children's first and most important teachers, making continuity between family and institutions a critical need" (Kagan, 1991). Families also experience the stress of change at transition times. Their concerns may range from questions about their child's ability to manage change, to worries about whether the new service providers will meet their child's needs. They may also be concerned about their relationship with the new service provider and whether they like and trust each other. A number of recent studies have assessed concerns expressed by families of young children following transitions into and out of preschool. A common finding by researchers is that families report that they experience some stress over the change in services, they prefer to be involved, and they want information about the process (Hamblin-Wilson & Thurman, 1990; Johnson et al., 1986).

Identifying Expectations, Goals, and Roles

Based on a study of family concerns about the transition of preschool children to kindergarten (Johnson et al., 1986), Fowler, et al. (1990) developed two written transition planners to assist 30 families in planning their children's change of placement by identifying expectations, goals, and roles. Parents used the first planner in the fall of their child's final year in preschool to identify skills that they wanted their child to acquire prior to preschool graduation, information that they needed about school options, and the extent to which they preferred to be involved in further transition planning. The planner provided an opportunity for parents and staff to discuss expectations regarding the child's development in the coming year, to clarify what readiness skills might be helpful for the child to acquire, and to address the family's concern over their future separation from the program. Many families selected several readiness skills to work on with their child at home (e.g., listening to stories, independently caring for some personal belongings, learning their street address and phone number). Nearly every family stated that they wanted an active role in planning their child's transition and identifying the next program. Parents indicated a willingness to attend planning meetings and to contact their neighborhood school to gather information about placement options. Goals that were identified as priorities were added to the child's Individual Education Program for the year. In the spring, parents used the second transition planner to identify priorities for the new program (e.g., location, integration of classrooms, half-day versus full-day schedule). They used the list developed from the planner as a guide when they visited programs and attended the placement decision meeting.

Similar recommendations for family participation in transition planning have been made by Diamond, Spiegel-McGill, and Hanrahan (1988) and Conn-Powers et al. (1990) for families whose children are entering kindergarten and by Hains et al. (1991) for families whose children are moving from early intervention to preschool services. In fact, federal law requires that the Individualized Family Services Plan used by early intervention programs contain steps to ensure a smooth transition to preschool services. The requirements include "a description of how the families will be included in the transitional plans" (Federal Register, 1992, p. 18998).

Departing and Entering

Learning to accommodate to change, including separation, is a critical competency for children. To ensure that early transitions between programs are positive experiences, children also should be prepared. Ziegler (1985) suggests that families and staff discuss with children concepts of time, growth, and change as natural and normal events before the transition. Examples of activities include using photographs of the children to show how they have grown over time; discussing how children's new shoes are bigger than their old shoes; and role-playing ways to make friends, enter new situations, and ask for help. Ziegler also recommends that children be encouraged to express worries, so that they can be addressed through discussion or a visit to the new school, where they can see their classroom, playground, bathroom, and cubby spaces for keeping their belongings. Likewise, introducing a child to a new classmate and arranging playtime together in advance of the new placement will provide the child with a familiar friend and most likely ease the child's entrance into the program.

Parental visits to the new program are frequently a component of transition plans. Parents may wish to meet with the new teacher to discuss ways in which they can follow up on their child's adjustment. Johnson et al. (1986) reported that one of the most difficult adjustments for parents of children entering kindergarten was the reduced home-school contact. In this study parents had reported eight or more contacts a month during preschool and only one or two per month in kindergarten. Some parents attributed the reduction to personal factors, such as the new teacher's not caring about them. Johnson et al. speculated that it was most likely a result of reduced opportunities for contact due to significantly larger classes and the fact that most parents were no longer transporting their children to the new program. It may also have reflected a different view regarding the role of families in the new school.

Follow-up by families on their child's adjustment to school should be encouraged. In fact, with parental permission, sending programs may wish to maintain occasional contact with the family and receiving program to support the family's transition and to answer unanticipated questions that arise. Follow-up interviews with families whose children had moved to kindergarten indicated that most families had developed an allegiance to the new program and felt comfortable about their child's adjustment within six to eight weeks of entering school (Johnson et al., 1986).

SUMMARY

Transitions represent change, for children, families, and staff. They also are inevitable, often tied to the calendar year or a child's actual birth date. In order to maintain continuity and quality in services between programs, transitions require planning. And they require a systemwide effort to ensure that the planning produces the necessary preparation, coordination, and accommodation in the sending and receiving programs. The role of the family in transitions must be acknowledged and considered, as it is the families who are the children's first and most important source of continuity.

REFERENCES

Appreciation is expressed to Ms. Jin Hee Hyun for her assistance with references.

Boyer, E. L. (1991). *Ready to learn: A mandate for the nation.* Princeton, NJ: The Carnegie Foundation for the Advancement of Learning.
Brinkerhoff, J., & Vincent, L. (1986). Increasing parental decision making at the individualized educational program meeting. *Journal of the Division for Early Childhood, 11,* 46–58.

Caldwell, B. M. (1991). Continuity in the early years: Transitions between grades and systems. In S. L. Kagan (Ed.), *The care and education of America's young children: Obstacles and opportunities* (pp. 69–90). Chicago: University of Chicago Press.

Carden-Smith, L., & Fowler, S. A. (1983). An assessment of student and teacher behavior in treatment and mainstreamed classes for preschool and kindergarten. *Analysis and Intervention in Developmental Disabilities, 3,* 35–57.

Carta, J. J., Atwater, J. B., Schwartz, I. S., & Miller, P. A. (1990). Applications of ecobehavioral analysis to the study of transitions across early educational settings. *Education and Treatment of Children, 13*(4), 298–315.

Chandler, L. K. (1992). Promoting children's social/survival skills as a strategy for transition to mainstreamed kindergarten programs. In S. L. Odom, S. R. McConnell, & M. A. McEvoy (Eds.), *Social competence of young children with disabilities: Issues and strategies for intervention* (pp. 245–267). Baltimore: Paul H. Brookes.

Conn-Powers, M. C., Ross-Allen, J., & Holburn, S. (1990). Transition of young children into the elementary education mainstream. *Topics in Early Childhood Special Education, 9*(4), 91–105.

Diamond, K. E., Spiegel-McGill, P., & Hanrahan, P. (1988). Planning for school transition: An ecological-developmental approach. *Journal for Early Intervention, 12,* 245–252.

Edgar, E., Heggelund, M., & Fischer, M. (1988). A longitudinal study of graduates of special education preschools: Educational placement after preschool. *Topics in Early Childhood Special Education, 8*(3), 61–74.

Edgar, E., McNulty, B., Gaetz, J., & Maddox, M. (1984). Educational placement of graduates of preschool programs for handicapped children. *Topics in Early Childhood Special Education, 4*(3), 19–29.

Epps, W. (1992). *The transition to kindergarten in American schools.* Final report of the National Transition Study. Washington, DC: U.S. Dept. of Education, Office of Policy and Planning.

Federal Register. (1989, January 13). Rules and Regulations, Department of Education (34 CFR Part 301). *Preschool Grants for Handicapped Children Program, 54,* 1642–1648. Washington, DC: U.S. Government Printing Office.

Federal Register. (1992, May 1). Notice of Proposed Rulemaking, Department of Education (34 CFR Part 303). *Early Intervention Program for Infants and Toddlers with Disabilities, 57,* 18986–19012. Washington, DC: U.S. Government Printing Office.

Fowler, S. A., Hains, A. H., & Rosenkoetter, S. E. (1990). The transition between early intervention services and preschool services: Administration and policy issues. *Topics in Early Childhood Special Education, 9*(4), 55–65.

Fowler, S. A., Schwartz, I., & Atwater, J. (1991). Perspectives on the transition from preschool to kindergarten for children with disabilities and their families. *Exceptional Children, 58,* 136–145.

Fowler, S. A., & Titus, P. E. (in press). Managing transitions. In P. Beckman & G. B. Boyce (Eds.), *Deciphering the system: A guide for families of young children with disabilities*. Boston: Brookline Books.

Hains, A. H., Fowler, S. A., Schwartz, I. S., Kottwitz, E., & Rosenkoetter, S. (1989). A comparison of preschool and kindergarten expectations for school readiness. *Early Childhood Research Quarterly, 4*, 75–88.

Hains, A. H., Rosenkoetter, S. E., & Fowler, S. A. (1991). Transition planning with families in early intervention programs. *Infants and Young Children, 3*, 38–47.

Hamblin-Wilson, C., & Thurman, S. K. (1990). The transition from early intervention to kindergarten: Parental satisfaction and involvement. *Journal of Early Intervention, 14*, 55–61.

Hanline, M. F. (1988). Making the transition to preschool: Identification of parent needs. *Journal of Early Intervention, 12*, 98–107.

Hanline, M. F., & Knowlton, A. (1988). A collaborative model for providing support to parents during their child's transition from infant intervention of preschool special education public school programs. *Journal of Early Intervention, 12*, 116–125.

Harbin, G. L., Gallagher, J. J., & Terry, D. V. (1991). Defining the eligible population: Policy issues and challenges. *Journal of Early Intervention, 15*, 13–20.

Hume, J., & Dannenbring, G. L. (1989). A longitudinal study of children screened and served by early childhood special education programs. *Journal of Early Intervention, 13*(2), 135–145.

Hurley, O. L. (1991). Implications of P.L. 99-457 for preparation of preschool personnel. In J. J. Gallagher, P. L. Trohanis, & R. M. Clifford (Eds.), *Policy implementation and P.L. 99-457: Planning for young children with special needs* (pp. 133–146). Baltimore: Paul H. Brookes.

Johnson, T. E., Chandler, L. K., Kerns, G. M., & Fowler, S. A. (1986). What are parents saying about family involvement in school transitions? A retrospective transition interview. *Journal of the Division for Early Childhood, 11*, 10–17.

Kagan, S. L. (1991). Moving from here to there: Rethinking continuity and transitions in early care and education. In B. Spodek & O. N. Saracho (Eds.), *Yearbook in early childhood education, Vol. 2: Issues in early childhood curriculum* (pp. 132–151). New York: Teachers College Press.

Katz, L. (1991). Pedagogical issues in early childhood education. In S. L. Kagan (Ed.), *The care and education of America's young children: Obstacles and opportunities* (pp. 50–68). Chicago: University of Chicago Press.

Ladd, G. W. (1990). Having friends, keeping friends, making friends, and being liked by peers in the classroom: Predictors of children's early school adjustment? *Child Development, 61*, 1081–1100.

Lazzari, A. M., & Kilgo, J. L. (1989). Practical methods for supporting parents in early transitions. *Teaching Exceptional Children, 22*, 40–43.

McCollum, J. A., & Bailey, D. B. (1991). Developing comprehensive personnel systems: Issues and alternatives. *Journal of Early Intervention, 15*, 57–65.

McGonigel, M. J., Kaufmann, R. K., & Johnson, B. H. (1991). A family centered process for the Individualized Family Service Plan. *Journal of Early Intervention, 15,* 46–56.

McLean, M., Smith, B. J., McCormick, K., Schakel, J., & McEvoy, M. (1991). *Developmental delay: Establishing parameters for a preschool category of exceptionality.* Position Statement, Division for Exceptional Children, Council for Exceptional Children, Reston, VA.

McNulty, B. A. (1989). Leadership and policy strategies for interagency planning: Meeting the early childhood mandate. In J. J. Gallagher, P. L Trohanis, & R. M. Clifford (Eds.), *Policy implementation and P.L. 99-457: Planning for young children with special needs* (pp. 147–168). Baltimore: Paul H. Brookes.

Mitchell, A., Seligson, M., & Marx, F. (1989). *Early childhood programs and the public schools: Between promise and practice.* Cited in B. M. Caldwell (1991), Continuity in the early years: Transitions between grades and systems. In S. L. Kagan (Ed.), *The care and education of America's young children: Obstacles and opportunities* (pp. 69–90). Chicago: University of Chicago Press.

National Association for the Education of Young Children. (1984). Accreditation Criteria and Procedures of the National Academy of Early Childhood Programs. Washington, DC: Author.

NEC*TAS — National Early Childhood Technical Assistance System. (1992, May). Section 619 Profile. Document, Frank Porter Graham Child Development Center, University of North Carolina, Chapel Hill.

Office of Special Education Programs. (1988). *Tenth Annual Report to Congress on the Implementation of the Handicapped Act.* Washington, DC: U.S. Government Printing Office.

Office of Special Education Programs. (1992). *Fourteenth Annual Report to Congress on the Implementation of the Handicapped Act.* Washington, DC: U.S. Government Printing Office.

Peterson, N. L. (1986). *Early intervention for handicapped and at-risk children: An introduction to early childhood-special education.* Denver: Love.

Peterson, N. L. (1991). Interagency collaboration under Part H: The key to comprehensive multidisciplinary, coordinated infant/toddler intervention services. *Journal of Early Intervention, 15,* 89–105.

Powell, D. R. (1991). Parents and programs: Early childhood as a pioneer in parent involvement and support. In S. L. Kagan (Ed.), *The care and education of America's young children: Obstacles and opportunities* (pp. 91–109). Chicago: University of Chicago Press.

Rice, M., Wilcox, K., & Hadley, P. A. (1991). *Promoting successful transitions into school: The role of language and social interaction skills.* Unpublished manuscript, University of Kansas, Kansas Early Childhood Research Institute.

Rule, S., Fiechtl, B. J., & Innocenti, M. S. (1990). Preparation for transition to mainstreamed post-preschool environments: Development of a survival skills curriculum. *Topics in Early Childhood Special Education, 9*(4), 78–90.

Sainato, D. M., & Lyon, S. R. (1989). Promoting successful mainstreaming transitions for handicapped preschool children. *Journal of Early Intervention, 13*(4), 305–314.

Salisbury, C. L., & Vincent, L. J. (1990). Criterion of the next environment and best practices: Mainstreaming and integration 10 years later. *Topics in Early Childhood Special Education, 10*(1), 78–89.

Schwartz, I. S., & Baer, D. M. (1991). Social validity assessments: Is current practice state-of-the-art? *Journal of Applied Behavior Analysis, 24*(2), 189–204.

Spodek, B. (1991). Early childhood teacher training: Linking theory and practice. In S. L. Kagan (Ed.), *The care and education of America's young children: Obstacles and opportunities* (pp. 110–130). Chicago: University of Chicago Press.

Stephens, P. (1991). *Early childhood transition.* Paper prepared for the Midsouth Regional Resource Center, University of Kentucky, Lexington, KY.

Strickland, B., & Turnbull, A. (1990). *Developing and implementing individualized educational programs.* Columbus, OH: Merrill.

Summers, J. A., dell'Oliver, C., Turnbull, A. P., Benson, H. A., Santelli, E., Campbell, M., & Seigel-Causey, E. (1990). Examining the Individualized Family Service Plan process: What are family and practitioner preferences? *Topics in Early Childhood Special Education, 10*(1), 78–99.

Thiele, J. E., & Hamilton, J. L. (1991). Implementing the early childhood formula programs under P.L. 99-457. *Journal of Early Intervention, 15*, 5–12.

Thurlow, M. L., Lehr, C. A., & Ysseldyke, J. E. (1987). Exit criteria in early childhood programs for handicapped children. *Journal of the Division for Early Childhood Education, 11*, 118–123.

Thurlow, M. L., Ysseldyke, J. E., & Weiss, J. A. (1988). Early childhood special education exit decisions: How are they made? How are they evaluated? *Journal of the Division for Early Childhood, 12*(3), 253–262.

Trohanis, P. L. (1989). An introduction to P.L. 99-457 and the national policy agenda for serving young children with special needs and their families. In J. J. Gallagher, P. L Trohanis, & R. M. Clifford (Eds.), *Policy implementation and P.L. 99-457: Planning for young children with special needs* (pp. 1–17). Baltimore: Paul H. Brookes.

U.S. Department of Health and Human Services, Administration for Children, Youth and Families. (1988). *Transition from Preschool to Kindergarten.* Chapel Hill, NC: Chapel Hill Outreach Training Project.

Vincent, L., Salisbury, C., Walter, G., Brown, P., Gruenewald, L., & Powers, M. (1980). Program evaluation and curriculum development in early childhood/special education. In W. Sailor, B. Wilcox, & L. Brown (Eds.), *Methods of instruction for severely handicapped students.* Baltimore: Paul H. Brookes.

Ziegler, P. (1985). Saying goodbye to preschool. *Young Children, 40*, 11–15.

CHAPTER 8

Young Children with Special Health-Care Needs

Nancy L. Peterson, Patricia A. Barber, and Marilyn Mulligan Ault

Traditionally, early childhood educators have not been responsible for working with infants or young children with complex medical needs, conditions for which they were sometimes termed "medically fragile." They were considered too ill or too vulnerable to participate in day care, preschool, or even early childhood special education (ECSE) programs. Health care and "getting well" were the first priority. Consequently, these youngsters were cared for by health-care professionals in hospitals or by their families at home. Whether due to reluctance of parents or of early childhood educators, these children were the least likely to be found alongside their typical peers in early childhood programs. These exclusionary practices are rapidly changing. ECSE programs now receive more referrals for these children, and the full-inclusion movement is resulting in more inquiries about their placement in regular preschools. Day-care providers are also more frequently contacted by parents seeking equal access to child care, especially since the enactment of the Americans with Disabilities Act. Many will attend programs in which nonmedical personnel will attend to their special needs.

INCREASING INCIDENCE AND VISIBILITY

Several factors contribute to the increased visibility of young children with complex health conditions and to our greater awareness of their needs. Children who had no hope of surviving 20 years ago now survive life-threatening conditions in our neonatal intensive care units

(NICUs), including many at very low birthweight or very premature and with congenital disorders, genetic and infectious disease, and serious traumatic injury. Dramatic progress has been made in preventing, controlling, and sometimes curing conditions once fatal (e.g., meningitis, pneumonia, diabetes, and lung disease). Organ transplants are possible for children whose liver or kidneys have not developed properly. Congenital heart defects can often be surgically corrected. Advances in neonatal and pediatric medical care are enabling most children with chronic or catastrophic illnesses to live to adulthood (Garrison & McQuiston, 1989; Hobbs, Perrin, & Ireys, 1985).

The number of children with chronic illness doubled between the mid-1960s and the mid-1980s (Newacheck, Budetti, & McManus, 1984), by 1985 totaling 10–15 percent of all children. The number, approximately 10 percent, with medically or physiologically severe conditions (Gortmaker, 1985; Surgeon General's Report, 1987) continues to rise due to such factors as drug-affected pregnancies, AIDS in children, interventions that prevent death in utero or sustain life during the most vulnerable first year, and treatments that bring certain childhood diseases into remission. Estimates are that 1–2 percent of all newborns have a disabling condition with health-care implications. Some 2.2 percent of children birth through age 5 have health problems that limit activities (Behrman, 1992). While medical advances save lives and ameliorate certain conditions, many young children still live with chronic illness.

Procedures that save children's lives are sometimes required to sustain their continued well-being. Some youngsters remain dependent, constantly or intermittently, on technology, traditionally provided only in the NICU or acute-care hospital, where sophisticated equipment was available. This imposed extreme restrictions on a child's mobility and deterred normal life activities, but to move technology-dependent children to their homes was considered unthinkable. Today, many professionals and parents consider it unthinkable that children should spend such an important period of their lives in a hospital apart from their families (Kohrman, 1991; Task Force on Technology Dependent Children, 1988).

With technological advances and new perspectives on children's developmental needs, drastic changes in methods of health-care maintenance have become a necessity. Devices are more portable, compact, and manageable for use outside the hospital. Life-sustaining equipment, some small enough to travel in an infant seat, stroller, or wheelchair, can go with a child. Microcomputer interfaces with equipment simplify care and can allow for automatic, computer-based decision making (e.g., medication dosage levels) by nurse or physician. Some procedures have been so simplified that they can be handled on an out-patient basis, at home by traveling nurses, or by parents or other caregivers. With training and supervision, nonmedical personnel handle some procedures formerly performed only by doctors and nurses (Merkins, 1991). This new compact, mobile technology makes children less vulnerable and enables them to enjoy the same home-life activities that others do. Infants and preschoolers who once spent months, even years, of their early lives in a small crib inside a sterile, restrictive hospital setting are returning more quickly to the much more nurturing environment of their homes. Even more significant is the fact that these children who once were either wholly "hospital-bound" or "home-bound" can now enter into more normal community participation (Kohrman, 1991; Parmelee, 1993).

Medical advances have greatly altered the impact of many serious health conditions. Certain conditions, once severely debilitating, are no longer so severe or life-threatening. For example, only 5–10 percent of children with severe asthma have difficulty carrying out daily routines. Only about 10 percent of those with chronic illnesses are severely affected. Most can experience normal life activities through assistive technology and medications that control symptoms and reduce risks associated with out-of-hospital care (Hobbs et al., 1985).

At the same time, medical advances are increasing the numbers of children with *serious multiple* health problems. These youngsters often require continuous, extensive medical treatment and health care, management of which can be, for some, very complicated due to the need to coordinate medications and medical procedures for each condition. Treatment requirements, combined with early education needs, transform professionals' roles with these children into a very different "ball game." While one child in 10 experiences a chronic health condition, this no longer necessarily means confinement or dependence on hospital care. With technology-assisted care provided at home and well-planned emergency care procedures, these youngsters are not the same severely ill, life-restricted individuals of the recent past (Caldwell & Sirvis, 1991; Long, Artis, & Dobbins, 1993).

Community-based Services: A Shift in Philosophy

Factors contributing to the shift to providing care in home and community settings include rising medical costs, effects of long-term hospitalization on young children, pressures on families when a child is under extended hospital care, and growing recognition of families' importance in a child's care plan and reluctance to replace them in their parenting roles. While new treatment approaches and technology have provided the tools for this shift to occur, this perspective is based on several key philosophical principles.

First, health-care and all other services for young children should be *family-centered*. This concept emphasizes the pivotal role of families in young children's lives and underscores a belief that services should support, not deter, families in their roles as primary caregivers and decision makers. Since the child's optimal development depends on optimal family functioning, health-care and other services should promote, not undermine, family independence and competence through working partnerships that support children and families (Shelton, Jeppson, & Johnson, 1987). A second principle, *community-based care*, emphasizes that children should live at home if possible and that removal from their natural homes is not a desirable option (Lantos & Kohrman, 1991). Special services needed (e.g., ECSE, nutrition services, financial support, transportation, respite care, therapies, medications, etc.) should be available and provided within the child's home community. *Coordinated care* reflects the reality that special care for a child with serious health conditions may involve a complex network of people and services, with the potential for fragmentation and redundancy. Conflicts in treatment that occur when multiple professionals and families work in isolation must be minimized. Coordinated care requires good communication, collaboration, and teamwork among all concerned.

Finally, *holistic care* encompasses the others and emphasizes that a health condition cannot be treated effectively without considering the child's overall quality of life and developmental status. Nor can a health problem become so dominant that it is treated as if it were the child's only characteristic or need. Holistic care implies treatment with a constant view of the broader arena in which the youngster must function (i.e., home, school, and community) and the child's overall development (Shelton et al., 1987). Coordination of medical treatment, general child care, and educational-social activities is essential so that a child's physical, social, emotional, and intellectual well-being are addressed.

EFFECT ON EARLY CHILDHOOD
EDUCATION AND DAY CARE

All programs serving young children face growing demands for services from increasingly diverse clienteles. Children with complex health conditions and their families, among other groups not previously served by early childhood (EC) programs, have become more visible, knocking at the doors of EC service providers and asking for equal access. The 1990s ushered in an era in which all families rely more heavily on alternative care for their children and support systems outside the home. For the many American parents of all socioeconomic levels, cultural groups, and educational backgrounds employed outside the home (National Commission on Children [NCC], 1991a), child care is a necessity, not a luxury; most 3- to 5-year-olds participate in preschool programs, with infant-toddler child care by persons other than a parent or immediate family member increasingly common.

Dramatic changes in the American family require greater availability of community support services. Over 25 percent of American children live with a single parent. The number of children under 6 with working mothers increased from 32 percent in 1970 to nearly 60 percent in 1991. Many of the nearly 10.9 million children under 6, including 1.7 million babies under one year and 9.2 million toddlers and preschoolers, with mothers in the work force spend significant time in day care. One in 5 children lives in a family with an income below the federal poverty level. Poverty is most glaring in one-parent families, 43 percent of which are poor, compared with 7 percent of two-parent families (NCC, 1991a, 1991b). Given these factors, the challenge for EC professionals is to assist families with more intensive and individualized yet affordable support services, while serving more children, including infants, and more diverse populations. It has important implications for how service systems support children with serious health problems and their families.

Legislation has contributed significantly to change. While levels of implementation vary, services provided under P.L. 99-457, Part H, are proliferating. As of 1993, 19 states were fully implementing programs, making comprehensive services available to eligible infants and toddlers and their families. Such programs open the door for many young children with serious health-care needs and their families. Since the very nature of serious health problems creates conditions that can interfere with development, they are among the indicators used to identify potential candidates for early intervention. Thus, increased survival rates of young children with special health-care needs is likely to result in greater numbers of children eligible for services under P.L. 99-457. Since eligible children cannot be denied services, staff will find themselves responsible for a growing number with special health-care needs (Graham & Bryant, 1993; Walker, 1986). And since *Least Restrictive Environment* (LRE) requires children with disabilities to be served, as much as possible, in environments where they would have been had they not required special services, it is likely that young children with special health-care needs will increasingly be in regular programs.

LRE for young children was further supported by encouragement from the U.S. Office of Special Education and Rehabilitative Services (OSERS) for school districts to develop linkages with community preschools and child-care centers. Head Start, which had long had policies in place to include children with disabilities, further affirmed their inclusion in its 1993 regulations, which stipulate that no child can be denied enrollment based on the nature or severity of a disability and which address needs for special equipment or personalized procedures, such as feeding, suctioning, catheterization, and so forth (Walsh, 1993).

WHO THESE CHILDREN ARE AND
WHAT THEIR SPECIAL HEALTH-CARE NEEDS ARE

When confronted with the medical terminology and diagnostic labels applied to this population, service providers typically want more information. What kinds of symptoms do they present? What kinds of health problems do they experience? Consider the following as a few examples of the tremendous range of children with special health-care needs:

Alisha is 5, but her size is that of a 3-year-old. Cerebral palsy makes her movements stiff and jerky, and she has intermittent seizures, largely controlled through medication. Since Alisha has difficulty chewing and swallowing without choking and pulling food into her lungs, food intake is a serious problem. She has been enabled to receive nourishment through a fundoplication, a procedure to prevent "gastroesophagal reflux," which causes food in her stomach to be involuntarily moved back up her esophagus, and a gastrostomy tube inserted in her stomach. She is unable to tolerate large amounts of food at a time, so a mechanical infusion pump regulates the continuous flow of nutrients. Eventually, it is hoped her feeding time can be reduced to a series of 30-, then 15-minute sessions. For now, Alisha remains connected to the infusion pump for 12 hours. In spite of these problems, Alisha seems very bright, alert, and determined to be part of activities around her.

Alex is a 2-year-old with severe multiple disabilities. He was a 28-week premature baby who weighed only 1 pound, 5 ounces. During his 7-month stay in the NICU, he had cardiac surgery, fought lung disease, and miraculously survived many other complications. He was on a respirator for a long time; he still has a tracheotomy and requires oxygen support. He is severely delayed, functioning at about the 8-

month level, and has poor strength and muscle tone. He is beginning to gain weight and show more responsiveness to auditory and some visual stimuli, though initially believed clinically blind, and now smiling socially. He accepts toys handed to him and will hand them back. He has no speech but responds with smiles, vocalizes when others talk to him, and mimics sound.

Yen Su was an active 3-year-old, attending preschool, learning English as a second language, and discovering the wonderful world of toys, when a cancerous brain tumor was diagnosed. Her behavior has changed dramatically as chemotherapy treatments have made her ill and sapped her energy, and she is seen by many strangers who do examinations, run CAT scans, and give medications. She has become shy and listless, much of the time simply watching what goes on around her. With limited insurance, both parents must maintain their jobs in order to pay medical bills. Between hospitalizations, she is enrolled in a day-care program. Her parents feel fortunate that staff were willing to deal with multiple medications, special food, predictable vomiting, and the extra rest and care and attention she needs.

Carly, age 4, was born to a 16-year-old, multisubstance-abusing teenager with HIV infection who abandoned him in the hospital. He has lived in foster care or in the pediatric ward for the past four years. Extensive medical records reflect repeated, prolonged hospitalizations for pneumonia, urinary tract infections, and other problems. Colds and ear infections are frequent, normal childhood diseases and flu linger much too long, and complications often follow. Between times of illness, Carly seems more like his age-mates, although he shows delay in gross and fine motor development and visual-motor integrative tasks. He is independent in most self-help skills, although occasionally has day and night bowel and urinary incontinence. He does small chores around the house and loves to play, usually with older youngsters. He is prone to wide mood swings and emotional outbursts, sometimes aggressive, violent tantrums. Since sleep at night is erratic, he is often tired and cranky. As a child with AIDS, his long-term prognosis is not good. However, the length of his young life is not clear, and for the moment he is alive, reasonably well, learning, and growing.

A Definition of the Population

Given such differences, numerous descriptive terms are found in the educational and medical literature, for example, *medically fragile, medically complex, chronically ill, technology dependent* or *technology assisted, health impaired,* and so forth (Lehr, 1990; Surgeon General's

Report, 1987). Such terms suggest inappropriate stereotypes and conno-
tations about the health issues these children represent. For example,
"medically fragile" may suggest children who are weak, nonresilient,
who might "break," while in reality many may be incredibly strong,
survivors of very adverse, sometimes catastrophic, conditions. The preferred terminology is *children with special health care needs*, recently
adopted by the Surgeon General (1987). This phrase places primary
emphasis on the child and then on special health-care needs as second-
arily related to a child's overall needs and status. While children labeled
with any of these terms do not present a single set of characteristics or
concerns for parents and professionals, medical conditions frequently
reported (Batshaw & Perret, 1992) include

- Hereditary diseases — cystic fibrosis, muscular dystrophy, diabetes, sickle cell anemia
- Congenital disorders — spina bifida, cardiovascular disorders
- Respiratory disorders — asthma, bronchopulmonary dysplasia in
  preterm newborns
- Neurological disorders — cerebral palsy, seizures
- Life-threatening diseases and serious infectious conditions — cancer, leukemia, HIV or AIDS, herpes, cytomegalic inclusion disease or CMV
- Major body deformities — cranial abnormalities, cleft palate, or
  malformation of limbs, digestive tract, heart, or other organs
- Conditions resulting from trauma — closed head injury, near
  drowning, ingestion of toxic substances that damage organs or
  destroy body tissue

Many other low-incidence disorders may affect the gastrointestial,
neurological, or musculo-skeletal systems, such as failure to thrive, disorders in metabolism of various nutrients, brittle bone disease, short
bowel syndrome, and conditions requiring technological intervention.
As many as 100,000 infants and young children may be *technology
dependent* or *technology assisted* (Office of Technology Assistance [OTA],
1987). Most dependent are those needing mechanical ventilators for
breathing, while others require intravenous feeding and mechanical
assistance for removal of waste through catheterization, kidney dialysis,
or modifications in digestive-elimination processes through a colostomy
or ileostomy. Others require such devices for respiratory or nutritional
support as a tracheotomy, suctioning, oxygen supplementation, or tube
feeding (Caldwell & Sirvis, 1991).
    Since these problems are very diverse, generalizations about this
population are difficult to make. Symptoms and levels of severity for a

single condition differ from one individual to another. Each condition presents a different set of health concerns that affect each child and family in unique ways, and every child reacts differently to a given condition. Family reactions also vary, which in turn affects the child's reactions to treatments and how much the condition interferes with other life functions. *All* children have health-care needs at some point in their development, for most (85–90 percent), limited to typical childhood diseases and acute or episodic trauma (e.g., broken arm, leg cuts, etc.). For them, health care is achieved successfully at home or through a brief visit to the pediatrician or clinic. Most conditions run their course, and children return to normal functioning. During such episodes, a child may be considered *acutely ill*, implying the short-term, transient nature of the illness (Parmelee, 1993). Some, however, experience long-term conditions that require special health-care procedures of varying levels of intensity and complexity. Their conditions significantly affect their ability to engage in activities that peers enjoy. These youngsters are considered to have a *chronic illness* and may experience or be at high risk for one or more disabilities. Thus, they are also *children with special health-care needs*, children who never become "well" in the typical sense.

A Description of Children's Health-care Needs

Figure 8.1 presents a model illustrating differences and similarities in illness conditions and care requirements between children with special health-care needs and children who are typically healthy. As Figure 8.1 indicates, an illness must first be described in terms of whether it is experienced as *chronic* or *acute*. The term *illness* defines a collection of symptoms with a specific etiology and is synonymous with the term *disease*. It does not imply lack of health or the presence of sickness in the common, vernacular sense, but rather suggests the presence of a functional disorder or disability related to health. In *chronic illness*, the impact of the illness is long term, that is, lasting longer than three months, often requiring daily treatment, medications, and sometimes hospitalization for more than a month per year. Chronic illness may involve acute episodes when a child is more seriously ill, thus *episodic* describes a fluctuating presentation of the characteristics of a chronic illness. Leukemia, cancer, and muscular dystrophy, for example, have periods of remission. The condition of children with special health-care needs associated with one or more chronic illnesses is a long-term presence, in contrast to typical childhood health problems, which may be acute but then gone. *Acute illness* is intensive and possibly life-threatening for only a short time. With treatment and management

Figure 8.1. Health-care Needs of Young Children with Chronic, Complex Health Conditions Compared to Those with Typical Acute Childhood Illnesses

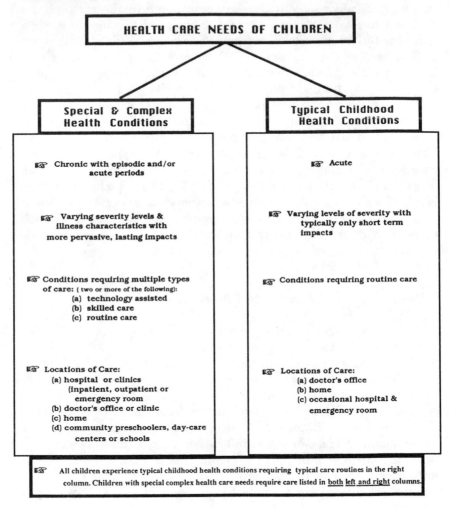

through medication, acute conditions are usually cured or controlled to the extent that they do not require continued care. Concerns for educational personnel are usually short-term and are quite different from those for children whose conditions continually affect their lives.

Severity involves the more invasive, pervasive, and lasting impacts of the illness. While acute illnesses of young children may show varying levels of severity, the illness itself is short-term, as is its impact. Severity of an illness can be defined in terms of whether the condition (1) is life-threatening or mainly a disruption of normal life routines; (2) carries *major or minor risk* for loss of function (i.e., is degenerative); (3) involves major or minor interference with the child's mental alertness and well-being; (4) involves minor-to-severe levels of discomfort, pain, or physical trauma; and (5) involves one or multiple problems affecting one or several bodily functions.

The *types of health care* required by children with special health-care needs, in addition to routine forms needed by other youngsters, are more extensive, complicated, and multiple. *Technology-assisted care* is care that requires "routine use of a medical device to compensate for the loss of a life-sustaining body function and may require daily and ongoing care and/or monitoring by trained personnel" (OTA, 1987, p. xiii). *Skilled care* is performed by a person with certified training, which may be specific to the child but delivered according to pre-scribed, systematic procedures (e.g., gastrostomy feeding, clean inter-mittent catheterization, medication administration, changing of ban-dages and more sophisticated dressing of body wounds). *Routine care* involves general health-related procedures like those needed by healthy children with typical childhood diseases and does not require specific or certified training of caregivers (e.g., cleansing of minor abrasions, cleaning and sanitation procedures when a child has diarrhea, adminis-tration of medications, or monitoring fever and infectious conditions). It is estimated that 15 percent of the overall issues surrounding health care for chronically ill children are specific to the condition, while 85 percent are common to the day-to-day requirements of chronic disor-ders (Gortmaker, 1985).

The *locations where health care is provided* are also more extensive for children with special and complex health-care needs, which often require multiple resources and numerous types of skilled and specialized personnel, as well as persons who can provide more intensive and exten-sive routine care. Care for healthy children who become sick usually occurs at home with occasional short visits to the doctor's office or hospital emergency room.

EFFECTS OF CHRONIC ILLNESS ON YOUNG CHILDREN AND THEIR FAMILIES

Educators often have questions concerning how these illnesses and their treatment may affect a child's development and participation in a preschool setting. Serious illness does change the lives of young children and their families. For some, the changes are no more than an inconvenience. For others, they are profound and lasting, a roller coaster of changing needs that is in many ways unique (Lynch, Lewis, & Murphy, 1993). A child with a chronic illness, as Hobbs et al. (1985) poignantly describe, is

> responsive to the world and needful of care and support. Yet recurrent events and experiences unknown to most other youngsters punctuate the lives of these children. The pain, anticipated and actual, of repeated medical procedures; the boredom of waiting for the doctor or lying in bed until one's body finally heals; the rage against an indifferent nurse or physician; the sense of gratitude for those who care in special ways; the fear of death in the midst of a frightening unpredictable crisis; the repeated separation from parents and family . . . ; the embarrassment of being physically different from other children; the relief when symptoms abate; the despair when the pain begins again: these are events that may occasionally touch all children, but they are well known only to those with a chronic illness. (pp. 70–71)

The social–emotional consequences for young children are largely defined by how the illness is handled by the family. Each child is first a child with ordinary needs for nurturance, sense of worth, and stimulation to promote development. Because illness can alter or disrupt normal interactions, child-adult interactions take on greater importance. How well does the family cope with the child's special health-care needs, added to those typical of any child at that age? How effectively do family members mediate to encourage as much independence as possible and enable the child to master age-appropriate developmental tasks?

Variables That Help Define How Health Conditions Affect Child and Family

Just as every child is unique, every family is different. A child's illness affects all family members and the family as a system, and altered interactions among members in turn affect the adjustment of each. Thus, Beckett (1989) stated bluntly that "if the child is to survive, the family must also survive" (p. 101). Many authors (e.g., Allen & Zigler, 1986; Burr; 1985; Patterson, 1988) have proposed models to explain the dynamic reciprocity among a child who is ill, the family, and the community. Many factors interact to shape the impact of serious health conditions. Figure 8.2 provides a conceptual framework for thinking about those multiple variables, describing the parameters of a

Figure 8.2. Variables That Collectively Define the Impacts of a Health Condition on a Child and Family

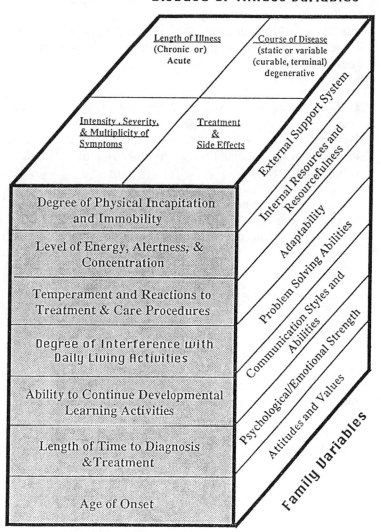

Disease or Illness Variables

Length of Illness
(Chronic or)
Acute

Course of Disease
(static or variable
(curable, terminal)
degenerative

Intensity, Severity,
& Multiplicity of
Symptoms

Treatment
&
Side Effects

External Support System

Internal Resources and
Resourcefulness

Adaptability

Problem Solving Abilities

Communication Styles and
Abilities

Psychological/Emotional Strength

Attitudes and Values

Degree of Physical Incapitation
and Immobility

Level of Energy, Alertness, &
Concentration

Temperament and Reactions to
Treatment & Care Procedures

Degree of Interference with
Daily Living Activities

Ability to Continue Developmental
Learning Activities

Length of Time to Diagnosis
&Treatment

Age of Onset

Family Variables

Child Variables

child's illness, and differentiating among seriously ill children to help service providers assess what forms of assistance are important for a particular child and family, based on variables associated with the disease itself, variables concerning the child, and variables within the family.

Variables connected with the illness define the potential impacts of a particular condition, depending on the unique experiences and reactions of child and family:

- Is the condition a short-term (acute) or long-term (chronic) illness?
- How will the disease progress (static or variable or degenerative) and what is the expected outcome (unknown or unpredictable, terminal, or curable)?
- What are the intensity, severity, and multiplicity of symptoms?
- What are the treatment requirements and the side effects of that treatment (e.g., is more than one condition present and, if so, are the needs, treatments, and progressions of the other conditions similar or different)?

Variables associated with the child represent a second set of considerations:

- What is the age of onset when symptoms affect the child's well-being?
- What difficulties were experienced in identifying the problem, and how much time passed before a diagnosis was made and treatment initiated?
- To what degree does the illness interfere with the child's progression through the normal developmental sequences and with learning processes typical of each age?
- How invasive is the illness or how much interference does the condition and its treatment impose on the child's activities of daily living?
- What is the child's overall temperament and reaction to care procedures?
- What is the child's level of energy, alertness, and ability to concentrate?
- What degree of physical incapacitation or immobility is imposed?

Finally, *variables within the family*, its unique "personality," influence how family members respond, individually and collectively, to the child's illness and its treatment:

- What are the values/attitudes of the family about the child and the illness?
- What psychological strength is evidenced within the family that affects how everyone copes with the situation?
- What are the styles and levels of communication among family members about issues or events that are important to individual members or the family as a whole?
- What are the problem-solving abilities of the parents and family as a whole?
- How adaptive are parents and family members, individually and collectively?
- What internal resources does the family have, and how resourceful are parents in getting assistance?
- What is the nature of the external support system the family has in place, or what supports and resources are available for them to access?

Perspectives about what is "best" for a child can be considerably different among the adults involved. Health professionals are most concerned about treating the illness, educators with assessing the child's developmental status and providing developmentally appropriate activities, parents with their child's overall quality of life and daily activities (Lynch et al., 1993). Increasingly, professionals adopt a more common set of concerns and a more global view of the child and family system. More attention is being given to how serious illness affects that family system and how the system alters the impact of the illness.

Impact on Children's Development and Life Experiences

A young child who is very ill may be observed to be quiet and listless or quite fussy and cranky, usually needing a lot of sleep and cuddling and comforting by a familiar adult. Small children seem insecure when ill, clinging and becoming more dependent on caregivers. Discomfort or pain associated with illness or its treatment can easily deter the child from typical activities. There is diminished interest in play, and the youngster may be less attentive to events and things in the environment that promote learning. As children grow older and are more able to understand what is happening to them, they are able to take more control over what is happening, to be sick yet engage simultaneously in other activities.

Severe illness during a child's formative years not only threatens life and physical health, but overall developmental progress is also vulnerable. Research suggests that children with chronic illnesses are more likely to show difficulties adjusting, the risk increasing for youngsters from poor and already stressed families (e.g., Bailey & Simeonsson, 1988); greater impacts are likely when conditions involve the central nervous system or result in physical disability (e.g., Allen & Zigler, 1986); and psychological adjustment is related not only to disease parameters but to the functional status and ability of the child to engage in daily activities (e.g., Stein & Jessop, 1984). Not all children are adversely affected. Rather, there are several points of vulnerability, suggesting a continuum of potential outcomes ranging from little or no impact to impact that is profound and lasting. In some cases, effects on a child's life may have positive elements. Potential effects of a serious, chronic health condition on young children, as described by many authors (e.g., Cerreto, 1986; Khan & Battle, 1987; Perrin & Gerrity, 1984; Peterson, 1987), are summarized below:

1. *Disruption in development and achievement of age-appropriate developmental tasks.* While for older children serious illness is most likely to affect social adjustment, young children's achievement of developmental tasks may be impeded. For example, repeated and sometimes traumatic separation from caregivers, accompanied by painful treatments, may not be conducive to developing *basic trust*, an important task of infancy. Illness can also interfere with attainment of *autonomy*, by restricting toddlers' control over what they do and what happens to them. Hospital confinement, restriction to a bed in a strange environment, and repeated painful treatments combined with loss of energy can impede *initiative* in a child who otherwise might be active, curious, and interactive.

2. *Disruption in interpersonal relationships and life experiences that promote learning.* Extended periods of bed rest and invasive medical procedures restrict activities of young children, limiting interaction with peers and increasing reliance on adults. Parent-child interactions can be affected in many ways. Extended separation from parents and siblings can affect emotional bonding. Also, adults (professionals as well as family members) sometimes react to the stress of illness, especially if life-threatening, by pulling back psychologically. Others focus all attention on the illness to the extent of perva-

sive overaccommodation and indulgence, affecting the child's sense of competence and independence. Some youngsters thrive on such attention, becoming more interactive verbally and more social, while others react by becoming demanding and difficult to manage. Others become very passive, with behavior often described as "learned helplessness."

3. *Physical limitations, reduction in energy, and side effects.* While caregivers may work overtime to provide stimulation, the sick child, not feeling good enough to respond, may be listless and passive. The more the condition can be controlled (e.g., through medication or technology, unless these create other disruptive side effects), the more physical limitations can be reduced. Some children experience a wide range of side effects, while others experience none. These additional impositions can themselves affect energy and alertness, inhibit activity, require long recuperative periods and bed rest, impose apparatus such as casts and braces or technological devices that affect body posture and comfort, or alter food intake and elimination processes.

4. *Effects on parents' child rearing practices and children's independence.* Since parents may hesitate to place demands on an ill child, disciplinary practices may become more relaxed, and typical parental guidance may be deemphasized, even skipped for a time. Conversely, constant proximity to adults may mean additional expectations placed on a child. These dimensions of appropriate control versus overcontrol, reduced discipline versus no discipline, and overprotection versus psychological distancing all impact a child's social–emotional adjustment and development. The very nature of illness makes young children more dependent on adults. Basic caregiving becomes more intensive. Toileting habits are likely to be altered at the very time a child is attempting to master basic self-care tasks. Feeding may be altered, especially if diet must be controlled or the child must be fed in bed. Thus, more dependency is imposed at the very time a young child is striving for independence and building a sense of self apart from caregivers, whose ability to maintain balance between the child's dependence and needs for independence depends on their skills, confidence and security in their role, and willingness to take the time to work through this sensitive issue.

5. *Potential emotional impact of illness.* Young children typically do not understand what is happening to them during medical treatment. Only as they gain experience with the procedures and as adults explain what is happening are they able to verbalize their thoughts about their sickness and treatments. Children often inter-

nalize illness as something bad or caused by something they have done, thus seeing treatments as punishment, rather than acts of caring or nurturance by adults. Sensitive explanations greatly mitigate the emotional impact of illness on children and its effect on their emerging self-image, and how adults deal with fears and anxieties influences the child's ability to deal with frightening events, as well as trust in adults.

Impact on Families

Many parents of young children with special health-care needs recount powerful stories concerning their questions, experiences, and complex feelings:

> The shock of the initial diagnosis and the urgent compelling need for knowledge, the exhausting nature of constant care unpredictably punctuated by crisis; the many and persistent financial concerns; the continued witnessing of a child's pain; tensions with one's spouse that can be aggravated by the fatiguing chronicity of care; the worries about the well-being of other children; and the multitude of questions involving the fair distribution within the family of time, money and concern—these are challenges that parents of a chronically ill child must face. (Hobbs et al., 1985, p. 80)

Families' responses to these circumstances vary greatly. Most cope despite obstacles encountered within the health-care system, with professionals who may be uninformed or impatient about parental concerns, or with communities insufficiently supportive at times when families need support most. Most families' resilience and strength are manifest in how they achieve their own personal "level of comfort" with their child's care. In some families, stress is severe and members pay a high emotional price. Families describe several impacts:

1. *Financial strains that affect family functioning.* Families often find that many expenses are not covered by their insurance or by social services programs. Costs of equipment, medications, deductibles, co-insurance, and so forth, for a single episode can be devastating, and financial strains are exacerbated when a parent, usually the mother, must leave the work force to care for the child. Security is threatened by the prospect of unending expenses, and required policy adjustments result in increased premiums or depletion of coverage. Ideally, national health-care reform will change these conditions, but problems are likely to continue (Freedman & Clarke, 1991).

2. *Heightened caregiving responsibilities and management issues.* Parenting any infant or preschooler is demanding and time-intensive, but additional demands are superimposed when a child is seriously ill. Major alterations in family routines and life-styles are often necessary to accommodate frequent visits to an array of specialists and intermittent hospitalizations. These, along with transportation issues, providing care at home, and management of other children and their schedules, combine to create a fast-paced, stressful way of life, with little or no time or energy left for personal needs and recreation. Moreover, to watch a child fight for each breath or experience pain or discomfort involves emotional strains that magnify family stress. Over time, families continually cycle through periods of adjustment and adaptation in order to respond to these ongoing stressors.

3. *Necessity of parent's acting as "ultimate case manager."*

> It's difficult to describe our home life to people. Mark's routine care starts at 7:00 A.M. when the nurse arrives. Twice a week, a physical therapist comes to our home. We schedule the preschool teacher to come once a week. Others constantly are in and out of the house — the medical equipment people, his case workers, the speech pathologist. Folks have to be scheduled around Mark's medical care routines, but apart enough to let him rest between sessions. We're constantly going from one end of the city to the other to some office to fill out forms, pick up medicine, meet with people, or do something. You'll find us at the doctor's office or hospital about 1–2 times a month. We're booked from morning to night and usually exhausted. When somebody doesn't keep the schedule or has to change appointments, it'll take us hours or days to unravel and rearrange the domino effect that happens.

While not all families face such complexities, many require an array of special services. Families become painfully aware that the "service system" is actually a set of service systems, often fragmented and uncoordinated, a situation substantially improving with the Individualized Family Services Plan (IFSP), services coordinator, and interagency collaboration provisions of Part H. Nevertheless, the family is actually the only "system" that maintains a truly holistic view of the child and his or her needs, maintaining a careful balance between what each individual service provider considers important and the child's overall well-being. Thus, parents cannot avoid being the ultimate "case manager" or "family services coordinator" for the myriad things impacting on their child and the family as a unit (Brotherson & Goldstein, 1992).

4. *Information and resource needs of families.* Parents experience many initial and continuing questions. What is this condition my child has? Could I have done something to avoid this? How will it affect my child? What treatments are best? Where can we go for help? How do we pay for this? The search can be exhausting and frustrating and information obtained often difficult to understand; sometimes differing opinions and recommendations must be sorted out. The search for resource — where to purchase the most economical and most palatable special foods, or toys appropriate during times of restricted activity — is ongoing. People who can provide understandable, timely information, or who help parents connect with helpful resources, are invaluable to families (Able-Boone, Sandall, Stevens, & Frederick, 1992).

5. *Need for a strong support system.* The impacts of a chronic illness are mediated in part by internal and external support systems, which represent *family resources* to the extent that they actually respond to needs experienced by families. What parents view as "support" takes many forms, such as opportunities to connect with other parents who have similar experiences and can share their experiences, availability of respite care, and supportive extended-family members, friends, and social, religious, or other organizations.

IMPLICATIONS FOR SERVICE PROVIDERS

With the complex array of needs across diverse client populations testing the capacity of agencies, major change is taking place in early education, health-care, and social service programs. How will greater numbers of young children with serious health conditions affect the roles and responsibilities of persons representing different disciplines, different agencies, and possibly very different viewpoints concerning what is "best" for the child?

A New Perspective on Professional Roles and Responsibilities

Service providers must be open and willing to make adjustments that allow young children with special health-care needs to be in the mainstream of family and community life. Added responsibilities to the scope of the service provider's work should be regarded as a positive challenge and a means to improve children's options (Briggs, 1991; Fauvre, 1988). The issue is not whether these children should have access to community programs that their healthy peers enjoy, but what resources should be tapped and what actions taken to make inclusion and participation in a more normal life-style possible for them and their families.

Professional and Interagency Collaboration and Teamwork

Since inevitably numerous professionals from various disciplines and agencies will be involved, they must become skilled in interdisciplinary and interagency collaboration processes. However, effective collaboration does not happen automatically, but requires: (1) communication and respect for each individual's interlinked roles and tasks; (2) full sharing of information; (3) sharing of resources in ways that maximize quality and efficiency of assistance to the child and family; and (4) sharing of power over critical decisions and joint decision making. Greater weight is placed on families' preferences and the overall welfare of the child than on professionals' preferences and standard agency practices (Brewer, McPherson, Magrab, & Hutchins, 1989; Klerman, 1985). Open, clear communication among everyone, including parents, is the bottom line for effective teamwork.

Specialized Individualized Planning About a Child's Unique Service Needs

The key role of the *family services coordinator* is especially critical when complex health-related services are involved. Multiple agency involvement also implies types of working relationships that may be new to most people (Hanson & Lynch, 1992; Lowenthal, 1992). Moreover, in addition to the IFSP or IEP, and individual transition plans, as discussed by Fowler and Ostrosky in Chapter 7, two other types of plans are needed. A *health-care plan* defines the child's special needs across environments, identifying such areas as nutritional or feeding requirements, technology, medications, and so forth. Such plans are subject to continuous change, and constant communication among service providers and with families is essential to monitor status and progress, adjust care procedures and educational programming, and support families. An *emergency plan* specifies steps under: (1) normal emergency situations (e.g., fire) that may require special handling for the child; (2) potential emergencies related to a child's unique condition and its treatment that may necessitate skilled and quick action; and (3) emergencies that occur if technology devices malfunction or are damaged (e.g., blockage of a tracheostomy tube, electricity failure).

Training and Preparation of Staff for
New Roles and Responsibilities

Three types of training are indicated: (1) general training, preservice or in-service, in the health-care needs of all young children in any setting to assure a safe environment and hygienic procedures; (2) training specific to a child's illness and symptoms, treatment regimen, and unique aspects outlined in the health-care plan, conducted by qualified health professionals in cooperation with family, and best acquired when one begins working with a child; and (3) training that prepares team members to collaborate within a service network for children and families, which is not limited to the boundaries of a single agency. All levels of training should be informed by new resources, with additional sources of information accessed as needs arise (Ault, Graff, & Rues, 1993; Lehr, 1990).

Incorporating Certain Qualities in Delivery of Services

Such familiar themes as individualized, family-focused, transdisciplinary, coordinated, comprehensive, normalizing, and so forth, become especially important when dealing with a child with a chronic illness (Bruder, 1993; Hobbs et al., 1985; Lehr, 1990). But the quality of *flexibility* is perhaps the most critical theme underlying services. Parents emphasize its importance because of the constant change typical of the ongoing saga of what chronic illness entails in a child's life. With such change requiring frequent communication to plan and replan how situations will be handled, it is not unusual for parents to be in daily phone contact with service providers. True flexibility requires an integrated perspective from multiple points of view, including those of the child and family, the professionals/service providers, and the agency. Situations commonly occur in which a child has particular needs, but rigid agency rules slow the work of service providers and make it difficult to deliver appropriate help in a timely way (Lynch et al., 1993). Flexibility involves mutual problem solving, negotiation, and compromise to achieve consensus concerning what best serves the child's needs. It is important to remember that, just as professionals are including parents in areas they have regarded as their domain, families are allowing professionals to enter into their life arena and private affairs (Dunst, Trivette, & Deal, 1988).

Discussion and Agreement on Important
Issues Affecting Services

Chronic health conditions require frequent decisions that affect these children's lives. Since chronic illness involves constantly changing conditions, the decisions cannot be considered permanent and unalterable, but rather "working agreements" that must be reconsidered as a child's health status and needs change or new variables come into play. New issues emerge as outcomes of each choice become apparent. A pervading, underlying issue concerns the *balance of risk*: How much risk should be taken versus what quality of life should the child enjoy? More specifically, how much should medical and other care procedures be allowed to alter normalcy and reduce the quality of a child's life? Conversely, how much should the desire for quality of life and normalcy change medical and health care procedures if the child faces symptoms that may worsen or greater risk for an acute attack, injury, or hastened death (Dennis, Williams, Giangreco, & Cloninger, 1993)?

The balance-of-risk issue arises in many forms. How much should the child be allowed to play with peers, if that exposure increases the chances for infection and potential for greater complications? How much therapy should be provided if giving the child what seems best means taxing the stamina of an already stressed 3-year-old? How many hours of play can be allowed, or should the child be kept in bed? How much should normal activity be restricted if it means that the lack of movement, activity, and stimulation will promote further developmental delay? Issues of liability, staffing, amount and intensity of services to be provided, activities in which the child can participate, and other pragmatic concerns build on decisions about this basic consideration. Personnel with little experience with young children with special health-care needs may be especially uncertain about how to create a balance between the "perfect, safe environment" and the child's right to participate in normal life experiences. There are no easy solutions to such conflicts faced by health-care providers, early childhood educators, and day-care providers, but parents are the final decision makers concerning their child's balance of risk.

Since the balance of risk constantly changes, each major decision requires a reevaluation of the child's developmental needs and of risks. Persons involved are constantly adjusting their perceptions of the child and willingness to accept risk according to the child's changing developmental and medical needs. Parents often waver on the continuum between caution and risk. Some people do not want to take any risks, some want to take too many, and some are not certain what to do. Some may not share ethics that emphasize quality of life over longevity. Some parents, unwilling or unable to take any steps that might adversely affect their child's health, may disagree with educators willing to provide normalizing activities for the child. Others may insist on more normalizing activities when service providers feel uncomfortable about the risks. It is the planning process that makes resolution of these issues possible and leads to individually appropriate programs that address the child's overall development and welfare (Dennis et al., 1993).

Another issue is liability: What happens if . . . ? Who is responsible if . . . ? What will we do if . . . ? There is no single set of right answers to these questions, but as educators and other service providers consider them, communication is critical. Liability risks *increase* when people work in isolation and fail to coordinate. Liability risks *decrease* when there is communication, plans for emergencies are in place, everyone concerned has agreed on procedures, and all are prepared for emergency situations. As one parent explained,

> It was so gratifying to see all these people and me sit together and plan how we'd all handle these situations we all were so concerned about. In one short hour, I felt more assured, more relieved about Andy's safety, than I've ever felt before. I'd been so uncertain, worried, uptight about things. I finally felt reassured that things would be okay.

While assembling the diverse services a child and family need and finding agreement among diverse individuals are difficult, equally challenging is the issue of funding services and resolving how cost sharing and payment will occur. Sharing and release of information about a child and family raise confidentiality issues. Differences in the rules and regulations of the various agencies must be resolved in determining procedures to be followed. Joint decision-making discussion and formal agreements are essential, but most important it must be remembered that resolving issues of confidentiality ultimately resides with parents. When professionals realize that, since parents are primarily concerned about the welfare of their children, confidentiality may not be a primary issue. Once parents give permission for information to be shared for something they believe will help their child, the real issue is how to streamline mechanisms within agency bureaucracies to make this possible.

Finally, children with special health-care needs are important young citizens who, like everyone else, need opportunity, appropriate care, and quality early education. They benefit from professionals who understand their need to be with their families and to be included with age-mates. They, too, need the opportunity to work toward their best potential, whatever it may be.

REFERENCES

Able-Boone, H., Sandall, S., Stevens, E., & Frederick, L. L. (1992). Family support resources and needs: How early intervention can make a difference. *Infant-Toddler Intervention, 2*(2), 93–102.

Allen, L., & Zigler, E. (1986). Psychological adjustment of seriously ill children. *Journal of the American Academy of Child and Adolescent Psychiatry, 25*, 708–712.

Ault, M. M., Graff, J. C., & Rues, J. P. (1993). Special health care procedures. In M. E. Snell (Ed.), *Instruction of students with severe disabilities* (4th ed., pp. 215–247). New York: Merrill.

Bailey, D. B., & Simeonsson, R. J. (1988). Assessing needs of families with handicapped infants. *The Journal of Special Education, 22*, 117–127.

Batshaw, M. L., & Perret, Y. M. (1992). *Children with disabilities: A medical primer* (3rd ed.). Baltimore: Paul H. Brookes.

Beckett, J. E. (1989). With a parent's eye. In R. E. K. Stein (Ed.), *Caring for children with chronic illness: Issues and strategies* (pp. 101–116). New York: Springer.

Behrman, R. E. (1992). *The future of children: U.S. health care of children.* Los Altos, CA: Center for the Future of Children, David & Lucille Packard Foundation.

Brewer, E. J., McPherson, M., Magrab, P. R., & Hutchins, V. L. (1989). Family centered, community-based, coordinated care for children with special health care needs. *Pediatrics, 83*(6), 1055–1060.

Briggs, M. H. (1991). Team development: Decision-making for early intervention. *Infant-Toddler Intervention, 1*(1), 1–10.

Brotherson, M. J., & Goldstein, B. L. (1992). Time as a resource and constraint for parents of young children with disabilities: Implications for early intervention services. *Topics in Early Childhood Special Education, 12*(4), 508–527.

Bruder, M. B. (1993). The provision of early intervention and early childhood special education within community early childhood programs: Characteristics of effective service delivery. *Topics in Early Childhood Special Education, 13*(1), 19–37.

Burr, C. K. (1985). Impact on the family of a chronically ill child. In N. Hobbs & J. M. Perrin (Eds.), *Issues in the care of children with chronic illness* (pp. 24–40). San Francisco: Jossey-Bass.

Caldwell, T. H., & Sirvis, B. (1991). Students with special health conditions: An emerging population presents new challenges. *Preventing School Failure, 35*, 13–18.

Cerreto, M. C. (1986). Developmental issues in chronic illness: Implications and applications. *Topics in Early Childhood Special Education*, 5(4), 23–35.

Dennis, R. E., Williams, W., Giangreco, M. F., & Cloninger, C. J. (1993). Quality of life as context for planning and evaluation of services for people with disabilities. *Exceptional Children*, 59(6), 499–512.

Dunst, C., Trivette, C., & Deal, A. (1988). *Enabling and empowering families: Principles and guidelines for practice*. Cambridge, MA: Brookline Books.

Fauvre, M. (1988). Including young children with "new" chronic illnesses in early childhood education settings. *Young Children*, 43, 71–77.

Freedman, S. A., & Clarke, L. L. (1991). Financing care for medically complex children. In N. J. Hochstadt & D. M. Yost (Eds.), *The medically complex child: The transition to home care* (pp. 259–286). New York: Harwood.

Garrison, W. T., & McQuiston, S. (1989). *Chronic illness during childhood and adolescence: Psychological aspects*. Newbury Park, CA: Sage.

Gortmaker, S. L. (1985). Demography of chronic childhood diseases. In N. Hobbs & J. M. Perrin (Eds.), *Issues in the care of children with chronic illness* (pp. 135–154). San Francisco: Jossey-Bass.

Graham, M. A., & Bryant, D. M. (1993). Developmentally appropriate activities for children with special needs. *Infants and Young Children*, 5(3), 31–42.

Hanson, M. J., & Lynch, E. W. (1992). Family diversity: Implications for policy and practice. *Topics in Early Childhood Special Education*, 12(3), 283–306.

Hobbs, N., Perrin, J. M., & Ireys, H. Y. (1985). Chronically ill children and their families. In N. Hobbs & J. M. Perrin (Eds.), *Issues in the care of children with chronic illness* (pp. 62–101). San Francisco: Jossey-Bass.

Khan, N. A., & Battle, C. U. (1987). Chronic illness: Implications for development and education. *Topics in Early Childhood Special Education*, 6(1), 25–32.

Klerman, L. V. (1985). Interprofessional issues in delivering services to chronically ill children and their families. In N. Hobbs & J. M. Perrin (Eds.), *Issues in the care of children with chronic illness* (pp. 420–440). San Francisco: Jossey-Bass.

Kohrman, A. F. (1991). Medical technology: Implications for health and social service providers. In N. J. Hochstadt & D. M. Yost (Eds.), *The medically complex child: The transition to home care* (pp. 3–14). New York: Harwood.

Lantos, J., & Kohrman, A. F. (1991). Ethical aspects of pediatric home care. In N. J. Hochstadt & D. M. Yost (Eds.), *The medically complex child: The transition to home care* (pp. 245–257). New York: Harwood.

Lehr, D. H. (1990). Providing education to students with complex health care needs. *Focus on Exceptional Children*, 22(7), 1–12.

Long, C. E., Artis, N. E., & Dobbins, N. J. (1993). The hospital: An important site for family-centered early intervention. *Topics in Early Childhood Special Education*, 13(1), 106–119.

Lowenthal, B. (1992). Interagency collaboration in early intervention: Rationale, barriers, and implementation. *Infant-Toddler Intervention*, 2(2), 103–111.

Lynch, E. W., Lewis, R. B., & Murphy, D. S. (1993). Educational services for children with chronic illnesses: Perspectives of educators and families. *Exceptional Children*, 59(3), 210–220.

Merkins, M. J. (1991). From intensive care unit to home: The role of pediatric transitional care. In N. J. Hochstadt & D. M. Yost (Eds.), *The medically complex child: The transition to home care* (pp. 61–78). New York: Harwood.

National Commission on Children. (1991a). *Speaking of kids: A national survey of children and parents*. Washington, DC: Author.

National Commission on Children. (1991b). *Beyond rhetoric: A new American agenda for children and families* (Final Report). Washington, DC: Author.

Newacheck, P. W., Budetti, P. P., & McManus, P. (1984). Trends in childhood disability. *American Journal of Public Health*, 74(3), 232–236.

Office of Technology Assistance, U.S. Congress. (1987). *Technology-dependent children: Hospital vs. home care—a technical memorandum*. Washington, DC: U.S. Government Printing Office.

Parmelee, A. H. (1993). Children's illness and normal behavioral development: The role of caregivers. *Zero to Three*, 13(4), 1–9. Washington, DC: National Center for Clinical Infant Programs.

Patterson, J. M. (1988). A conceptual model of chronic and life-threatening illness and its impact on families. In C. S. Chilman, E. W. Nunnally, & F. M. Cox (Eds.), *Chronic illness and disability* (pp. 17–68). Newbury Park, CA: Sage Publications.

Perrin, E. C., & Gerrity, P. S. (1984). Development of children with a chronic illness. *Pediatric Clinics of North America*, 13, 13–32.

Peterson, N. J. (1987). *Early intervention for handicapped and at-risk children: An introduction to early childhood special education*. Denver: Love.

Shelton, T. L., Jeppson, E. S., & Johnson, B. H. (1987). *Family centered care for children with special health care needs*. Washington, DC: Association for the Care of Children's Health.

Stein, E. K., & Jessop, D. J. (1984). Psychological adjustment among children with chronic conditions. *Pediatrics*, 73, 169–174.

Surgeon General's Report: U.S. Department of Health and Human Services. (1987). *Children with special health care needs: Campaign '87*. Washington, DC: U.S. Government Printing Office.

Task Force on Technology Dependent Children. (1988). *Fostering home and community-based care for technologically-dependent children: Report of the Task Force on Technology Dependent Children* (Vols. 1–2). Washington, DC: U.S. Government Printing Office.

Walker, D. K. (1986). Chronically ill children in early childhood education programs. *Topics in Early Childhood Special Education*, 5(4), 12–22.

Walsh, S. (1993). Head Start Disability Regulations released. *DEC Communicator*. Logan, UT: Center for Persons with Disabilities.

CHAPTER 9

Promoting the Development of Young Children Through Use of Technology

Philippa H. Campbell, Gail McGregor, and Ellen Nasik

Many educators have been inspired to explore computer applications with young children through technology-mediated approaches to teaching logic and problem solving (Papert, 1980). References to developmental gains attributed to early computer use are evident in the marketing campaigns of hardware manufacturers and also child-care providers seeking to boost enrollment by incorporating computers into their program (Anselmo & Zinck, 1987). There is growing use and documentation of successful technological applications with young children in a variety of skill areas (e.g., Haugland, 1992), although predictions that all preschools would be using computers by 1989 were a bit optimistic (Chin, 1984).

Computers are increasingly becoming a part of early education programs, allowing young children to learn how to operate and use computer applications in their learning. Computers provide an instructional modality that is enjoyable, as well as educationally beneficial for young children. For children whose development is delayed or different in some way, technology plays an even more critical role. Physical and cognitive access to education that has not otherwise been possible can be provided through assistive technology (Burnette, 1990; Lahm, 1989). Assistive-technology use facilitates the participation and full inclusion of young children with disabilities into community settings, including child-care and early education programs (Parette, Van Biervliet, & Parette, 1990). Various types of equipment, devices, and adaptations can enable infants and young children with disabilities to move around their environments, speak and communicate with others, and participate in developmentally appropriate activities that might not be possible without technology.

TECHNOLOGY ACCESS FOR YOUNG CHILDREN

While many preschool children can access technology directly through electronic toys, switch interfaces, keyboards, or standard keyboard bypass devices such as a mouse or track ball (Butler, 1988; Davidson, 1989), others may require special adaptations that compensate for developmental skill limitations. Switches can be interfaced with toys, appliances, games, audiovisual equipment, and computers. The value and range of assistive-technology applications for young children with disabilities is directly attributable to the variety of ways through which computer equipment and other materials can be accessed. A Touch Screen, for example, allows a child to access a computer by bypassing the computer keyboard, although it is not reliable when two or more children are using a computer interactively (Clements, 1991).

Single-Switch-Interface Devices

Technology-mediated intervention has been used with children who experience slow or restricted motor development by providing them with opportunities to interact with objects through switch-interface devices, simple devices that a teacher or a parent can fabricate out of commonly available materials (e.g., Burkhart, 1987; Wright & Samaras, 1986) or that can be purchased commercially through a variety of suppliers (see Figure 9.1 for examples of suppliers of switch-interface devices and adapted toys). These switches can be operated by movement of any body part or area. For example, a child can operate a switch by kicking, turning the head, blinking an eye, sucking, moving the chin, or hitting with a hand. Many different types of switch interfaces are available so that a switch can be matched to whatever movement a child can make. Most young children, even with the most severe physical limitations, have some movement of the head, arms, or legs to enable them to operate a switch. (Adults with physical disabilities may use more complicated switches, such as those operated through eye movements or muscle contractions.) The switches, in turn, can be connected to battery-operated toys, tape recorders, televisions or VCRs,

Figure 9.1. Primary Resources for Adapted Toys and Switches

Ablenet 1081 10th Avenue, S.E. Minneapolis, MN 55414 (612) 379-0956	**Handicapped Childrens Technological Services** Box 7 Foster, RI 02825 (401) 397-3420
Cinta Therapeutic Toys, Inc. 91 Newberry Road East Haddam, CT 06423 (203) 873-9509	**Maddak, Inc.** Bel-Art Products 6 Industrial Road Pequannock, NJ 07440 (201) 694-0500
Crestwood Company 6625 N. Sidney Place Milwaukee, WI 53209-3259 (414) 351-0311	**Kapable Kids/The Able Child** 227 Knickerbocker Avenue, #4 Bohemia, NY 11716 (516) 563-7176
Jesana Ltd P.O. Box 17 Irvington, NY 10533 (800) 443-4728	**Toys for Special Children** 385 Warburton Avenue Hastings, NY 10706 (914) 478-0960
TASH Unit 1 91 Station Street Ajax, ON L3R 4C2 Canada (416) 686-4129	**The Capable Child, Inc.** S. Herkimer Avenue Hewlett, NY 11557 (513) 872-1603

computers, or a variety of special devices to facilitate children's competence and inclusion into typical environments and activities (Esposito & Campbell, 1993).

Computer Access

Many infants and young children are interested in computers and enjoy playing games and other activities through age-appropriate software (Chevat, 1992; Clements, 1991). Some older preschoolers easily use a regular computer keyboard (Killian, Nelson, & Byrd, 1986; Williams, 1984), but the youngest children are better introduced to the computer using such peripherals as a mouse or adaptations that allow access while bypassing the regular keyboard. Some software programs for young children use a regular keyboard but operate by use of only selected keys, such as the arrow keys or the return key (e.g., Davidson, 1989). These are less complicated for young children to operate independently than those that require letter or number discrimination or the manipulation abilities necessary to activate an isolated key. A number of methods are available to assist young children to use a computer, many of which bypass physical, visual, or cognitive disabilities (Hutinger, 1986). Children able to successfully use an augmentative communication aid may be able to access a computer directly from the aid, in essence using their communication aid as a substitute for the computer keyboard (Behrmann, Jones, & Wilds, 1989). Selection of a particular access method may be necessary for a child with a disability to ensure that it sufficiently accommodates a child's needs in computer access. The general types of access methods most likely to be useful with infants and young children are listed in Table 9.1. The most common types of keyboard bypass devices used with young children include the Touch Screen, which allows access by directly touching the computer monitor screen, and a variety of membrane keyboards, such as the Muppet Keys, where children touch large keyboards that include either letters, graphics, or pictures. The Adaptive Firmware Card allows many software programs to be operated through scanning where the child can access the computer via a switch interface. The particular type of access device that will assist a young child with disabilities to use a computer and software can be determined by an assistive-device specialist or someone familiar with the technological options and adaptations.

TECHNOLOGY AS A TOOL
TO ENHANCE PLAY AND LEARNING

Infants and young children acquire information about their physical and social worlds through interactions with objects and materials, adults, and other children in their environments that permit them to experiment with ideas and concepts. Technology plays an instrumental role for children by providing a modality to facilitate interaction and learning (Behrmann et al., 1989). Access devices and adapted toys provide an interface between a child and the events, people, and activities in the environment, thus increasing a child's capacity to learn through interactions. Play also provides children with opportunities to imitate actions and activities that they have observed others doing as well as with opportunities to learn social relationships and rules, as Linder notes in Chapter 4. Computers can help structure children's interac-

Table 9.1. Computer Input Modalities and Assistive Devices

Input Source	Student Response Requirements	Variations and Adaptations
1. Conventional keyboard * space bar * key press	Child depresses designated location on keyboard	Responses made by hitting key in given area of keyboard, e.g., keyboard divided into quadrants or halves Responses made by hitting any key Color code keys used for responses in a program Add keyguard to maximize chances of depressing correct key
2. Game paddle	Typically, child is required to press button or move joystick	Paddles can be mounted or positioned to accommodate child's motor patterns
3. Single switch		All switches can be mounted or positioned to accommodate individual needs Multiple switches can be used
* Activated by extremities (fingers, hands, feet, elbows)	Child depresses switch with given body part	Push-button switch Paddles & levers Pillow switch
	Child pushes stick off center in any direction to activate	Wobblestick Joystick
	Child pushes/pulls switch to slide along track	Sliding or trolley switch
	Child pokes pointer into hole or indentation on switch	Poke switches
	Child tilts switch in one direction for "on" and the other for "off"	Tilt or tip switches

Input Source	Student Response Requirements	Variations and Adaptations
* Switches a specific body part	Child uses lateral head rotation	Head switch
	Child squeezes switch between chin and chest	Chin switch
	Child raises eyebrows	Eyebrow switch
	Child moves knee	Knee switch
	Child presses tongue against switch molded to fit in the palate	Palate switch
	Child uses tongue movement	Tongue switch
	Child depresses thumb	Thumb switch
	Child rotates wrist	Wrist switch
* Pneumatic switch	Air movement is created by the child's blowing	
4. Voice input	Child activates through sound production	
5. Touch screen	Child has physical contact with screen, but no physical pressure	
6. Light pen	Child holds pen; directs it to designated location on screen	
7. Membrane keyboard	Child directs body part or device to designated location on keyboard	Response locations on keyboard vary in size from small squares to quadrants of the keyboard

Reprinted with permission from McConville, L., McGregor, G., Panyan, M., & Tobin, D. (1986). Educational matching: Microcomputer applications in the education of handicapped children. In P. Campbell and G. Fein (Eds.), *Young children and microcomputers* (pp. 145–156). Englewood Cliffs, NJ: Prentice Hall.

tions with both objects and people or can be used as learning devices to support preschool curriculum (Buckleitner & Hohmann, 1987; Burns, Goin, & Donlon, 1990).

Single-Switch-Activated Play

Children who are unable to get around their environments independently or manipulate objects are limited in their abilities to use play effectively as a context for learning. A particular difficulty for children with limited manipulation is the fact that play involves toys and other objects. To learn, for example, that an action such as turning a knob results in music, children need to be able to manipulate the knob on a music box. To learn social rules and relationships within a play context may require manipulation and other motor skills in order to use the housekeeping center, do an art activity, or use outdoor play equipment. Technology can facilitate children's participation in a wide range of play activities, thus providing them with opportunities to use play as a context for learning cognitive, social, and other skills.

Switch-Activated Toy Play. Toy play provides children with opportunities to learn that performing an action results in an outcome and by experimentation children learn to manipulate toys in ways that produce various outcomes. A switch interface removes the need for manipulation or fine motor skills typically required in toy play by allowing certain types of toys to be activated electronically (Hanline, Hanson, Veltman, & Spaeth, 1983). Almost any switch interface can be hooked up to a battery-operated toy, and many common toys such as trucks, trains, music boxes, and busy boxes either have been adapted by suppliers to activate by switch interfaces or can be modified by an adult with knowledge of simple electronics (Burkhart, 1986; Torner, 1986). Rather than turn the knob on the music box or pump the handle of a top, a child activates a switch that electronically turns the music on or makes the top spin. Through switch-activated toy play, children are able to play independently, self-direct their actions, and discover simple relationships between switch activation and outcome (Schaeffler, 1988) that involve concepts of causality and means-end.

There are both benefits of and limitations to single-switch-activated toy play. Of primary importance is a child's curiosity about the toy and interest in the result that occurs when the toy is activated. Since switch-activated toy play enables a child to manipulate a toy in only one way, however, the toy may quickly become boring to a child who understands the result of activation or who is no longer interested in the outcomes (Warren & Horn, 1987). Most toys are seldom manipulated by children in the same ways again and again, nor are they likely to be interacted with in exactly the ways the toys were designed to be used. A child may, for example, spin the wheels while holding a truck upside down or roll it across the ground, choosing whether to put objects into the truck and what kinds of objects. Switch-activated toy play does not provide the same opportunities for learning that children have when manipulating toys in a variety of ways. Nevertheless, the switch operates to allow a child with limited manipulation skills at least to activate a toy in one way.

Since they have a variety of interests and enjoy a variety of outcomes, children need to be excited by and interested in what the toys do when activated. Sometimes these outcomes can be produced electronically. For example, children who enjoy a toy that moves can explore these interests easily through switch-activated toys. Other electronic toys marketed for young children (e.g., Cabbage Patch Talking Kids, Fred the Stuffed Dog) are activated by a child's vocalizations (Mittler, 1988), and provide normalized play experiences without requiring special switch adaptations. It is therefore important to have a variety of toys that can be operated by switches or by vocalizations. Single-switch-activated toys enhance toy play to the extent that opportunities are provided for children to pursue their own interests and to learn about outcomes resulting from activating different types of toys. Such activities can also be a first step in the development of skills used in learning contingency relationships, achieving mobility, using computers for learning and expression (e.g., writing), or, for children who are non-speaking, operating more complex expressive communication devices (Musselwhite & St. Louis, 1989).

Switch-Activated Activity Participation. While toys are central to young children's play, even very young children use materials other than toys or participate in activities other than toy play, such as art, cooking, and literacy activities. While the most common use of switch-activated play involves use of a single switch to activate a toy, switch interfaces can be incorporated into a broad array of activities to facilitate children's participation (Levin & Enselein, 1990). Switch interfaces are best incorporated into activities when children are otherwise unable to participate, even partially (York, Nietupski, & Hamre-Nietupski, 1985), and should not be used as the activity (Garner & Campbell, 1987). Activities into which switches can be incorporated are those typical for a child of similar age and important in the settings in which the child participates, determined by a family's choice for child care

and family activities. Toddlers, for example, are more likely to participate in such settings as library story hour or parent-infant-toddler or
family day-care play groups, whereas preschoolers may attend nursery
or child-care programs where activities are more structured (e.g., art,
music, playtime).

Switches can enhance children's activity participation in many
ways. An answering machine tape (i.e., a fixed loop tape) can be recorded with appropriate phrases (such as "my turn now") so that a child
can participate more fully in an opening circle or group activity or be
the helper responsible for telling the other children to clean up, using a
tape recorder and a fixed loop tape. Any number of phrases appropriate
within an activity can be recorded, and children can use several tapes
that have been individualized to suit particular activities (Place &
Soukup, 1992). A child with a switch-activated tape recorder might be
responsible for turning on the music during a gross motor activity such
as musical chairs. A switch can activate a drum so that a child has an
instrument during music or a battery-operated Spin-Art to create a
picture during art. Many battery-operated games can be modified and
interfaced with switches to allow a child with limited manipulation
abilities to play the game alone or with other children. Children can
also amuse themselves by listening to tape-recorded stories.

While the basic switch and battery-operated toy or tape recorder
can be wired together easily, some uses of switch interfaces to facilitate
activity participation can require more complex technology. Switch
interfaces can be connected to such AC current appliances as a blender
through a switch-control unit so that a child can assist with meal preparation or help with snack in a preschool or child-care setting. A televi-
sion, VCR, slide projector, music system, or any small appliance can be
connected to a switch through a control unit so that children can select
and control their own entertainment. When AC rather than battery
current is required, a control unit must be added to ensure safety (e.g.,
Burkhart, 1987). Teachers and parents may need to work with therapists, rehabilitation engineers, or adaptive-device specialists to identify
ways to adapt an activity or part of an activity through technology use.

Contingency-Learning Experiences

Many children with disabilities may be physically able to activate
a switch, but determining the extent to which children understand the
contingent relationship between switch and toy can be more difficult
(Campbell, 1993; Esposito & Campbell, 1993). The term *contingency*
relates to an understanding of a relationship, or causality, between two

events. Infants are believed to learn about response-outcome object contingencies on the basis of knowledge of results of their motor actions such as kicking, swatting, or batting, or manipulation schemes such as banging, squeezing, poking, twisting, or crumpling (Sullivan & Lewis, 1990). Infants and young children whose manipulation abilities are limited due to physical dysfunction or whose manipulation competence is delayed may be at a disadvantage for learning response-outcome contingencies related to objects. Contingency-learning experiences provide opportunities for children to become aware of and actively control the relationships between their own responses and outcomes. Such learning enables infants to begin to make sense out of their physical and social worlds. For children with severe disabilities, such learning is an essential step toward using more sophisticated types of technology for such functional skills as communication, mobility, or recreation and play.

The most researched contingency-learning curriculum for infants and young children has been developed for infants with disabilities, with whom it has been effective in providing opportunities to acquire contingency learning (Brinker & Lewis, 1982a, 1982b, 1982c; Sullivan & Lewis, 1990, 1993). This curriculum uses a computer to combine several switch interfaces and toys in order to provide contingency learning activities. Parents use the curriculum at home in twice-weekly sessions. The curriculum includes six levels of contingency-learning activities: (1) basic contingency awareness; (2) specific contingency mastery; (3) contingency variation; (4) additional contingencies and variation; (5) contingency puzzle; and (6) additional contingencies. Children are presented with two switch interfaces (e.g., a kick switch, an arm-pull switch), only one of which activates a toy. The computer monitors the child's responses and reverses the contingent switch about halfway through the session. A home teacher visits weekly to monitor and alter curriculum levels as child data warrant. Most of the infants with whom the curriculum has been used to date have had diagnoses of Down syndrome. Children with delayed development or with cerebral palsy have been less frequent research subjects and may require considerable skill on the part of the teacher or early intervention team to ensure proper positioning, sufficient response availability, and adequately motivating outcomes when toys are activated (Sullivan & Lewis, 1993).

Contingency-learning opportunities require a computer and software in order to provide children with successively more complex "problems" to solve and to learn cognitive concepts that typically developing children acquire through object manipulation. The use of a computer program provides opportunities for children's acquisition of contingency learning to be determined on the basis of inspection of response data under a variety of conditions (Behrmann & Lahm, 1984; Esposito & Campbell, 1993). The opportunity for professionals to judge children's learning on the basis of response data is critical when children have severe disabilities, limited motor responses, low rates of motor response, or a limited number of toys or outcomes of switch activation in which they show interest. These children may be able to use a standard contingency learning curriculum only with systematic attention to positioning, motivating outcomes, and responses (Campbell, 1989; Campbell & Place, 1993).

Computers and Learning

With the introduction of microcomputers have come controversies about the ages at which they should be introduced to children and the ways in which computers are incorporated into preschool programs. Empirical evidence, although limited, indicates that even the youngest children are fascinated by the computer and view it as a form of play when software and peripherals are available that allow children to manipulate objects on a screen or use computers to solve problems (Clements, 1991). Incorporated into early childhood classrooms as a learning station, they have been reported to provide children opportunities to choose the computer among several available activities appropriate for young children's learning interests (Buckleitner & Hohmann, 1987). Girls and boys have been found not to differ in their selection of a computer activity, and the computer is no more likely to be selected than other learning centers, such as the housekeeping, art, or block areas (Clements & Nastasi, 1988). Since they create the environments in which computers are introduced and provide support for children as they learn to interact with the computer, adults play an important role. Adults need to be easily available when children get frustrated and to reinforce children's interactions (Shade, Nida, Lipinski, & Watson, 1986). When these conditions are met, even very young preschool-age children can acquire skills, such as problem solving, and information, such as concepts, through interactions with computers (Clements, 1987, 1991; Haugland, 1992).

Several types of software are available for use by toddlers and preschool children, including computer-assisted instruction (CAI), computer-managed instruction (CMI), and tools (e.g., Logo programming; drawing programs) (Davidson, 1989). Very few software programs that use CMI are available for young children. The majority of software packages are either of the CAI, drill-and-practice variety, or provide children with opportunities to use the computer as a tool for music, writing, drawing, painting, or robotic control (Clements, 1991). Drill-and-practice software provides children with experiences that are similar to activities such as completing written worksheets and are thus not likely to capitalize on young children's learning styles and interests (Clements, 1991). Children prefer programs that give them opportunities to interact with and have some degree of control over the computer (Haugland, 1992; Hutinger, 1986). Use of CAI drill-and-practice software with young children may result in boredom (Buckleitner & Hohmann, 1987; Clements, 1986). However, in one study (Haugland, 1992) comparing time spent with developmental (i.e., tool) and nondevelopmental (CAI) software, 4- and 5-year-old children spent more time with the latter. Children who spent time using this drill-and-practice software showed decreased scores on a measure of creativity but increased scores in concentration and short-term memory.

Young children's use of Logo programming has been explored widely with children as young as 3 and has been found to increase children's thinking abilities (e.g., Clements, 1986; Clements & Gullo, 1984; Emihovich & Miller, 1988). This programming language allows children to teach the computer to do tasks such as moving an external turtle device or making graphic designs. Children teach the computer by writing commands (or programs) using the Logo computer language (Davidson, 1989). Tool software programs also allow children to control the computer through word processing, drawing, painting, or playing music. Software that provides children with opportunities to control the computer in unique ways is more easily integrated into early childhood settings than are CAI programs that offer drill and practice of a particular concept. A frequent recommendation for use of computers in early childhood classrooms is for the software on the computer to be matched with actual experiences and activities that allow for manipulation of real objects (Buckleitner & Hohmann, 1987). Accompanying computer manipulation with manipulation of real objects has been found to result in gains in problem solving, abstraction, and conceptual skills not demonstrated when children used computer-only manipulations (Haugland, 1992).

While young children with disabilities are likely to enjoy software that allows them to use the computer as a tool, they may benefit more than their peers who do not have disabilities from drill-and-practice programs. Children with attention deficit disorder, for example, learn to concentrate and demonstrate increased attention spans when working with drill-and-practice software (Hutinger, Johnson, & Clark, 1993). Children with poorly coordinated fine motor skills can increase speed and precision by interacting with software that provides practice in simple manipulation skills. Even scanning skills can be increased through certain software training programs. Use of computers with young children with disabilities has been based largely on a premise of replacing a function that the child cannot (or is unlikely to) perform, such as speaking, writing, playing games, or experiencing environmental control (Butler, 1988). Most applications of computers to learning have related to contingency learning, where the role of the computer is to control the learning circumstances rather than to have the child gain control over the computer. Software that allows children to manipulate objects on the screen may provide learning experiences that approximate actual physical manipulation (Clements, 1991), a finding with important implications for children with physical disabilities who may not be able to manipulate objects or who may do so at such a slow rate that reduced learning opportunities result. Generally, however, investigation of computer use as a means of facilitating learning of young children, and that of children with disabilities, has been very limited, compared with the study of its impact on children's creativity, problem solving, or thinking.

TECHNOLOGY AND SOCIAL INTERACTIONS

The adaptability of technology as well as the wide array of entertaining software available for young children provides an ideal context in which practices known to promote child-child interaction and cooperation can be embedded (McCormick, 1987). Computers can provide a cooperative learning environment (Baron, 1991), although many educators have feared that they might foster isolation. The extent to which technology promotes cooperative interaction or isolation depends in part on the social context in which it is used. When computers are introduced into preschool programs through learning stations, for example, two or more children can be encouraged to work together cooperatively (Clements, 1991). The most important factor in promoting cooperative interaction among young children is the role of the teacher, who can promote interaction by structuring social requirements such as turn-taking, promoting question answering and problem solving, and generally supporting cooperation and reinforcing participation (Dickinson, 1986). That teachers play an instrumental role in fostering cooperation and interaction among children using a computer is not surprising, since it is similar to their role in connection with other types of play and activities.

Young children have been found to prefer to work at a computer with other children rather than alone (Shade et al., 1986). Selection of appropriate software is also important in promoting cooperation. Open-ended programs that allow children to create or explore using the computer as a tool and that are designed to facilitate participation in typical group activities are more likely than drill-and-practice programs to facilitate interaction. For example, such software as the UCLA/Los Angeles Unified School District programs are designed for use by children in groups and to promote social interaction around games and action-oriented songs (Behrmann et al., 1989). The computer has been found to facilitate socially directed behavior of young children with multiple disabilities (Spiegel-McGill, Zippiroli, & Mistrett, 1989), although reactive toys and materials have been found superior to computer programs in increasing social behavior of young children who are typical or who have mild disabilities (Bambara, Spiegel-McGill, Shores, & Fox, 1984).

Peripherals can be used to create the positive interdependence quality of cooperative learning environments. For example, a concentration-type game can be easily structured to accommodate diverse skill levels and promote interaction through use of an alternative input device and a minor change in rules (McGregor, 1988). Rather than defining a "turn" as a two-step process of uncovering a box and finding its match, a child without number and memory skills can make the first response of uncovering the box and a more capable child makes the match. The responses of both are required for "success" within a structure that places the visual-memory burden of the task on the second child. A second modification involving the *Adaptive Firmware Card* enables the first child to make his or her numerical selection from a string of numbers displayed on the bottom of the screen by hitting a single switch. The number highlighted by a scanning cursor at the time the switch is depressed is accepted by the computer as numerical input just as if the numbers had been depressed on the standard keyboard. A comparison of this cooperative structure with a baseline phase that involved merely placing two children together at the computer revealed a shift from negative or "helping" interactions to more positive social interactions between the two children (McGregor, 1988).

Assistive devices that enable children to play, speak, or move around the environment facilitate their inclusion in activities and routines (Mistrett, Raimondi, & Barnett, 1990). Assistive technology is one means of facilitating physical and social inclusion of toddlers and preschoolers in regular child care, nursery school, or other educational environments as well as in home and community activities and routines

(Campbell, 1993; Spiegel-McGill et al., 1989). However, in order for these devices to be maximally effective, parents and other family members, teachers, and other children must structure the physical and social environment, and especially provide opportunities for their use. Many adults do not wait for children to respond using communication devices and/or miss children's attempts to initiate communication, particularly when children are using devices that do not speak (i.e., the adult or another child must look at a picture or symbol). Teachers and parents must think creatively about ways in which switches and other types of interface devices can be used promote children's inclusion in play and other types of activities.

Accomplishing speech, play, mobility, and other activities by means of assistive devices is better than not being able to accomplish them at all. For example, young children unable to use speech are not likely to interact with other children, ask questions, or express their feelings. Although not as ideal as being able to speak, an assistive-communication device expands children's capabilities for both spoken and written expression. The communication device must be accessible to the child, in working order, easy to move around, and easy to use in order to fully replace natural speech. Similarly, mobility devices need to be easily transportable, able to traverse a wide variety of terrains, usable within a classroom and rooms in a house, and in working order for their use to replace walking and running. Environments may have to be structured physically (e.g., place furniture in a room so that a child can use a mobility device) and socially (e.g., provide opportunities for children to initiate communication using a device) by adults in order to ensure their maximal benefit as one means of including young children with disabilities in age-appropriate typical environments.

TECHNOLOGY AND COMMUNICATION

The roots of language and cognitive and social learning lie in an infant's early physical and vocal interactions. As children grow older and acquire greater competence in language, speech is used both to exercise control over and to acquire information about the world. While difficulty with movement may impede interactions with the environments, some children have difficulty learning language or with speaking or writing. Technology provides a variety of alternative and augmentative forms of communication for children who are unable to speak or to speak clearly or quickly enough. Communication aids are activated by a child's response and produce output that is either visual or auditory (or both). A light may scan a series of pictures and/or words, and the child may stop the scanner on the desired word (or phrase). The person with whom the child is interacting, in turn, "reads" the picture or words, or a child may stop a scanner on the desired word or phrase, and the aid may "say" what the child has indicated. The most common communication aids in use today produce speech output through digitized speech, which can be programmed to speak in male or female, adult or child voices.

Most technological communication aids require an understanding of contingencies, and those that provide a child with pictures that, when selected, speak words or phrases are usable by children who understand symbols (i.e., that the picture represents a particular word or phrase) as well. Those that use letters, words, or phrases require children to understand these symbols and, in some instances, to be able to combine them in order to speak. Various motor abilities are also required, at the minimum the ability to stop and start a switch interface or to point to a particular place on the board with fingers, a pointer, or a light pointer. Thus, the cognitive understandings and motor control required to operate augmentative communication aids often restrict their use to children who are 2 or older (Behrmann et al., 1989; Butler, 1988), although the use of dedicated communication devices with non-speaking children as young as 2 and 3 has been well established (Hutinger, 1986).

Some clinicians view single-switch-activated toy play as a way to prepare children to use a communication device, particularly children likely to access the device through a single switch (e.g., Burkhart, 1987; Musselwhite & St. Louis, 1989). The steps in one training sequence (Butler, 1988) are (1) use of switches to produce interesting effects; (2) use of single and dual switches to initiate a scanning array and stop the scanner at a desired location; and (3) progression to more complex scanning techniques, focused on facilitating a speedy choice selection in the context of a vocal communication output device. Others suggest experiences with switch-activated tape recorders to teach children predictable interactions with people in their environment (Place & Soukup, 1992). Using computers with communication software (e.g., Touch-Com) with membrane access devices can be effective in introducing young children to communication but, due to the computer's lack of portability, is useful as a communication mode only in the most structured circumstances (e.g., Behrmann et al., 1989).

Teachers, parents, or speech language pathologists can program the access device into as many blocks as a child can touch accurately, place whatever symbols are desired onto the blocks, and program the computer software to speak a word, phrase, or sentence that relates to the symbol. The recent introduction of more sophisticated communication devices that contain their own computer chips has extended their use to younger children because of their adaptability in both input mode and symbolic representation. Various aids are distributed by different suppliers (see Table 9.2 for listings).

For many children, aids that use Minspeak technology (exclusively distributed by Prentke-Romich Company) may offer the greatest range of variety. These devices can be accessed through audio or visual scanning and a switch, a light pointer, or direct selection. The device speaks for the child using digitized speech. Each is programmable to include information unique to a particular child, and the most sophisticated devices can be used to input into a computer.

Many more toddlers and young children could benefit from communication devices than are now provided them at an early age (Van Tatenhove, 1987). Reluctance to recommend such devices is sometimes due to cost, unfamiliarity with what is available, or an expectation that a child will eventually speak. There are many ways of communicating that rely neither on speech nor on technologically based devices. Children can use simple communication devices (such as the switch-fixed loop tape described above) or can point to object or picture communication boards (Burkhart, 1987). Others may learn to use sign language, and many will communicate using a combination of sign, vocalizations, and technological or nontechnological aids. Selecting a communication device for a child requires knowledge of motor control, of language development and functioning, and of technology. The rapid and continuing development of dedicated communication aid technology means that new and more sophisticated devices are introduced regularly. While most companies have loan-rental programs, and in some states assistive device centers have materials for loan, most devices are too expensive to allow for selection or purchase mistakes. Teachers and parents need to work together with speech language pathologists, rehabilitation engineers, product consultants, or assistive-technology specialists to determine the best approach for a particular child.

TECHNOLOGY AND MOBILITY SKILLS

Mobility provides young children independence and child-directed access to people and objects in the environment. Parents and therapists have traditionally been reluctant to use a mobility device with young children due to concerns about the length of time it may be needed

Table 9.2. Selected Examples of Resources for Technology Software and Peripherals for Young Children

Company	Products
ABLENET 1081 10th Avenue, S. E. Minneapolis, MN 55414-1312 (800) 322-0956	Games/toys (e.g., *Bed Bugs*) Switches (e.g., *Big Red, Jelly Bean Switch*) Communication Devices (e.g., *SpeakEasy*)
Don Johnston Development Equipment P.O. Box 639 1000 North Rand Road, Bldg 115 Wauconda, IL 60084 (312) 526-2682	Specialized Computer Input (e.g., *Touch Window*) Computer Interfaces (e.g., *Adaptive Firmware Card, Ke:nx*) Switch Games (e.g., *Interaction Games, Join the Circus*)
Innocomp 26210 Emery Road Warrenville Heights, OH (216) 464-3636	Communication Devices (e.g., *Say-It-All, Say-It-Simply Plus, Scan-It-All*)
Macomb Projects Western Illinois University 27 Horrabin Hall Macomb, IL 61455 (309) 298-1634	Communication Software (e.g., *EasyCom*) Switch Training Software (e.g., *Master Blaster, Switch'N See*)
Toys for Special Children 385 Warburton Avenue Hasting, NY 10706 (914) 478-0960	Battery-operated Toys (e.g., *Musical Toys, Sesame St. Toys*) Specialized Switches (e.g., *Button Switch, Computer Keyboard Switch*)
Prentke Romich Company 1022 Heyl Road Wooster, OH 44691 (800) 642-8255	Communication Devices (e.g., *Liberator, TouchTalker, LightTalker*) Communication Training Aids (e.g., *Versascan*)
UCLA/LAUSD Micropcomputer Software Department of Pediatrics 1015 Gayley Avenue, #1079 Los Angeles, CA 90024 (213) 825-4821	Software Games (e.g., *Dinosaur Game, This is the Way We Wash Our Face, The Wheels on the Bus*)

(e.g., the child may learn a more independent form of mobility), concern that device use may impede mobility development, availability and cost of motorized chairs for young children, and safety. That children as young as 18 to 24 months can learn to use a motorized vehicle has been demonstrated in a number of studies (Butler, 1984; Butler, Okamoto, & McKay, 1983) where both the types of training strategies and the effects of mobility on young children's overall development have been investigated (e.g., Verburg, Snell, Pilkington, & Milner, 1984). Young children have been trained to operate motorized wheelchairs as well as toy vehicles adapted to provide powered mobility.

The single most important training factor is the time that toddlers and young children need to spend operating the chair or vehicle to learn about control of their own mobility. Creating opportunities to provide sufficient time can be a challenge in preschool programs or family activities. More open environments, such as a gym or playground, provide opportunities to learn to activate, stop, and steer and maneuver the device. Most children can learn fundamental skills (e.g., start/stop and basic steering) safely in these environments with approximately 6 to 10 hours of use (Butler, 1988). Opportunities for this length of training time are not likely to occur naturally within typical functional activities. Children provided with powered mobility vehicles within an integrated preschool program used them to move between activities and rooms (e.g., to the classroom, between the classroom and gym). The total length of time activation switches were used, automatically recorded by timer devices placed on the vehicles, averaged less than three hours over a 15-week period.

Physical or occupational therapists are likely to be familiar with the wider range of powered mobility chairs becoming available to help young children become mobile as early as possible. These are expensive, often bulky, and may not fit under typical preschool tables, requiring modifications either in children's seating or in the physical environment of a classroom. Modified toy vehicles (e.g., Barbie's car, jeep) offer alternatives to more costly powered mobility devices and may be more motivating for young children to learn to operate. While a limited number of already modified vehicles are available through suppliers, a wide range of vehicles can be purchased through toy stores or catalogues and modified to physically position or support a child, as well as electronically. However, modification requirements represent a limitation, since activation devices (e.g., switch interface) may be difficult to alter, and it may not be possible to change the steering mechanism. Ultimately, young children who will use powered mobility permanently will use motorized wheelchairs. These can be operated through a variety of switch interfaces, but most typically with a joystick interface to stop, start, and steer the chair. Since very few toy vehicles are equipped with joystick interfaces, a young child who learns to use a vehicle through some other switch interface and/or steering mechanism may later have to relearn skills required to operate a motorized chair.

Most young children can move independently and competently through most environments by the age of 2, able to move to locations they choose, access a wide variety of objects and situations, and explore relatively free from adult control. Young children delayed in learning to move independently are denied such opportunities for self-directed exploration. While powered mobility vehicles and chairs may not provide the full range of options possible through walking and other movement skills (e.g., climbing), children can gain independence and a sense of control of themselves and their actions. For this reason alone, powered mobility should be made possible for children with disabilities as early as possible.

ASSISTIVE-TECHNOLOGY RESOURCES FOR YOUNG CHILDREN

The use of technology by infants and young children has gained acceptance during the past decade. Early childhood programs report increased purchase and use of computers (e.g., Buckleitner & Hohmann, 1987; Clements, 1991), which children clearly must learn to use to participate fully in their current and future worlds. For children with disabilities, the rapid development in technology has yielded innovative devices that assist play, communication, and mobility in ways not previously possible. Support for the importance of technological use by children with disabilities has been provided both through research and clinical applications that demonstrate positive benefits and through public policy requiring the use of technology to enhance children's participation in home, school, and community environments.

Many resources are available to provide parents and professionals with information about computers and technology use with young children. While companies come and go quickly in the area of technology, the resources listed in Table 9.2 represent long-standing sources of quality information and products for technology use with young children and particularly for those with disabilities. This list is intended for use by educators and related services personnel interested in obtaining catalogues and product information from these sources.

Other resources are available to aid professionals and families in learning about computers, assistive technology, and adaptations. Many computer companies and organizations support the use of computers and assistive technology with young children. Assistive-technology centers or resource programs have been established in many states and can be located by contacting a state department of education's special education or early childhood education division. In other states, technological resources are available through regional instructional materials centers operated by the state's special education division. Figure 9.2 lists some of the resources available for finding out more about technology use with young children.

Figure 9.2. A Sampling of Organizations/Publications Related to Technology and Persons with Disabilities

Apple Computer, Inc. Worldwide Disability Solutions Group 20525 Mariani Avenue Cupertino, CA 95014 (408) 974-7910	**Electronic Learning** Scholastic, Inc. 730 N. Broadway New York, NY 10003-9538 212-505-3000
Technology and Learning Peter Li, Inc. 330 Progress Road Dayton, OH 45449 513-847-5900	**IBM Special Needs Systems** P.O. Box 1328 Boca Raton, FL 33429-1328 (800) 426-4832 (for information) (800) 426-3388 (to order)
Closing the Gap P.O. Box 68 Henderson, MN 56044 (612) 248-3294	**RESNA-Association for the Advancement of Rehabilitation Technology** 1101 Connecticut Avenue, NW, Suite 700 Washington, DC 20036 (202) 857-1199
Communication Outlook Artificial Language Laboratory Michigan State University 405 Computer Center East Lansing, MI 48824-1042 (517) 353-0870	**U.S. Society for Augmentative & Alternative Communication** Barkley Memorial Center P.O. Box 830732 Lincoln, NE 68583-0732 (402) 472-3956
Council for Exceptional Children (CEC) Center for Special Education Technology Information Exchange 1920 Association Drive Reston, VA 22091 (800) 345-8320	

Effective use of technology with all young children requires skills that many parents, teachers, related services personnel, and other adults may not have, especially competence in the use of technology, such as computers; knowledge of software and how it can be used to enhance children's learning and participation; and knowledge of assistive devices in a wide range of areas such as communication, mobility, or environmental control. In today's rapidly changing marketplace, any one person is unlikely to possess all of the required skills. Specialists in assistive devices, related services personnel familiar with device use related to their specialty area (e.g., speech language pathologists who know about augmentative communication), rehabilitation engineers, and other specialists may be valuable resources for parents and early childhood educators seeking to use technology to support children's learning or to promote independence of children with disabilities.

In the last 15 years, the microcomputer has revolutionized the way in which we do business, communicate with others, and generally conduct our lives. The impact of this technology has opened many doors for people with disabilities. Digitized speech has made communication devices understandable by other people, and the design of new chips has enabled computer technology to be embedded within these devices. The popularity of computers has been extended to allow even the youngest children with disabilities to use them and other forms of technology as media for learning and for gaining inclusion within typical environments. Even with all these advances, the full potential of technology for young children or for those with disabilities has yet to be realized. The continued development of more sophisticated and user-friendly devices, new software, and new teaching strategies can only serve to enhance the lives of all young children, and especially of those with disabilities.

REFERENCES

Anselmo, A., & Zinck, R. A. (1987). Computers for young children? Perhaps. *Young Children, 42*, 22–27.

Bambara, L. M., Spiegel-McGill, P., Shores, R., & Fox, J. J. (1984). A comparison of reactive and nonreactive toys on severely handicapped children's manipulative play. *JASH, 9*, 142–149.

Baron, L. J. (1991). Peer tutoring, microcomputer learning and young children. *Journal of Computing in Childhood Education, 2*, 27–40.

Behrmann, M. M., Jones, J. K., & Wilds, M. L. (1989). Technology intervention for very young children with disabilities. *Infants and Young Children, 1*, 66–77.

Behrmann, M. M., & Lahm, L. (1984). Babies and robots: Technology to assist learning of young multiply disabled children. *Rehabilitation Literature*, 45, 194–201.

Brinker, R. P., & Lewis, M. (1982a). Discovering the competent handicapped infant: A process approach to assessment and intervention. *Topics in Early Childhood Special Education*, 2(2), 1–16.

Brinker, R. P., & Lewis, M. (1982b). Making the world work: A learning prosthesis for handicapped infants. *Exceptional Children*, 49, 163–170.

Brinker, R. P., & Lewis, M. (1982c). Contingency intervention in infancy. In J. Anderson (Ed.), *Curricula for high risk and handicapped infants* (pp. 37–41). Chapel Hill: University of North Carolina, Technical Assistance and Development System.

Buckleitner, W. W., & Hohmann, C. F. (1987, June). Technological priorities in the education of young children. *Childhood Education*, pp. 337–340.

Burkhart, L. (1986). *More homemade battery devices for severely handicapped children with suggested activities*. Millville, PA: Burkhart.

Burkhart, L. J. (1987). *Using computers and speech synthesis to facilitate communicative interaction with young and/or severely handicapped children.* College Park, MD: Author.

Burnette, J. (1990, April). *Assistive technology design in special education.* Reston, VA: Council for Exceptional Children, ERIC Clearinghouse on Handicapped and Gifted Children.

Burns, M. S., Goin, L., & Donlon, J. T. (1990, January). A computer in my room. *Young Children*, pp. 62–67.

Butler, C. (1984). Effects of powered wheelchair mobility on self-initiative behaviors of two-and-three-year-old children with neuromusculoskeletal disorders. In *Proceedings of the Second International Conference of Rehabilitation Engineering* (pp. 167–177). Ottawa.

Butler, C. (1988). High tech tots: Technology for mobility, manipulation, communication, and learning in early childhood. *Infants and Young Children*, 1, 66–73.

Butler, C., Okamoto, G., & McKay, T. (1983). Powered mobility for very young disabled children. *Developmental Medicine and Child Neurology*, 25, 472–474.

Campbell, P. H. (1989). Students with physical disabilities. In R. Gaylord-Ross (Ed.), *Integration strategies for persons with handicaps* (pp. 53-76). Baltimore: Paul H. Brookes.

Campbell, P. H.(1993). Physical management and handling procedures. In M. E. Snell (Ed.), *Instruction of students with severe disabilities* (4th ed., pp. 248–263). New York: Merrill.

Campbell, P. H., & Place, P. L. (1993). Contingency learning with young children with multiple disabilities. Manuscript submitted for publication.

Chevat, R. (1992, June). Laptop learners: What you need to know about computers and your child. *Sesame Street Parents' Guide*, pp. 24–26.

Chin, K. (1984). In the school room "A" for access. *Info World*, 6, 26–27.

Clements, D. H. (1986). Effects of Logo and CAI environments on cognition and creativity. *Journal of Educational Psychology, 78*, 309–318.

Clements, D. H. (1987). Longitudinal study of the effects of Logo programming on cognitive abilities and achievement. *Journal of Educational Computing Research, 3*, 73–94.

Clements, D. H. (1991). Current technology and the early childhood curriculum. In B. Spodek & O. N. Saracho (Eds.), *Yearbook in early childhood education Vol. 2: Issues in early childhood curriculum* (pp. 106–131). New York: Teachers College Press.

Clements, D. H., & Gullo, D. F. (1984). Effects of computer programming on young children's cognition. *Journal of Educational Psychology, 76*, 1051–1058.

Clements, D. H., & Nastasi, B. K. (1988). Effects of computer environments on social-motional development: Logo and computer-assisted instruction. *Computers in the Schools, 2*(2–3), 11–31.

Davidson, J. I. (1989). *Children and computers together in the early childhood classroom.* Albany, NY: Delmar.

Dickinson, D. K. (1986). Cooperation, collaboration, and a computer: Integrating a computer into a first-grade writing program. *Research in the Teaching of English, 20*, 357–378.

Emihovich, C., & Miller, G. E. (1988). Talking to the turtle: A discourse analysis of Logo instruction. *Discourse Processes, 11*, 183–201.

Esposito, L., & Campbell, P. H. (1993). Computers and the physically and severely handicapped. In J. Lindsey (Ed.), *Computers and exceptional individuals* (rev. ed., pp. 105–124). Columbus: Merrill/Macmillan.

Garner, J. B., & Campbell, P. H. (1987). Technology for persons with severe disabilities: Practical and ethical considerations. *Journal of Special Education Technology, 21*, 122–132.

Hanline, M. F., Hanson, M. J., Veltman, M. A., & Spaeth, D. M. (1983). Electromechanical teaching toys for infants and toddlers with disabilities. *Teaching Exceptional Children, 18*(1), 20–29.

Haugland, S. W. (1992). The effect of computer software on preschool children's developmental gains. *Journal of Computing in Childhood Education, 3*, 15–30.

Hutinger, P. L. (1986). *Activating children through technology (ACTT) curriculum.* Macoomb: Western Illinois University.

Hutinger, P. L., Johnson, J., & Clark, L. (1993, August). Illinois Head Start children achieve computer literacy. *Early Childhood Report: Children with special needs and their families, 4*(8), 6–8.

Killian, J., Nelson, J., & Byrd, D. (1986, August/September). Child's play: Computers in early childhood programs. *The Computing Teacher*, pp. 13–16.

Lahm, E. A. (Ed.). (1989). *Technology with low incidence populations: Promoting access to education and learning.* Reston, VA: Center for Special Education Technology.

Levin, J., & Enselein, K. (1990). *Fun for everyone: A guide to adapted leisure activities for children with disabilities.* Minneapolis: Ablenet.

McCormick, L. (1987). Comparison of the effects of a microcomputer activity and toy play on social and communication behaviors of young children. *Journal of the Division for Early Childhood, 11,* 195–205.

McGregor, G. (1988). *The effect of cooperative learning structures on the academic performance and peer interaction of students with mild disabilities during CAI* (Unpublished technical report). Baltimore, MD: Johns Hopkins University Center for Technology in Human Disabilities.

Mistrett, S. G., Raimondi, S. L., & Barnett, M. P. (1990). *The use of technology with preschoolers with handicaps.* Buffalo, NY: Preschool Integration Through Technology Systems.

Mittler, J. (1988). Electronic toys and robots. In M. Behrmann (Ed.), *Integrating computers into the curriculum* (pp. 79–102). Boston: College Hill Press.

Musselwhite, C., & St. Louis, K. (1989). *Communication programming for persons with severe handicaps: Vocal and augmentative strategies* (2nd ed.). Boston: Little, Brown, & Co.

Papert, S. (1980). *Mindstorms: Children, computers and powerful ideas.* New York: Basic Books.

Parette, H. P., Van Biervliet, A., & Parette, P. C. (1990). Young children with respiratory problems and assistive technology needs: A nursing care perspective. *Issues in Comprehensive Pediatric Nursing, 13,* 167–191.

Place, P., & Soukup, C. (1992). Easy as 1-2-3: A first augmentative communicative system. *Hearsay.*

Schaeffler, C. (1988). Making toys accessible for children with cerebral palsy. *Teaching Exceptional Children, 20*(3), 26–29.

Shade, D. D., Nida, R. E., Lipinski, J. M., & Watson, J. A. (1986). Microcomputers and preschoolers: Working together in a classroom setting. *Computers in the Schools, 3,* 53–61.

Spiegel-McGill, P., Zippiroli, S. M., & Mistrett, S. G. (1989). Microcomputers as social facilitators in integrated preschools. *Journal of Early Intervention, 13,* 249–260.

Sullivan, M. W., & Lewis, M. (1990). Contingency intervention: A program portrait. *Journal of Early Intervention, 14,* 367–375.

Sullivan, M. W., & Lewis, M. (1993). Contingency, means-end skills, and the use of technology in infant intervention. *Infants and Young Children, 5*(4), 58–77.

Torner, R. S. (1986). A switch for education: Utilizing simplified microswitch technology. *Journal of Special Education Technology, 8*(4), 25–31.

Van Tatenhove, G. (1987). Teaching power through augmentative communication. *Journal of Childhood Communication Disorders, 10,* 185–199.

Verburg, G., Snell, E., Pilkington, M., & Milner, M. (1984). Effects of powered mobility on young handicapped children and their families. In *Proceedings of the Second International Conference of Rehabilitation Engineering* (pp. 172–175). Ottawa.

Warren, S. F., & Horn, E. M. (1987). Microcomputer applications in early childhood special education: Problems and possibilities. *Topics in Early Childhood Education, 7,* 72–83.

Williams, R. A. (1984, April). Preschoolers and the computer. *Arithmetic Teacher,* pp. 39–42.

Wright, J. L., & Samaras, A. S. (1986). Play worlds and microworlds. In P. F. Campbell & G. Fein (Eds.), *Young children and microcomputers* (pp. 73–86). Englewood Cliffs, NJ: Prentice-Hall.

York, J., Nietupski, J., & Hamre-Nietupski, S. (1985). A decision-making process focusing microswitches. *The Journal of the Association for Persons with Severe Handicaps, 10*(4), 214–223.

CHAPTER 10

Issues and Emerging Practice in Preparing Educators to Be Early Interventionists

Jeanette A. McCollum
and Susan P. Maude

The recent past has witnessed growing attention to early intervention, birth–age 3, as a powerful way to influence the developmental and learning outcomes of young children, including those with disabilities and developmental delays. Part H of P.L. 99-457, passed by Congress in 1986 and reauthorized by the passage of P.L. 102-119 in 1991, emphasized in law and subsequent policy a combination of practices viewed as being the most likely to lead toward these outcomes: a family focus, coordinated interagency resources, and integrated, interdisciplinary services. Despite the relatively small amount of funding attached to these congressional initiatives, states generally have responded with enthusiasm, if also with trepidation, to the opportunity to put into place early intervention service systems that are truly responsive to very young children with special needs and their families.

Under the federal legislation, any state choosing to participate in the Part H program must develop and implement policy related to two different personnel components. First, standards for early intervention personnel from a wide array of relevant disciplines (e.g., education, occupational therapy, nursing) must be delineated. Second, a comprehensive system for personnel development must be implemented by each state to ensure that personnel have opportunities to become qualified to deliver early intervention services. These opportunities may range considerably in type (e.g., preservice, in-service), in extensiveness (e.g., one class session to full program), and to which discipline(s) they are provided. However, both preservice and in-service training are to occur on an interdisciplinary basis when appropriate, and must respond specifically to the interrelated nature of development in infants and toddlers (McCollum & Bailey, 1991).

As with all new human service systems, the ability to meet intended goals is dependent on the availability and quality of personnel; thus, as the new birth–age 3 legislation has moved toward full implementation, personnel issues increasingly have loomed among the major roadblocks to achievement, with each state addressing at least the following questions:

- Who will deliver early intervention services?
- What should be included in training for early intervention personnel?
- Does this differ across disciplines?
- Are there enough personnel to meet our needs?
- What certification or licensing is relevant for these personnel?
- How should states go about meeting the need for an increasing number of qualified personnel?

There is now general agreement that professionals working with infants and toddlers with disabilities and their families, regardless of their disciplines, require unique knowledge and skills in addition to or different from those required to work with other populations. In addition, a body of literature defining this unique content, as well as recommended practice for teaching it, has emerged and continues to grow and evolve (Fenichel & Eggbeer, 1990). Many states either are adding new training requirements over and above existing licenses, or are defining new occupational categories that more directly address early intervention needs, in order to ensure that personnel are appropriately and adequately prepared and trained (Bruder & McCollum, 1991).

New training systems are being put into place across multiple disciplines to provide options that enable both current and future personnel to meet these new standards (McCollum & Bailey, 1991). In the discipline of education, new programs developed to prepare personnel for the birth–age 3 level may differ substantially from those in place prior to this new legislation. Increasingly, development of these new programs is in turn bringing about reexamination of older preparation programs in both special education and early childhood education. This impact is particularly evident with regard to the major underlying themes of the new legislation and the service delivery approaches that have emerged from it: a family focus, interdisciplinary teaming, and interagency collaboration.

It is for these reasons that the preparation of early childhood special educators for roles in early intervention settings has been selected as the focus of this chapter, thereby necessitating the exclusion of other important issues that would require chapters of their own. We will examine the emerging role of the early childhood special educator from the perspective of the role of this discipline within a larger multidisciplinary team of early interventionists. The legislative history of early childhood special education as a field is closely tied to the federal special education system (Shonkoff & Meisels, 1990), with activities at the national level playing a critical role in the emergence and 25-year evolution of this field (McCollum & Maude, 1993). A definition of the role of the educator as a member of the early intervention team has emerged within this same context, but has been enriched substantially by increasing collaboration with collateral disciplines from the health, allied health, and social service fields, as well as by an increasingly broad research base in infant development. This chapter therefore will begin with a review of legislation influencing and supporting personnel preparation in early childhood special education, as well as a brief history of professional certification in this field, with particular emphasis on the birth–age 3 level. We will then examine in more depth the evolution of personnel preparation for the birth–age 3 level, and how it contrasts with preparation for working with older children. We will end by speculating on coming changes in the field and their potential impact on future personnel preparation.

PERSONNEL PREPARATION IN ECSE: A BRIEF HISTORY

The development of programs preparing educators in early childhood special education, and subsequently in early intervention, has paralleled the history of federal legislation affecting programs for young children with disabilities. Initially, legislation and policy were designed for the sole purpose of supporting direct services for young children. Later, they expanded to include training or technical assistance for professionals, with allocation of financial resources for staff development, training, and dissemination activities.

The passage of P.L. 90-538 in 1968 provided a dramatic turning point in the development of early childhood special education, establishing the Handicapped Children's Early Education Program (HCEEP). HCEEP, a federal initiative now entitled Early Education Programs for Children with Disabilities (EEPCD), provided funds for the development of model demonstration programs throughout the country. This was the first federal initiative that focused solely on this very young population of children with disabilities and developmental delays. Soon after the establishment of the HCEEP program, the Bureau of Education for the Handicapped (BEH), federal headquarters for all government-funded programs in special education, developed a national technical assistance network designed to provide technical assistance to all HCEEP recipients. As the HCEEP projects began to achieve maturity and to disseminate their methods, in-service became more widely available, more cohesive, and more firmly grounded in experience.

While provisions for preservice personnel training were not a part of this early legislation, the model demonstration programs influenced early childhood personnel development in important ways. First, one major goal of these programs was to disseminate the models developed; technical assistance to other programs became a primary activity of the programs, and in the initial years of early childhood special education, were the major source of training for many personnel across the country. Second, the knowledge that derived from these programs provided the framework for much of what came to be included in university programs preparing early childhood special educators. Since many of the early demonstration programs were housed in university settings, these became practicum settings for university students. The central role of families in the intervention process, as well as the emphases on individualization, interdisciplinary team process, and integrated settings, grew from the experiences of these early programs.

P.L. 94-142, passed in 1975, mandated free, appropriate education services for children with disabilities ages 5 through 18, and provided incentive funds to states should they choose to offer services to children with disabilities ages 3 through 5. A major provision of P.L. 94-142 was the requirement that each state education agency develop its Comprehensive System for Personnel Development (CSPD) for all professionals providing special educational services for children. Therefore, should a state elect to provide such services for children ages 3 through 5, the state CSPD plan would be required to include staff development activities for these personnel as well.

In 1976, the Office of Special Education Programs (OSEP, a new name for the old BEH), funded state implementation grants to encourage states to further expand their services for young children with disabilities (Hebbeler, Smith, & Black, 1991). Included as a requirement for these funds was the provision of in-service staff-development activities. Hence, at the same time that a knowledge base in early childhood special education was emerging from the HCEEP projects and increasingly from university settings, P.L. 94-142 and state planning efforts were providing a major impetus for establishing university training programs to address the development of personnel qualified as early childhood special educators. Moreover, federal competitions for training grants in special education were expanded during the mid-1970s to include programs focused on early childhood. Universities funded through these grants became the major centers within which early childhood special education was developed into an integrated, comprehensive body of knowledge that soon yielded its own textbooks and journals.

Developments related to the provision of early intervention services for children from birth to age 3 therefore represented a next major step in the emergence of personnel efforts in this new field (McCollum & Maude, 1993). Significant impact on early intervention services occurred in 1986 with the passage of P.L. 99-457. As an amendment to P.L. 94-142, this law not only increased the impetus for direct service, but also contained specific provisions related to personnel.

Compared with the rapid development of national and state policy supporting direct services and technical assistance at the preschool and early intervention levels, relatively little movement initially occurred in the development of certification standards for personnel, including early childhood special educators, who would be certified to work with this population (Smith & Powers, 1987). In 1982, seven years after the passage of P.L. 94-142, the National Association of State Directors of Special Education reported that only four states had established a certificate in early childhood special education. Instead, most states utilized teachers having certification in either special education, early childhood education, or both. In 1987, Smith and Powers reported that 15 states had developed early childhood special education requirements.

The personnel requirements of P.L. 99-457 stimulated renewed interest in developing specialized standards for professionals working with young children, with particular emphasis on the birth–age 3 level. Five years after passage of the legislation, Bruder, Klosowski, and Daguio (1991) reported on current state certification requirements for educators and other disciplines for the birth to age 3 and 3- to 5-year-old age groups. Their results indicated that 23 states held some type of licensing requirement (certification, registration, endorsement) for early childhood special educators working with the 3–5 age group, while 19 had requirements for the birth–age 3 group. A more recent report (Hebbeler, 1992) indicated that 23 of 48 states reporting (including the District of Columbia and Puerto Rico) had some form of birth-through-5 or birth to primary certification requirement, whereas an additional 9 reported requirements for the 3–5 or 3–primary age groups, and an additional 10 reported that endorsements for this age group are added to other certificates. Hence, it appears that as of the date of collection of data for this study, it was no longer common for states to have no requirement in place for working with young children with special needs, although only 23 states had requirements specifically linked to the infant/toddler period. As the field of early childhood special education has continued to expand and develop, the need to develop training that is more responsive to the particular population has increasingly been reflected in the development of new certification standards.

To support states as they pursued efforts to develop specialized certification in early childhood special education, the Division for Early Childhood (DEC) of the Council for Exceptional Children (CEC) in 1989 published a position paper providing recommendations for the certification of early childhood special educators (McCollum, McLean, McCartan, & Kaiser, 1989). Building on open discussion that began among interested members of DEC beginning in 1986, this paper recommended that certification be developed specifically for practitioners in early childhood special education, birth–age 5, with additional specialization at either the infant/toddler or the preschool level. Through this paper, DEC strongly advocated that training content be provided that was uniquely suited to very young children with special needs, to include coursework and extensive field experience not only with this population of children, but also with families and interdisciplinary teams. In 1988, the Association of Teacher Educators (ATE) established the Commission on Early Childhood Teacher Education to develop a position paper on the preparation of teachers for young children through age 8 (Association of Teacher Educators and National Association for the Education of Young Children, 1991; Miller, 1992). A subsequent addendum to the ATE paper (*Early Childhood Special Education Teacher Certification*, 1991) recognized the need for specialized training of personnel to work with young children who have disabilities. Agreement between these papers is substantial, and although important differences remain, both efforts are indicative of the recognition that something new is needed, as well as of the commitment of both professional organizations to work together to better define this new area of study. This collaboration is an emerging, welcome trend.

Ascertaining the exact number and location of universities offering programs in early childhood special education is not an easy task. The most complete source of information on special education programs that contain this emphasis is a directory published periodically by the Teacher Education Division (TED) of CEC, listing personnel programs in special education. The data are collected by surveying all colleges and universities in each state, and are updated routinely (Teacher Education Division, 1982, 1987, 1992). In 1983, the TED directory documented 74 Institutions of Higher Education (IHEs) offering training in this area, with an increase to 83 by 1987. The most recent TED directory (1992) shows that the number of programs again increased, from 83 to 130, during the intervening period. No similar information source is available on university programs in early childhood education or in child development that also may have developed early childhood special education as a program of study. Nevertheless, these data clearly demonstrate the rapid development of preservice programs throughout the 1980s and early 1990s, in parallel with the changes in legislation supporting the provision of services to this population.

PRESERVICE PREPARATION FOR
EARLY INTERVENTION, BIRTH–AGE 3

Part H of P.L. 99-457 was the culmination of several years of discussion and political action by professionals and parents interested in providing early intervention services for infants and toddlers with special needs and their families. Within this larger early intervention policy context, notable advances also had been made prior to 1986 with regard to the preparation of personnel for early intervention, birth–age 3. As noted above, these advances were tied at least in part to legislative initiatives. Conversely, however, the personnel components of the new legislation were highly influenced by the thinking that already had taken place.

Defining the Issues

The first formal work undertaken to clarify the roles and training needs of professionals at the birth–age 3 level occurred in 1984, at a meeting organized jointly by the federal Office of Special Education Programs and the Department of Special Education at George Washington University (GWU). Notably, those present represented a variety of disciplines from the education, social service, and health fields. For the first time, attention was clearly focused on personnel issues related to working with children from birth to age 3 with special needs and their families. For early childhood special education, as for the other disciplines present, the GWU meeting was the beginning of what truly became a revolution in thinking about the roles and training needs of personnel in settings serving very young children with disabilities and their families, with participants addressing issues related to

- Delineating the disciplines that work in early intervention settings
- Defining the roles of these disciplines with this population
- Distinguishing among roles of individuals from different disciplines
- Identifying differences in values and approaches among and within disciplines

From this meeting there emerged a view of the roles of the early interventionist as highly complex and multifaceted, and as clearly diverging from the roles of interventionists working with older age levels. In addition, many of these roles were seen as being held in common across disciplines, as well as requiring different perspectives within each discipline; importantly, no one discipline was identified as being able to provide early intervention services alone. A closer look at training content and process therefore was clearly seen as an issue for all disciplines involved in early intervention. The year 1985 also witnessed the first year of funding, through the Division of Personnel Preparation of the Office of Special Education Programs, of a special grant competition for programs preparing personnel to work at the birth–age 3 level. Thus, even prior to the legislation, the field had begun to address the roles and training needs of personnel working with this unique population.

Since 1986, personnel issues have received increasing attention as states have begun to implement wide systems changes in early intervention services. The availability and quality of personnel have come to be seen as key components of these systems (McCollum & Bailey, 1991). For instance, in 1987, a broad-based set of policy recommendations advanced by the Division for Early Childhood, Council for Exceptional Children, contained statements and recommendations as to federal and state roles in ensuring the availability and quality of personnel in multiple disciplines, including the recommendation that licensing standards be reviewed and/or developed for all disciplines serving on early intervention teams (Division for Early Childhood [DEC], 1987). DEC's recommendations for certification of early childhood special educators, birth–age 5 (McCollum et al., 1989) were intended not only to make decisions about the scope and sequence of preservice preparation and certification, but also to help clarify the discipline of early childhood special education. Issues addressed included the unique contributions that the early childhood special educator brings to the interdisciplinary team; early childhood special education as a field distinct from other education fields; and the need for specialized training for more narrowly defined age ranges within the larger early childhood period. Most significant to this chapter was the recommendation that early childhood special educators, prepared for the broader birth–age 5 age range (or if the state so chose, for the birth–age 8 age range), specialize beyond the entry level to work with infants and toddlers and their families.

Simultaneous with these efforts in policy development, new personnel preparation models funded through the Division of Personnel Preparation were helping to further clarify issues, and to translate emerging areas of agreement into practice. Also of considerable impetus to this developing field of early intervention was a five-year national research institute, the Carolina Institute for Research on Infant Personnel Preparation, founded in the late 1980s and funded by OSEP to study preparation at the birth–age 3 level and to assist in identifying and addressing training issues (Bailey, Palsha, & Huntington, 1990). The institute was able to draw on the emerging cross-disciplinary expertise within the early intervention field, providing a framework and support for continuing discussion and study.

Historically, then, a number of different efforts merged in the latter part of the 1980s to yield an initial definition of early intervention, of the roles of early interventionists, and of the implications of these new roles for personnel preparation. Early childhood special educators played an active role in these efforts, and in the process learned a great deal about their own discipline. Despite these changes, however, and irrespective of the changes in certification noted above, programs offering specialized preparation related to the birth–age 3 population do not exist in every state, nor are they well dispersed across disciplines. Availability of higher education programs offering early intervention preparation is often dependent on outside funding (Klein & Campbell, 1990), and may not tie directly to state certification. Ironically, another factor weighing against the development of programs is the lack of state certification, with states being loath to develop such certification where there already exists a lack of personnel to fill current positions. Hence, access to specialized preparation at the preservice level remains limited in many states.

Clarifying Roles: The Content of Personnel Preparation

One of the first major activities of the new Carolina Personnel Institute was to sponsor a three-day working conference with the goal of defining roles, discussing training issues, and prioritizing training needs both within and across disciplines. Prominent professionals from each of 10 disciplines participated. Early childhood special education was represented by nine individuals actively involved in infant personnel preparation. This group agreed that the mission of the early childhood special educator in early intervention settings was "to ensure that environments for handicapped infants and preschoolers facilitate children's development of social, motor, communication, self-help, cognitive, and behavioral skills, and enhance children's self-concept, sense of competence and control, and independence" (Bailey et al., 1990, p. 49). Roles identified as important to and supportive of this mission included the following:

- Conducting screening and child-find programs
- Assessing children's developmental competence
- Planning and providing developmental intervention/services
- Coordinating interdisciplinary services
- Integrating and implementing interdisciplinary team recommendations
- Assessing family needs and strengths
- Planning and implementing family support services or training
- Coordinating services from multiple agencies
- Evaluating program implementation and effectiveness of overall services for young children and their families
- Advocating for children and families
- Consulting with other professionals, families, and other caregivers
- Working effectively as a team member

Although it is evident that many of these roles may be held in common with professionals from other disciplines, the group identified three areas of expertise as unique to the early childhood special educator:

1. Integrating goals from multiple developmental domains within the context of activity-based intervention
2. Using a comprehensive and systematic approach in which as-

sessment, intervention, and evaluation are combined into a coordinated whole

3. Advocating for children and families

Fenichel and Eggbeer (1990) noted that the daily practice of the early
childhood special educator undoubtedly will be working with child and
parent together in a center, a hospital, or a home. Mirroring Bailey et
al.'s (1990) delineation of roles, they note that the early childhood special educator "will use her relationship with the family and resources in
the environment to create experiences for the baby that will offer specific as well as general opportunities to develop social, motor, communication, self help, cognitive and behavioral skills" (p. 15), as well as
contributing actively to a multidisciplinary team. Thus, the educator's
roles in providing early intervention are likely to go beyond those of
classroom-based teachers in several ways. Geik, Gilkerson, and Sponseller (1982) summarized these roles as advocate, program developer, educator, team member, and consultant, emphasizing both child and parent as recipients of these services. More recently, as thinking has evolved
toward a family-centered perspective on service delivery (Dunst &
Trivette, 1988, 1989; Shelton, Jeppson, & Johnson, 1987), roles with
regard to families have become increasingly more clearly delineated.
Winton (1989), for example, summarized family-related roles (and areas of professional competence) as engagement, professional collaboration, assessment, collaborative goal-setting, and implementation.

Although roles are increasingly clear, it is also the case that the
application of any particular role may be extremely varied, depending
on where the early interventionist is employed. Early intervention programs differ from one another on multiple dimensions, all having implications for roles and therefore for the preparation of personnel. As
already noted, early intervention services may be affiliated with a variety of health, social service, or educational agencies or organizations.
Within any setting, services will vary considerably in where the services
generally occur (home, center); whether they involve the infant, the
parent, or both; whether they are provided individually or in groups;
the criteria for eligibility used by the program; who is seen as the
primary recipient of services (parent or child); and other disciplines
available. The teaming model defined by the program also may play a
major part in how the role of the early childhood special educator is
defined (McCollum & Hughes, 1988). When services are based on a
family-centered perspective, the configuration of services will vary considerably even within a particular early intervention program, with

each family receiving a unique configuration of services designed to address their own priorities and concerns. Hence, flexibility may be an overarching quality to be fostered within preservice preparation (Thorp & McCollum, 1988).

A number of studies indicate that early childhood special educators play particularly critical roles in early intervention programs. McCollum and Hughes (1988), in a national study designed to identify teaming practices, found that the educator was often not only the primary or only service provider, but was also the service coordinator, responsible for integration of services from multiple disciplines. This discipline was the one most consistently present in the largest number of programs. A more recent within-state study (McCollum, Cook, & Ladmer, n.d.) found the same patterns. Educators were represented in more programs, and served a wider variety of roles, than professionals from any other discipline. Educators were also more likely to be hired in regular staff positions (as opposed to contracted positions), and more likely to be hired for a larger percentage of time, than individuals from any other discipline.

Thorp and McCollum (1988) described the knowledge and skill base of the early childhood special educator working in early intervention as being comprised of three parts: (1) that which is common across all disciplines working in early intervention (e.g., knowledge of family systems); (2) that which defines the generalist roles that may be filled by any discipline (e.g., service coordination); and (3) that which defines the unique roles of early childhood special educators. The common infancy core includes competencies that fall into four broad categories:

1. Infant-related (e.g., ability to learn from observation, understanding of normal and atypical development)
2. Family-related (e.g., awareness of family systems, understanding of sources of vulnerability in families, supporting and assisting parent competence)
3. Team-related (e.g., common vocabulary, joint planning strategies)
4. Interagency advocacy-related (e.g., knowledge of state legislation, coordination of IFSP across agencies)

Personal qualities of flexibility, maturity, independence, willingness to share, and tolerance were also identified as critical to the successful functioning of any early interventionist.

With regard to the unique training needs of early childhood special

educators functioning as early interventionists, infant-related competencies identified included expertise in infant cognitive, social, and affective development, as well as skills in developmental assessment, design of learning environments, strategies that promote engagement and
interaction, and skills in data collection and evaluation. Unique family-
related competencies included strategies for including family members
in planning and intervention, and for promoting interaction between
parent and child. The latter is emerging as an especially important
area as the field continues to develop (Shonkoff & Meisels, 1990); thus,
whereas in the past programs tended to identify themselves as either
child- or parent-focused, a joint focus constitutes an emerging, powerful theme (Meisels, 1992). Since the educator is likely to be the primary
agent for delivery of services, he or she will gain a particularly intimate
knowledge of the family, and must be able to balance confidentiality
with the need to share information among team members. Teaming
competencies of special relevance to the educator include skill in integrating the knowledge and recommendations of multiple disciplines
into everyday activities that blend into the child's and family's daily
routines.

     It is clear that the nature of infancy impacts both roles and training
needs. The infancy period is unique in the human life span as one of
rapid change in all developmental systems. Two aspects of early life
have particularly direct implications for the training needs of personnel. First, the younger the child, the more intertwined and interdepen-
dent are different domains of development. Second, early development
and learning are inextricably imbedded within the transactional process
between infant and primary caregivers. Program values and practices
must not only take these into account, but must build on and strengthen
these characteristics. The crucial role of family relationships and environments requires that family members be integral members of early
intervention teams, and respect for families and their abilities is essential. The unique characteristics of services for infants and toddlers with
disabilities and their families were clearly recognized in P.L. 99-457,
which had as its major themes the delivery of services that were family-
oriented, interdisciplinary, and interagency. The skill and knowledge
base provided through personnel preparation programs therefore must
support developmental, family-centered, and interdisciplinary perspectives. For the early childhood special educator, early intervention roles
mean increasingly close links to the knowledge bases that define medical and social service disciplines, as well as to the expanding research
base in normal and atypical development.

Early Intervention Training: How Are We Doing?

The best source of data on the evolution of programs preparing personnel for early intervention roles is the Office of Special Education Programs. OSEP's Division of Personnel Preparation conducts annual national competitions to fund university programs to prepare special education and related service personnel. Lists indicating current recipients of grants related to young children with special needs have been compiled and disseminated on an informal basis. Prior to 1985 the emphasis in most funded projects was on preschool-age children, although some programs provided some work related to birth–age 3 (M. Bryan, personal communication). Between 1985 and 1991, special competitions were held for the infant/toddler period. Then, in the 1991–1992 competitions, the entire early childhood period, birth–age 8, was combined into the same competition, separate from the larger special education competition. The number of programs funded specifically to prepare early intervention personnel has increased substantially as a result, increasing from 66 in 1986 to 176 in 1990 (M. Bryan, personal communication).

Given early agreement on the importance of specialized training at the birth–age 3 level, the interest in early childhood special education broadened to the study of how well university programs were already addressing this need. A 1984–1985 national sample of 43 faculty teaching in university programs (primarily special education, child study, educational psychology, and early childhood education) preparing students for work as early childhood special educators found a good deal of consistency among programs in the content areas included in the curriculum as well as in a recognition of the importance of extensive field experiences (Bricker & Slentz, 1988). However, there was considerable variation among programs in the extent to which infant, family, and team content was addressed either through coursework or through field experience. Coursework specifically geared to young children with special needs ranged from one course to a full year or more, and field experience with the population of children from birth–age 5 ranged from none to over 300 clock hours. The primary factor contributing to these differences appeared to be requirements for state certification: For the most part, programs were preparing students for certification other than early childhood special education, necessitating that the majority of program time be spent addressing state requirements related to those certificates. Thus, work at the birth–age 3 level was added within programs directed toward other certification.

A study of 40 federally funded projects in infant personnel preparation for the years 1984–1987 (Bruder & McLean, 1988) yielded similar results. Only 28 of the programs had specific coursework on families. Twenty included coursework on infancy, 16 addressed medical issues, and 4 had coursework in interdisciplinary teaming. Furthermore, only 29 of these federally funded infancy programs contained work in assessment, and only 26 in intervention techniques, related specifically to the infancy period. Thus, even among programs specifically funded to prepare personnel for the birth–age 3 level, areas generally agreed to be important for all disciplines involved in early intervention were not well represented.

A major activity of the Carolina Personnel Institute in 1990 was to complete a national survey of personnel preparation programs in eight disciplines. The goal was to identify the infant/family content included in (1) the general curriculum of a typical student in the particular discipline and (2) curricula designed specifically to provide a birth–age 3 specialization (Bailey, Simeonsson, Yoder, & Huntington, 1990). All programs listed in the national TED directory of special education programs, programs funded through the Office of Special Education Programs, and other programs known to the researchers were included in a telephone survey addressed toward the first goal. (The limitations of this sample should be noted, since programs that might have been in place but not obtainable from these sources were not included. For instance, a notable omission was programs in early childhood education or child development, unless included on one of the above lists.) The second goal was addressed through a more in-depth written survey of programs known to offer a course of study directed specifically toward early intervention. The results indicated that students not enrolled in a specialized curriculum received very little information about the infancy period, about working with families, or about legislative, policy, and implementation issues related to this age period (Bailey, Palsha, & Huntington, 1990). While some programs provided opportunities for students to obtain field experience with children from birth–age 3 and their families, few students took advantage of these experiences unless required to. For both coursework and field experience, variability within disciplines was as great as that among disciplines. Even within early childhood special education programs with infancy specializations, the extent of coursework and field experience differed substantially (Bailey, Palsha, & Huntington, 1990). Clock hours of instruction in normal infant development, for instance, ranged from 4 to 80, whereas work in family services ranged from 0 to 80. In comparing programs providing an infancy focus with those providing a preschool focus, these authors found that students in infancy programs received more instruction in both normal and atypical infant development, infant assessment, and infant intervention. Although the two types of programs provided about equal exposure to family-related content (program models, assessment, services, communication skills) and to case management, both options provided approximately twice as much infant-related content as family-related content. Required clock hours of field experience also differed between these two options, with infant specializations requiring an average of approximately 115 additional hours. Students in infant-related field experiences spent more time in home- and hospital-based programs, although students in both types of programs spent more time in center-based settings than in other settings.

At least three states (California, Illinois, and Louisiana) have completed individual studies similar to the national study by Bailey, Palsha, and Huntington, but also have included early childhood education as a separate discipline of study. Results in each state have been highly congruent with those from the national study (Bevins, in preparation; Hanson, 1990). In Illinois, for instance, the number of clock hours spent in coursework related to child development ranged from 0 to 40 for programs in departments of special education, and from 40 to 250 for programs in early childhood education, whereas clock hours in infant intervention ranged from 0 to 50 and from 2 to 45 for these same two types of programs. As in the national study, considerably more infant- and family-related content was found in the few programs offering a birth–age 3 specialization.

Results from all of these studies indicate that universities may be having difficulty in providing infancy content to preservice students. Current program and university structures, as well as the lack of expertise of current faculty in early intervention content, have been identified as severe barriers standing in the way of such training (Gallagher & Staples, 1990; McCollum & Bailey, 1991). In some disciplines, it may not be feasible to add content related to infancy to already crowded curricula, particularly when the existing program of study is directed toward a specific professional license or certificate. Gallagher and Staples (1990) also found that deans of colleges of education were unwilling to consider the addition of new tracks of study without some indication from the state that they would lead toward state certification.

Whereas there is emerging agreement on the training content needed by early interventionists from multiple disciplines, less attention has been paid to the process of training and the ways in which this new content may require different processes. It is clear, however, that the major themes of the legislation (family focus, interdisciplinary, inter-agency) must be mirrored not only in content but also in process. The National Center for Clinical Infant Programs (Fenichel & Eggbeer, 1990) has identified four variables that are critical to preparing infancy personnel:

1. The provision of a knowledge base concerned with infants, tod-dlers, and their families
2. Opportunities for direct observation and interaction with a va-riety of children under 3 and their families
3. Individualized supervision that allows the trainee to reflect on all aspects of work with infants, families and colleagues from a range of disciplines
4. Collegial support, both within and across disciplines, that be-gins early in training and continues throughout the prac-titioner's professional life

A collaborative, interdisciplinary approach to training must be a criti-cal feature of programs designed to train early intervention personnel. Interdisciplinary approaches to training are strongly supported in Part H of P.L. 102-119. This will require interaction among faculty from different disciplines as part of the development and implementation of the training process. These new models for preservice training may not necessarily fit within the traditional disciplinary lines along which programs currently are organized (McCollum & Thorp, 1988). Bailey (1989) has noted that this may be accomplished in several ways, from combining programs into courses of study leading to dual certification to creating new interdisciplinary courses that can be used across depart-ments. Families, too, may become a major part of the training process, acting as co-faculty, as practicum sites, or as curriculum developers in helping students to achieve a family-entered perspective. Finally, a variety of new field experiences may be needed to enable students to achieve competence with infants and toddlers with disabilities and their families; these in turn may necessitate new approaches to the supervi-sion process, as students are supported in achieving self-knowledge and interaction strategies that match their new roles with families and col-leagues.

LOOKING FORWARD

Preservice programs preparing early childhood special educators for work in birth–age 3 settings have developed, and will continue to develop, not only within the context of federal and state policy, but also within the context of emerging trends in service delivery and in personnel preparation. Currently, the greatest challenge for states, in a time of existing personnel shortages in many early intervention disciplines, is to provide enough personnel to meet the needs of increasing numbers of families while also ensuring that personnel are trained to meet the unique needs of this new population. Each state must develop and implement policy in two areas: clarifying and/or setting standards for entry-level personnel and providing personnel training alternatives to ensure that these standards can be met not only by future personnel, but also by current personnel who may not be fully qualified. Hence, states must develop broad-based, comprehensive systems of personnel development that cross multiple disciplines and types of personnel, and in addition provide alternatives at the preservice, in-service, and continuing education levels. The resulting tension between the need for numbers and the desire for quality is, in many states, being addressed by short-term training (Bruder & McCollum, 1991; McCollum & Bailey, 1991). Longer term planning for preservice programs, in contrast, has received less attention, although it is these programs that will ensure the long-term stability of a labor force for early intervention. As one early intervention discipline, early childhood special education may present particular challenges, since roles of this discipline tend to be not only broader than those trained for in traditional preservice programs in education, but also quite different in many respects (e.g., primacy of family-centered services). Although there is general agreement that the knowledge and skill base needed for these roles differs to the extent that specialized training is necessary, there are significant barriers to providing such training. Hence, to date, a comprehensive early intervention focus is available through very few preservice programs, and certainly is not geographically available to the extent needed to meet states' needs with regard to preparation of this important member of the early intervention team. Thus, much remains to be done in developing appropriate training for this position.

Because early intervention is still very much a field in development, continuing changes in service delivery also will impact preservice preparation. One of the most powerful among current trends is the movement toward seamless services (*Early Childhood Reporter*, 1990). Whereas the federal special education legislation has divided services at the birth–age 3 and preschool levels from one another in terms of funding, authority, and rules and regulations, the feeling in the field is that this separation is a disservice to children and families. Advocates are calling for an upward extension to the preschool level of many of the policies put into place through Part H (*Early Childhood Reporter*, 1990). For instance, at least one state (Pennsylvania) has adopted state policy to support this, and local interagency councils in many other states (such as Illinois and Pennsylvania) have as a primary mission the coordination of services across the age span of birth–age 5. This trend, as well as the many benefits seen in Part H, has instigated a reexamination of practices at the preschool level, with the result that some preschool programs now use Individualized Family Services Plans (IFSP) rather than Individual Education Programs (IEP), and provide a more family-centered approach to service delivery. The definition of family involvement that has traditionally guided educators is no longer adequate.

From a different perspective, policymakers have begun to look at horizontal seamlessness as well. Not only is a broader range of families receiving specialized services, but young children with disabilities and delays are increasingly being served in regular early childhood settings. Although not the focus of this chapter, new roles are called for in these contexts as well, with a resulting need for new attitudes, knowledge, and skill. Horizontal seamlessness has brought about examination within the early childhood community of the similarities and differences between regular and special early childhood programs, and has increased the call for collaboration between these two disciplines in both service provision (Carta, Schwartz, Atwater, & McConnell, 1991; Mallory, 1992) and personnel preparation (Burton, Hains, Hanline, McLean, & McCormick, 1992; Miller, 1992). Here, as with respect to early intervention, questions remain as to how to achieve the amount of specialized training needed for these new roles within the context of broader training programs.

Early childhood special education as a field had its beginnings in 1968 with the passage of federal legislation funding the Handicapped Children's Early Education Program (McCollum & Maude, 1993). From that point, practice emerged essentially in parallel to the two primary fields from which it developed, early childhood education and special education, while drawing on and maintaining close ties with each of these. Although personnel roles within service programs mirrored emerging practice, personnel preparation remained fairly well imbedded within one or the other of these two parent fields. From the beginning, it was evident that early childhood special education served children who did not fit within the definitions of "education" as traditionally defined by either of these two types of teacher education programs. Typically, graduates of special education programs, while well-versed in disabilities and in the use of specialized and systematic instructional processes, have had little or no training related to child development, or to curriculum and methods for young children. Conversely, whereas graduates from early childhood education programs have had the latter, they do not have the former. Neither have had direct experience with young children with disabilities or their families, or with the emerging body of literature related specifically to the birth–age 3 population.

Thus, university faculty have looked beyond these two fields to expand the content and process of personnel preparation. It was the passage and implementation of P.L. 99-457 that forced early childhood special educators not only to reexamine critically the values and practices of each of its two parent fields as they apply to young children with special needs, but to recognize the value of knowledge, skills, and practices from an array of noneducation disciplines as well. Health (Shonkoff & Meisels, 1990) and social service (Halpern, 1990) fields have had extensive influence on early intervention practice, including that of early childhood special educators. Rapid growth in developmental research with very young children, including children with disabilities, also has contributed a broader understanding of the various biological and environmental conditions that foster or impede development. From family research has come knowledge of the roles of families in supporting the child's development and learning. With this new knowledge and these new roles have come broad challenges for personnel preparation programs preparing early childhood special educators for work in early intervention settings. As conversations between and among disciplines continue, there will undoubtedly be broad implications for personnel preparation programs in both regular and special early childhood education.

A final theme that must receive increased attention as early intervention personnel preparation becomes more widespread is the processes to be used for training (Fenichel & Eggbeer, 1990; McCollum & Thorp, 1988). Early intervention services represent a shift not only in service-delivery patterns, but in attitudes and values with regard to families and colleagues. These, as well as the need to develop personal qualities that enable one to work in complex environments with other adults, call for different approaches to training. In some cases, these new values may stand in direct opposition to current practice. Thus, personnel preparation programs of all disciplines must pay close attention to developing processes that will support self-examination, self-knowledge, and flexibility in thinking. While this certainly is not a new issue in education, and in fact is close to the call for reflective practice at all levels of education, it does represent a different focus, demanding that we look at the origins of our own family and personal histories and values with regard to their implications for our relationships with families and colleagues.

High expectations go hand in hand with the potential for disappointment (Burke, McLaughlin, & Valdivieso, 1988). To date, however, work toward the vision embodied in P.L. 99-457 has yielded increased professional collaboration among disciplines and between disciplines and families. From this process have emerged strong advocates. The challenge of the near future is to maintain this process of growth in the face of substantial barriers created by dwindling resources and multiple bureaucracies. Continued collaboration, flexibility, and creativity will be key components.

REFERENCES

Association of Teacher Educators and the National Association for the Education of Young Children. (1991). Early childhood teacher certification: A position statement. *Young Children, 47*(1), 16–27.

Bailey, D. B. (1989). Issues and directions in preparing professionals to work with young handicapped children and their families. In J. J. Gallagher, P. L. Trohanis, & R. M. Clifford (Eds.), *Policy implementation and P.L. 99-457* (pp. 97–132). Baltimore: Paul H. Brookes.

Bailey, D., Palsha, S. A., & Huntington, G. S. (1990). Preservice preparation of special educators to work with handicapped infants and their families: Current status and training needs. *Journal of Early Intervention, 14*(1), 43–54.

Bailey, D. B., Simeonsson, R. S., Yoder, D. E., & Huntington, G. S. (1990). Infant personnel preparation across eight disciplines: An integrative analysis. *Exceptional Children, 57*(6), 26–35.

Bevins, S. B. (in preparation). *Early intervention content in Illinois' institutions of higher education.* Unpublished master's thesis, Department of Special Education, University of Illinois at Urbana-Champaign.

Bricker, D., & Slentz, K. (1988). Personnel preparation: Handicapped infants. In M. C. Wang, M. C. Reynolds, & H. J. Walbert (Eds.), *Handbook of special education: Research and practice* (Vol. 3, pp. 319–345). Elmsford, NY: Pergamon Books.

Bruder, M., Klosowski, S., & Daguio, C. (1991). A review of personnel standards for Part H of P.L. 99-457. *Journal of Early Intervention, 15*(1), 66–79.

Bruder, M. B., & McCollum, J. (1991). *Analysis of state applications for Year 4: Planning for the personnel components of Part H of IDEA.* Chapel Hill, NC: National Early Childhood Technical Assistance System.

Bruder, M. B., & McLean, M. (1988). Personnel preparation for infant interventionists: A review of federally funded projects. *Journal of the Division for Early Childhood, 12,* 299–305.

Burke, P. J., McLaughlin, M. J., & Valdivieso, C. H. (1988). Preparing professionals to educate handicapped infants and young children: Some policy considerations. *Topics in Early Childhood Special Education, 8*(1), 73–80.

Burton, C., Hains, A., Hanline, M., McLean, M., & McCormick, K. (1992). Early education policy, practice, and personnel preparation: The urgency of professional unification. *Topics in Early Childhood Special Education, 11*(4), 53–69.

Carta, J. J., Schwartz, I. S., Atwater, J. B., & McConnell, S. R. (1991). Developmentally appropriate practice: Appraising its usefulness for young children with disabilities. *Topics in Early Childhood Special Education, 11*(1), 1–20.

Division for Early Childhood. (1987). *Position statement and recommendations relating to P.L. 99-457 and other federal and state early childhood policies.* Reston, VA: Council for Exceptional Children.

Dunst, C. J., & Trivette, C. M. (1988). A family systems model of early intervention with handicapped and developmentally at-risk children. In D. R. Powell (Ed.), *Parent education as early childhood intervention: Emerging directions in theory, research and practice* (pp. 131–179). Norwood, NJ: Ablex.

Dunst, C. J., & Trivette, C. M. (1989). An enablement and empowerment perspective of case management. *Topics in Early Childhood Special Education, 8*(4), 87–102.

Early Childhood Reporter. (1990). *1*(8), 1–4.

Early childhood special education teacher certification. (1991). A position statement of the Association of Teacher Educators and the National Association for the Education of Young Children. Reston, VA: Association of Teacher Educators.

Fenichel, E. S., & Eggbeer, L. (1990). *Preparing practitioners to work with infants, toddlers and their families: Issues and recommendations for educators and trainers.* Washington, DC: National Center for Clinical Infant Programs.

Gallagher, J. J., & Staples, A. (1990). *Available and potential resources for personnel preparation in special education: Dean's survey.* Chapel Hill: Carolina Policy Studies Program, University of North Carolina.

Geik, I., Gilkerson, L., & Sponseller, D. (1982). An early intervention training model. *Journal of the Division for Early Childhood, 5,* 45–52.

Halpern, R. (1990). Community based early intervention. In S. Meisels & J. Shonkoff (Eds.), *Handbook of early childhood intervention* (pp. 469–498). New York: Cambridge University Press.

Hanson, M. J. (1990). *Final report: California early intervention personnel model, personnel standards, and personnel preparation plan.* San Francisco: California Early Intervention Personnel Study Project, Department of Special Education, San Francisco State University.

Hebbeler, K. M. (1992). *State certification practices for infant specialists and early childhood special educators*. Alexandria, VA: National Clearing-house for Professions in Special Education.

Hebbeler, K., Smith, B., & Black, T. (1991). Federal early childhood special education policy: A model for the improvement of services for children with disabilities. *Exceptional Children, 58*(2), 104–112.

Klein, N., & Campbell, P. (1990). Preparing personnel to serve at-risk and disabled infants, toddlers, and preschoolers. In S. Meisels & J. Shonkoff (Eds.), *Handbook of early childhood intervention* (pp. 679–699). New York: Cambridge University Press.

Mallory, B. L. (1992). Is it always appropriate to be developmental? Convergent models for early intervention practice. *Topics in Early Childhood Special Education, 11*(4), 1–12.

McCollum, J. A., & Bailey, D. B. (1991). Developing comprehensive personnel systems: Issues and alternatives. *Journal of Early Intervention, 15*(1), 51–56.

McCollum, J. A., Cook, R., & Ladmer, L. (n.d.). Status of current personnel in Illinois' early intervention programs. Submitted for publication.

McCollum, J. A., & Hughes, M. (1988). Staffing patterns and team models in infancy programs. In J. Jordan, J. Gallagher, M. Karnes, & P. Hutinger (Eds.), *Early childhood special education: Birth–3* (pp. 147–162). Reston, VA: Council for Exceptional Children.

McCollum, J. A., & Maude, S. P. (1993). Early childhood special education: Theories, issues and emerging practice. In B. Spodek (Ed.), *Handbook of research and the education of young children* (pp. 352–371). New York: Macmillan.

McCollum, J. A., McLean, M., McCartan, K., & Kaiser, C. (1989). Recommendations for certification of early childhood special educators. *Journal of Early Intervention, 13*(3), 195–212.

McCollum, J. A., & Thorp, E. (1988). Training of infant specialists: A look to the future. *Infants and Young Children, 1*(2), 55–65.

Meisels, S. J. (1992). Early intervention: A matter of context. *Zero to Three, 12*(3), 1–6.

Miller, P. (1992). Segregated programs of teacher education in early childhood: Immoral and inefficient practice. *Topics in Early Childhood Special Education, 11*(4), 39–52.

Shelton, T., Jeppson, E., & Johnson, B. (1987). *Family-centered care for children with special health care needs*. Washington, DC: Association for the Care of Children's Health.

Shonkoff, J. P., & Meisels, S. J. (1990). Early childhood intervention: The evolution of a concept. In S. Meisels & J. Shonkoff (Eds.), *Handbook of early childhood intervention* (pp. 3–32). New York: Cambridge University Press.

Smith, B., & Powers, C. (1987). Issues related to developing state certification policies. *Topics in Early Childhood Special Education, 7*, 12–23.

Teacher Education Division. (1982). *National directory of special education *teacher preparation programs.* Reston, VA: Council for Exceptional Children.

Teacher Education Division. (1987). *National directory of special education teacher preparation programs.* Reston, VA: Council for Exceptional Children.

Teacher Education Division. (1992). *National directory of special education teacher preparation programs.* Reston, VA: Council for Exceptional Children.

Thorp, E., & McCollum, J. (1988). Defining the infancy specialization in early childhood special education. In J. Jordan, J. Gallagher, P. Hutinger, & M. Karnes (Eds.), *Early childhood special education: Birth-3* (pp. 147–161). Reston, VA: Council for Exceptional Children.

Winton, P. (1989). *Outline of core competencies for working with families in early intervention.* Chapel Hill, NC: Author.

CHAPTER 11

Early Childhood Education and Early Childhood Special Education: A Look to the Future

Bernard Spodek and
Olivia N. Saracho

The previous chapters in this book give an indication of the extent to which the field of early childhood special education has changed in recent years. They also indicate the extent to which the two fields — early childhood education and early childhood special education — have been moving closer to each other. These fields share some common elements of history, as indicated in Chapter 1. The work of Maria Montessori, for example, who significantly influenced early childhood education, grew out of the previous work of Periere, Itard, and Sequin, all of whom were concerned with children with disabilities, as well as out of the work of Froebel, who created the kindergarten. Margaret Macmillan, who pioneered the nursery school, was concerned with a population of children we would today characterize as being "at-risk."

The two fields, however, evolved in very different directions. Early childhood education, at least until the 1960s, was a field that was primarily concerned with educating typical middle-class children. The "child development point of view" (Hymes, 1955) that was reflected in the programs of that time was founded on a normative, maturationist conception of development. Nursery schools were concerned with nurturing individual children and supporting their development. Teachers were expected to set the stage for children's activities, but the activities themselves were to be initiated by the children rather than the teacher. While mental health was seen as an important goal, intellectual stimulation was not considered important.

CHANGING FIELDS

That view of early childhood changed in the 1960s as early childhood educators became aware of constructivist views of development and as they became more responsive to the needs of children in poverty. These views suggested that intellectual development is not totally determined by heredity, but that environmental stimulation was important too (Hunt, 1961). It was also noted that changes in environmental stimulation could have a greater impact on developing children if it was provided in the early years of life (Bloom, 1964). Experimental programs demonstrated that good early childhood education could make a difference in the present lives of children as well as in their future school careers. Project Head Start, a comprehensive child development program designed for children in poverty, was created. Head Start's focus on the whole child, on the family, and on the community in which the children are growing up significantly affected all of early childhood education. Increasing evidence contributed to the realization that early childhood programs can make a significant difference in children's lives — a realization that led to the almost universal enrollment of America's 5-year-olds in kindergarten and the increased availability of prekindergarten programs in the public schools. Changes in the structure of families and in the nature of the work force also dramatically increased the number of young children — children below age 5 — attending child-care centers.

Early childhood special education, as noted in Chapter 5, had a different recent history from that of early childhood education. The field developed more as a downward extension of special education for school-age children. Learning theory, rather than developmental theory, influenced the evolving programs. Intervention, often behavioral in nature, was considered a basic element of these programs. Thus, a set of goals, a teaching methodology, a philosophy, and even a vocabulary developed that were different in significant ways from those that were shared by early childhood educators. All too often, though, the disability or "handicap" was seen as more important and more focal to the program than the children themselves. Early childhood educators concerned with children with disabilities made little use of the knowledge that could be garnered from the field of early childhood education for children without disabilities (Spodek, 1982).

Just as early childhood education was shown to be effective in changing the lives of young children in poverty, so early childhood special education was shown to be effective. P.L. 94-142 and P.L. 99-457, later amended under the title *Individuals with Disabilities Edu-*

cation Act, required that public schools be responsible for educating all school-age children as well as children with disabilities down to age 3. Opportunities were also provided for states to offer programs for children from birth–age 3. These children were to be educated in the least restrictive educational setting, which meant that the majority of children would be enrolled in regular classes, with specific program modifications made or with children with disabilities pulled out of the regular classroom for special instruction. Thus, for many if not most children with disabilities, early childhood special education was to be provided while children were enrolled in regular classroom programs. This move towards "mainstreaming" or "inclusion" required that all teachers serve children with disabilities. All teachers became potential teachers of children with disabilities, and special educators spent more time serving as resource teachers and consultants rather than as teachers of self-contained classes. This was not the first move in this direction, for even earlier, the Head Start program required that at least 10 percent of the children enrolled be children with disabilities.

At present, young children with disabilities are integrated into regular classes at least in the kindergarten and primary grades. In many school districts children with disabilities below kindergarten age are still segregated into special classes since these districts do not provide education for children below age 5 who have no disabilities. Children with disabilities are also included in early childhood programs in child-care centers.

The consequence of this inclusion of children in regular classes is that early childhood educators and early childhood special educators are required to work together more closely than ever before. This is one factor that led to the closer cooperation of early childhood educators and early childhood special educators, but there are other influences as well.

From a theoretical perspective, early childhood special education programs began to change. As the goals of special education became the integration of persons with disabilities into the larger society, educators began to look at the generalizability of skills taught in intervention programs. They had also been looking at the research on the impact of including children with disabilities in regular classes as compared with segregating children with disabilities into their own classes. The evidence strongly suggested that many of the special intervention techniques that the field had developed are no more effective than regular classroom practices. In addition, because children learn a great deal from one another, those children with disabilities who were included in regular classes functioned more like their nondisabled peers than did those children who remained in segregated classes (Spodek & Saracho, 1994). Questions were raised about alternative, nonbehavioral approaches to the education of children with disabilities. As noted in Chapter 5, constructivist approaches were developed for these children, which were more consistent with the approaches of early childhood educators. Even the Individual Educational Program (IEP) that must be developed for children with disabilities, as has been noted in Chapter 6, can be written in nonbehavioral terms. Thus both programmatically and theoretically, the two fields of early childhood education and early childhood special education have moved considerably closer together.

THE FUTURE

It is reasonable to assume that the changes that have taken place in early special childhood education and early childhood education will continue. While it is not expected that these two fields will merge, it should be expected that the collaboration that has begun will increase. The major organizations in the two fields will continue to cooperate, and probably this cooperation will also increase. In addition, the basic concepts that underlie the two fields have always been compatible to some extent, and they could be expected to become more compatible.

The concept of "inclusion," or the integration of children with disabilities into regular classrooms, is consistent with the concept of diversity and the responsibility to modify curriculum in response to individual and group differences found in early childhood classrooms (Zimiles, 1991). The importance of the family in serving young children that is highlighted in programs for young children with disabilities can be found in all early childhood programs, but especially in family-centered programs (Galinsky & Weissbourd, 1992). These are but a few of the many examples that could be cited.

The changes that have brought these two fields closer together have significant implications for practitioners, scholars, and teacher educators in these fields. Early childhood teachers will continue to have primary responsibility for the education of all children in their classes. The growing move toward inclusion means that these teachers will have increasing responsibility for larger numbers of children with disabilities. This will require all teachers to know more about the education of children with disabilities. They will have to be aware not only of teaching strategies, but of ways of dealing with the health and welfare needs of these children and their families. Resources are presently available to help early childhood teachers learn more about children with disabilities (for example, Safford, 1989; Sheridan, Foley, & Radlinski, 1994; Spodek & Saracho, 1994). But teacher education programs seldom provide early childhood teachers with much beyond an understanding of characteristics of children with different kinds of disabilities.

Teachers will have to become aware of the resources in schools and in communities that can serve children with disabilities. Teachers will become increasingly responsible for coordination of services rather than for direct delivery of services. Increasingly teachers of children with disabilities are learning about the resources available in the regular classroom. They are becoming more a part of a team that includes the classroom teacher. However, in programs for the very young—for infants and toddlers and in some cases for preschoolers—these teachers continue to be isolated from the regular early childhood teachers. It is hoped that in the future, as early childhood services and programs expand, there will be more opportunities for collaboration between early childhood education and early childhood special education with these children.

REFERENCES

Bloom, B. S. (1964). *Stability and change in human characteristics*. New York: Wiley.

Galinsky, E., & Weissbourd, B. (1992). Family-centered child care. In B. Spodek & O. N. Saracho (Eds.), *Issues in child care: Yearbook in early childhood education, Vol. 3* (pp. 47–65). New York: Teachers College Press.

Hunt, J. McV. (1961). *Experience and intelligence*. New York: Roland Press.

Hymes, J. (1955). *The child development point of view*. New York: Prentice-Hall.

Safford, P. (1989). *Integrated teaching in early childhood*. White Plains, NY: Longman.

Sheridan, M., Foley, G., & Radlinski, S. (1994). *The supportive play process*. New York: Teachers College Press.

Spodek, B. (1982). What special educators need to know about regular early childhood classes. *Educational Forum, 46*, 295–307.

Spodek, S., & Saracho, O. N. (1994). *Dealing with individual differences in the early childhood classroom*. White Plains, NY: Longman.

Zimiles, H. (1991). Diversity and change in young children: Some educational implications. In B. Spodek & O. N. Saracho (Eds.), *Issues in early childhood curriculum: Yearbook in early childhood education, Vol. 2* (pp. 21–45). New York: Teachers College Press.

Index

Abelson, R. P., 55
Able-Boone, H., 184
Acceptance, of child's disability, 31
Accountability, 104, 112
Activity Based Intervention (ABI; Bricker & Cripe), 82, 109, 111–112
Acute illness, 173–174
Adaptive Firmware Card, 195, 205
Adcock, C., 101
Adelson, E., 86
Adult-child ratio, 153–154
Affleck, G., 36
Age appropriateness, 101–103
Age-expectancy norms, 16–17
Aiello, B., 13
Akers, J., 31
Alcanta, B., 19
Alessandri, S. M., 58
Algozzine, B., 99
Allen, L., 176, 180
Almy, M., 75
Alpert, K., 82
American Association for the Care of Children's Health, 26
American Psychological Association, 11
American Sign Language (ASL), 98
Americans with Disabilities Act (1990), 4, 13, 165
Anagnos, Michael, 98
Anastasiow, Nicholas J., 4, 7–25, 14–15, 20, 107
Anderson, S., 47
Anselmo, A., 192
Antia, S. D., 81, 83
Apolloni, T., 76, 77
Applied behavioral analysis (ABA), 106
Arnaud, S. H., 87
Artis, N. E., 167
Asher, S. R., 46, 51, 57
Assessment of Peer Relations (APR; Guralnick), 59–60
  Inventory of Resources, 59–60, 61
Assessment scales, 16
  developmental, 109

family needs, 29, 34
for social competence, 47–49, 58–60
Assistive devices, 196–197, 205–206
Association of Teacher Educators (ATE), 223
Athey, I., 75, 79, 83
Attachment, 21
Atwater, J. B., 102, 103, 120, 150, 154, 236
Auld, P. A. M., 58
Ault, Marilyn Mulligan, 5, 104, 165–191, 186
Autism, 14, 33, 76, 88–89
Avila, D. L., 38
Ayers, A. J., 88

Baer, D. M., 22, 152
Bagnato, S., 131
Bailey, D. B., 27, 29, 32, 34, 37, 39, 58, 101, 102, 106, 109, 110, 119, 120, 149, 180, 219, 225–228, 232–235
Bakeman, R., 47
Baldwin, James Mark, 9, 15, 18
Bámbara, L. M., 205
Bandura, A., 18, 22
Banet, B., 108
Barber, Patricia A., 5, 29, 34, 165–191
Barkley, R. A., 65
Barnett, M. P., 205
Baron, L. J., 204
Baron-Cohen, S., 65
Bates, E., 19, 46
Batshaw, M. L., 12, 32, 172
Battle, C. U., 180
Bauer, A. M., 26
Becket, J. E., 176
Beckman, P. J., 27, 61, 77, 108
Beeghly, M., 64, 123
Behavioral approach, 17–18, 105–106
  constructivist approach versus, 119, 130–131
  effectiveness of, 121–122
Behl, D., 31
Behr, S. K., 29
Behrman, R. E., 166

About the Editors
and Contributors

Nicholas J. Anastasiow is Thomas Hunter Professor in the department of Special Education of Hunter College and the program in Educational Psychology at the City University of New York. He received his B.A. from the University of California at Berkeley and his Ph.D. from Stanford University. He has had post graduate work in neurology at Columbia University College of Physicians and Surgeons. He has been an early childhood and elementary school teacher and principal, a director of research for a school district, a program director of an early childhood and elementary program for children who reside in economic poverty, and Director of the Institute for Child Study at Indiana University. He is an author of several books, and over 100 articles. In special education he has been President of the Division of Early Childhood Special Education. He is currently the co-author of *Educating Exceptional Children*, with S. Kirk and J. J. Gallagher; and *The At-Risk Infant* (3rd ed.) with S. Harel.

Marilyn M. Ault is Courtesy Assistant Professor in the department of Special Education at the University of Kansas where she teaches in the area of severely/multiply handicapped and deaf-blind. She is currently Co-director of two projects to help teachers work with children who have multiple disabilities and special health-care needs. Dr. Ault has co-authored a book and numerous other publications concerning health care for children with disabilities, teaching children with severe/multiple disabilities, health care–nutrition for children with disabilities, and implementing health care procedures for children in classroom settings. She has also worked as a head teacher in a preschool for severely/multiply handicapped children at the University of Kansas Medical Center and as a parent training coordinator for a program for children with autism.

Patricia A. Barber is a Post-Doctoral Fellow at the Juniper Gardens Children's Project in Kansas City and Courtesy Assistant Professor in the Department of Special Education, University of Kansas. She has served as the Executive Coordinator of the Kansas Interagency Coordinating Council on Early Childhood Developmental Services and as Director or Co-director of various research projects concerning family and child support services for children who are medically fragile, technology dependent, or have severe disabilities. Her studies focus on educational services for children who are ventilator assisted, parental adjustment to birth of a child with disabilities, and parent decision-making in the treatment of newborns with disabilities. She has also been a preschool early intervention teacher.

Philippa H. Campbell is an occupational therapist and educator whose interests relate to families, infants and toddlers, and children with severe disabilities. Dr. Campbell is Associate Professor for Early Childhood at Temple University and the Director of Child Development and Early Intervention for Temple University's Center for Research in Human Development and Education where she directs a number of research, training, and service provision programs. Before coming to Temple University, Dr. Campbell directed the Family Child Learning Center, a collaborative programs operated jointly by Children's Hospital Medical Center of Akron and Kent State University.

Christine Cook is Family Services Coordinator for the early childhood centers of the Cuyahoga County Board of Mental Retardation and Developmental Disabilities, in Cleveland, Ohio, and a doctoral candidate at Kent State University, specializing in Early Childhood Special Education. She is a member of the Executive Committee of the Ohio Subdivision of DEC, the Division for Early Childhood of Council for Exceptional Children. Her research interests involve the implications for intervention of parent-infant interaction.

Susan A. Fowler is Professor and head of the Department of Special Education at the University of Illinois. She received her doctorate in Developmental Psychology from the University of Kansas. Much of her research and writing has focused on the transition of young children with disabilities and their families into preschool and kindergarten. She is especially interested in the inclusion of children with disabilities in community preschool programs. Dr. Fowler has been active in a number of national organizations; in 1992 she served as President of the Division of Early Childhood within the Council for Exceptional Children.

Michael J. Guralnick is Director of the Child Development and Mental Retardation Center and Professor of Psychology and Pediatrics at the University of Washington. Over the years, Dr. Guralnick has conducted research and demonstration projects in early childhood intervention, mainstreaming, social skills development, peer relations, and pediatric education. He is a former president of the Division of Early Childhood of the Council of Exceptional Children and of the American Association of University Affiliated Programs. Dr. Guralnick is also a former Chair of the Mental Retardation Research Center Programs.

Toni Linder is a Professor and Coordinator of Graduate Studies in the College of Education at the university of Denver. She also directs the Early Childhood Special Education and the Child and Family Studies programs within the College of Education. Dr. Lindner has experience as an educator, administrator, researcher, and consultant with regard to early childhood issues. In addition to numerous articles, she is the author of *Early Childhood Special Education: Program Development and Administration* (1983), *Transdisciplinary Play-based Assessment* (1990, 1993), and *Transdisciplinary Play-based Intervention* (1993).

Gerald Mahoney is currently Director of the Family Child Learning Center, an early intervention research and training center which is sponsored by Kent State University and Children's Hospital Medical Center of Akron. Dr. Mahoney has worked for 20 years in the field of early intervention, including teacher training, research, and programs development. Much of the research that he has conducted has focused on factors that contribute to the cognitive, language, and motor development of young children with disabilities. Current research projects are focused on designing social and instructional conditions that encourage children's involvement in constructive activities.

Susan P. Maude is a project coordinator at the Research, Training, and Evaluation division of St. Peter's Child Development Centers in Pittsburgh, where she is working on statewide evaluation issues related to early intervention. She completed her doctorate in early childhood special education at the University of Illinois at Urbana-Champaign following several years as a classroom and home-based early intervention educator. During her doctoral studies she coordinated a federally funded personnel preparation project and completed a dissertation designed to identify the views of faculty and practitioners with regards to the competencies in multiple disciplines needed by early intervention personnel. She continues to pursue her interest in preservice and inservice personnel issues as part of her current position.

Jeanette A. McCollum is a Professor of Education at the University of Illinois where she co-directs the programs in Infancy and Early Childhood Education. Dr. McCollum has been active at both the state and national levels in the development of policy related to personnel preparation, with a particular focus on interdisciplinary and family-centered approaches to preparing personnel to work with birth–3 year olds with disabilities and their families. She has served as the personnel representative on the State Interagency Council for Early Intervention in Illinois and as chair of the personnel committee. Under her direction, Illinois developed a portfolio credentialing system for early intervention personnel. Dr. McCollum's primary areas of research include personnel preparation and parent-infant interaction.

Gail McGregor is Associate Professor in the College of Professional Studies at the University of Wisconsin–Stevens Point. At the time of this writing she directed an assistive technology resource center at Temple University where she was overseeing assistive technology training, evaluation, information and referral, and research services. She is currently involved in a two-year research project to document effective uses of assistive technology in school, home, and community settings throughout Pennsylvania.

Ellen Nasik is a school psychologist in the Minneapolis Public Schools and a doctoral student in School Psychology at Temple University. At the time of writing, she was an intern in the Early Childhood Evaluation Center in the Center for Research in Human Development and Education at Temple University.

Christine Nucci is Assistant Professor of Early Childhood Education at the College of Staten Island of the City University of New York (CUNY). She earned her Ph.D. in Educational Psychology at CUNY's Graduate School and University Center with a concentration in Human Development. Dr. Nucci has taught at the early childhood and elementary levels. She has done research in early cognition, in mathematical learning and teaching, and in microcomputer education as well as in applications of Fischer's Skill Theory in early childhood.

Michaelene M. Ostrosky is Assistant Professor of Special Education at the University of Illinois at Urbana-Champaign. She received her doctorate in Special Education with emphasis on Early Childhood Education from Vanderbilt University. Her research has focused on the social and communicative interactions between children with and without special needs, parent-implemented language interventions, and the transitions of young children between the multiple programs in which they are enrolled.

Nancy L. Peterson is Chair of Special Education at the University of Kansas where she also has served as Coordinator of Personnel Training Programs in Early Childhood Special Education. She has also served as Director of the KU Early Intervention Demonstration Program for young children with disabilities as well as of a variety of federally funded projects dealing with services for young children with disabilities and their families, personnel training, and the integration of special needs children with their typical peers in preschool settings. Dr. Peterson is currently appointed by the Kansas Governor as Chair of the

Kansas Interagency Coordinating Council for Early Childhood Developmental Services.

Philip L. Safford is Professor and former chair of Special Education at Kent State University. Prior to earning his Ph.D. through the Combined Program in Education and Psychology of the University of Michigan, he had taught children and youth with severe emotional disabilities. He subsequently joined the education faculty of Case Western Reserve University, where he directed an EPDA funded training program, the first of many grants he has directed or co-directed to support interdisciplinary early intervention training. In 1980, he was co-initiator of the Family Child Learning Center, a collaborative program of Children's Hospital Medical Center of Akron and Kent State University providing early intervention services, training, and research. His publications dealing with young children with disabilities include three earlier books, and he is co-author, with K. Cushner and A. McClelland, of *Human Diversity in Education.*

Olivia N. Saracho is Professor of Education in the Department of Curriculum and Instruction at the University of Maryland. Her areas of scholarship include cognitive style, teaching, and teacher education in early childhood education. Dr. Saracho's most recent books are *Right From the Start: Teaching Children Ages 3 through 8* (1994), *Dealing with Individual Differences in the Early Childhood Classroom* (1994), both with Bernard Spodek, and *Foundations of Early Childhood Education* (1987, 1991) with Bernard Spodek and Michael J. Davis. She is also editor, with Roy Evans, of *Early Childhood Teacher Education: An International Perspective* (1992). Dr. Saracho is co-editor of the Yearbook in Early Childhood Education Series.

Maria Sargent is a doctoral candidate at Kent State University, specializing in Early Childhood Special Education. She is also an instructor, teaching courses in both Early Childhood and Special Education, and coordinating the Parent Infant Toddler program of the Paul Jones Child Development Center of Kent State University. Her particular interests include ECSE curriculum and play adaptations to provide for young children with disabilities in developmentally appropriate preschool programs.

Bernard Spodek is Professor of Early Childhood Education at the University of Illinois where he has taught since 1965. He received his doctorate in Early Childhood Education from Teachers College, Columbia University. His research and scholarly interests are in the areas of curriculum, teaching, and teacher education in early childhood education. Dr. Spodek's most recent books are *Right From the Start: Teaching Children Ages 3 through 8* (1994), *Dealing with Individual Differ-*

ences in the Early Childhood Classroom (1994), both with Olivia N. Saracho, the *Handbook of Research on the Education of Young Children* (1993), and *Foundations of Early Childhood Education* (1987, 1991) with Olivia N. Saracho and Michael J. Davis. Bernard Spodek is co-editor of the Yearbook in Early Childhood Education Series.

Judy I. Stahlman is an Associate Professor at Cleveland State University where she developed and coordinates the College of Education's Early Childhood Special Education's Master's Degree Program. Earlier in her career she worked as an early childhood interventionist with infants and toddlers who were disabled or "at risk" and their families. She also served as Program Administrator for a federally funded Handicapped Children's Early Education Program demonstration project. Most recently, Dr. Stahlman has collaborated on the conceptualization and implementation of Ohio's ECSE Personnel Preparation Project which has focused on the training needs of professionals implementing P.L. 99-457. In addition to a number of publications in the field, she has served as Co-research Coordinator and Co-senior Editor of the Project PREPARE training modules series designed to provide comprehensive, competency-based, inservice training in early childhood education.

Amy Powell Wheatley is Associate Director of the Family Child Learning Center where she is currently directing a model demonstration project entitled "Developmentally Appropriate Practices for Preschool Children with Disabilities." She previously worked at the University of Connecticut Health Center and the High/Scope Educational Research Foundation. She has written a number of publications examining elements of the Developmentally Appropriate Practices Model that can be applied to children with disabilities. She has also conducted numerous workshops and seminars on the use of Developmentally Appropriate Practices with young children with disabilities.

7010